Serge Storms leaves the world breathless

"Hilarious . . . Serge Storms is, **hands down, one of the most original and just-plain-captivating characters in modern crime fiction**."
Booklist

"**I almost exploded with laughter as I read**. It's manic, hysterical, and puts Dorsey well up there with the cream of comic writers satirizing America in the 21st century."
Independent

"In Serge Storms, the convivial, schizoid torturer with an encyclopedic knowledge of Florida, Dorsey has created **a truly lovable loon**."
Birmingham Post

"**Twisted hilarity . . . a compelling page-turner** . . . a book that, if it was not funny, would be very, very frightening."
Belfast News Letter

"Dorsey's prose scampers at a rate just this side of manic . . . **Fans of the fast-read, you have met your match**."
Tampa Tribune

"**A newer, nuttier individual is introduced on practically every page** . . . It's a sweet relief to discover that Dorsey can keep up with himself. Heaven knows nobody else can."
Orlando Sentinel

"**Irreverent and loving at the same time** ... leaves the reader gasping for breath."
Washington Post Book World

CLOWNFISH BLUES

A SERGE STORMS ADVENTURE

Tim Dorsey

This edition published in 2018 by Farrago,
an imprint of Prelude Books Ltd
13 Carrington Road, Richmond, TW10 5AA, United Kingdom

www.farragobooks.com

First published by William Morrow in 2017

Copyright © Tim Dorsey 2017

The right of Tim Dorsey to be identified as the author of this Work has been asserted by him in accordance with the Copyright, Designs & Patents Act 1988.

All rights reserved. No part of this publication may be reproduced, stored in a retrieval system, or transmitted, in any form or by any means, without the prior permission in writing of the publisher.

This book is a work of fiction. Names, characters, businesses, organizations, places and events other than those clearly in the public domain, are either the product of the author's imagination or are used fictitiously. Any resemblance to actual persons, living or dead, events or locales is entirely coincidental.

ISBN: 978-1-911440-88-8

Have you read them all?

Treat yourself again to the first Serge Storms adventures—

Florida Roadkill
Local trivia buff Serge Storms loves eliminating jerks and pests. His drug-addled partner Coleman loves cartoons.

Hammerhead Ranch Motel
There's a different schemer or slimeball behind every door. And then there's Serge—who has stopped keeping up with his meds.

Orange Crush
The Republicans' "golden boy" seems a virtual shoo-in for re-election. That is, until he undergoes a radical personality shift.

Turn to the end of this book for a full list of the series, plus—on the last page—the chance to receive **further updates** on Serge Storms.

For Clark and Deedra Mullennix

Prologue

ANOTHER TYPICAL DAY IN PARADISE

A large, clear plastic ball rolled across the Atlantic Ocean off Miami Beach.

It approached a yacht. A hatch on the side of the ball opened. A head popped out. "Which way to Bermuda?" Three deep-sea sports fishermen pointed. "Thank you." The hatch closed. The ball resumed rolling.

Back ashore, a whiskered man dove onto the sidewalk next to U.S. Highway 1, capturing another iguana under his T-shirt. The reptile was hog-tied with rubber bands and hung from the handlebars of a Schwinn bicycle, joining five other similarly dangling reptiles all wondering how life had come to this.

High above the road, workers on a scaffold updated the jackpot on a billboard for the Florida lottery. Motorists stopped texting to slam their brakes as a Marilyn Monroe drag queen ran into the street, chased through traffic by a JFK impersonator. There were fistfights, fender benders, free clinics, firecrackers that people thought were gunfire, and gunfire that people thought was firecrackers.

A man with no known address was thrown out of a Chinese restaurant after trying to sell iguanas to the kitchen staff during the lunch buffet special. He was soon arrested in the parking lot but escaped during an increasingly bitter jurisdictional feud between Animal Control and the health department. A bullet-riddled body lay unnoticed behind a Dumpster as a nearby SWAT team surrounded a group of small boys lighting fireworks.

The sun climbed toward noon. Heat waves rose from the pavement. People slowed down. A bicycle rolled quietly past Caribbean trawlers docked along the banks of the Miami River. Six swaying iguanas looked up from the handlebars at a dilapidated office building and an unimpressed man in a fedora staring back at them from a second-story window.

The man in the window removed the hat and wiped his brow as the cyclist pedaled out of sight. Then he returned to his chair and the conversation with himself: "The name's Mahoney, and if I had a dime for every shanghaied lizard on this river, I could buy the B&O Railroad and not have to pass Go. But they don't pay for that kind of information in these parts, and until they do, I use up oxygen with my feet propped on a desk that has coffee stains older than all the cops in this town, and most of the hookers. The chipped gold letters on the window of my office door say I'm a 'PRIVATE INVESTIGATOR,' but from this side of the glass, I'm a 'ROTAGITSEVNI ETAVIRP.' Been called worse. As long as the money's green, except that's not a popular shade in this economy. Is business slow? My bartender stopped letting me hock cuff links for Cutty Sark, the bookies treat me like an IRS agent at a dice game, and the client chair on the other side of my desk has been empty so long it's starting to have that new-car smell. Guess it's just that time of year again in Miami. Summer, that is, when the road tar outside is hotter than a stolen pinkie ring at a mob wedding. Most people can't take this heat ..."

Rapid footsteps came pounding up the hallway. The door flew open. A Marilyn Monroe drag queen burst in and locked the door behind her. "I can't live like this anymore! You have to help me!"

Mahoney replaced the fedora on his head. "Then again, some like it hot."

It remained quiet and still outside a private detective's office on the Miami River. Suddenly, from high in the sky, the thunderous whapping of a Coast Guard helicopter that had just rescued someone drifting out to sea in a human-sized hamster ball. It continued north toward its air station in Opa-locka, flying over the horse track and a desolate, industrial stretch of Hialeah.

Down below sat a small, squat concrete pillbox of a building. Used to be the office of a high-mileage used-car lot. Now a lawyer's shingle hung over the door. Inside, two people sat on opposite sides of a desk. One wore a tailored French suit. The other, shorts, flip-flops, T-shirt. They stared at the ceiling, waited for the helicopter racket to fade. Then:

"Okay, I got you off on a technicality this time, but you need to be more careful."

The client didn't speak.

"I can't *legally* tell you to break the law," continued the attorney, kicking off his flip-flops. "But hypothetically, if someone absolutely had to transport weed for personal use, they should get a rental car and pull the most tightly packed buds from their stash. Now this is the most important part: no baggie. That's where they get fingerprints. And since you can't get prints off individual buds, just stick them here and there in various spots in the trunk. Even if the cops find your stuff, what can they do? Arrest you because the rental company didn't thoroughly vacuum after the previous customer?"

The man in the French suit slowly began to nod with understanding. "Cool." He stood up, revealing the extent of an athletic frame that made him one of the most popular players for the Miami —. He pulled a platinum money clip from his pocket and peeled off C-notes.

"But you already paid me."

"This is a tip." He formed a wad just north of two G's and passed the currency across the desk, then gave the lawyer an interlocking-thumb, freak-power handshake.

The player left. His lawyer remained behind the desk, counting the cash and sticking it in a bottom drawer before lighting an incense stick. Ziggy. Ziggy Blade, attorney to the ... well, it was different every day, about to become even more so. The entire office was one room, divided in half by a curtain of hanging beads. The walls were covered with taped-up posters: the Constitution, Vietnam napalm plumes, Frank Zappa in concert.

Ziggy had just fired up a joint when the front door opened. He quickly stubbed it out, swatting the incriminating smoke away from his face as the beads parted and someone walked in. Then someone else. And another. And another. So on, until there was no breathing room. Serious mouths, briefcases, guns, dreadlocks.

Ziggy sat with wide, stoned eyes. His T-shirt said: EVERYONE REMAIN CALM. LET THE P.E. TEACHER HANDLE IT. The leader of the group gave a slight nod, which was all the communication needed for the others to set their briefcases on the desk and open them in succession.

Ziggy had never seen so much cash, even on TV. He looked up with even bigger eyes. "You sure you have the right lawyer?"

The leader nodded. "You come highly recommended."

Outside the concrete-block law office in Hialeah, a bicycle rolled by with dangling iguanas. It continued on and approached one of Florida's most popular supermarkets, like Publix, except not Publix.

A dozen cars circled the parking lot for elusive spots. Crammed shopping carts crossed the crosswalks. Inside the automatic doors, all the checkout lines were full, even the registers at the customer-service counter, which were usually shortest of all and the last refuge of the one-item shopper. Except now they were the longest lines in sight because ...

Bright lights flooded the front of the store. A TV correspondent cheerfully raised a microphone. "*This is Bianca Blanco reporting live for* Action Eye Live Eyewitness Five at Five *from one of Florida's most popular supermarkets, where the short lines at the customer-service counter are now preposterously long due to an outbreak of lottery fever, and since we've gone three weeks without a winner, the jackpot has rolled over to a whopping record that is being updated by the hour ... Excuse me, sir, why are you willing to wait so long to buy lottery tickets?"*

"It gives my life meaning ..."

Behind the counter, employees worked frantically to dispense tickets and process the occasional grocery purchase. The staff all had little green plastic name tags. Two of them: SERGE and COLEMAN.

Another customer stepped up to the counter. "Six quick-picks, please."

"Jesus, don't buy lottery tickets," said Serge. "The store won't tell you this because they're in on it, but the whole thing is a fool's bet. It's a tax on people who are bad at arithmetic."

"What the hell's going on here? Just give me the tickets!"

"Buy food instead," said Serge. "That's a sure thing."

"I *am* buying food." The man set an item on the counter.

Serge gasped. "Not that!"

"I'm buying chips."

"But you're buying the twelve-pack of small individual bags! It's the worst possible cost-per-ounce scenario! Work the numbers, man!"

"I can afford it."

"That's not the point!" said Serge. "Think of all the extra Fritos!"

"Do I need to get the manager?"

Serge sighed and hit buttons. "It's your road to ruin."

The customer snatched tickets and chips. "Wacko ..."

At the next register, an employee popped a can of soda.

"Six quick-picks, please."

"Sure thing." The worker lowered the can and furtively manipulated something in his other hand. Then he chugged while pressing buttons on the lottery console.

"Are you drinking?" asked the customer.

"What?"

"I just saw you pour a miniature bottle of vodka into that can of Sprite."

Coleman stared a moment. "No, I didn't."

"Whatever. Just give me my tickets."

"Here you go."

"Hold on." The customer looked at his stubs. "These are Fantasy Five. I wanted Lotto. Where's your supervisor?"

"Wait! It's cool! It's cool!" Coleman quickly pressed more buttons, canceling the previous sale and spitting out correct tickets. "There you go. Have a nice day."

The customer gave him a cold stare before leaving.

Coleman took a deep breath, followed by an extra-long chug. "The pressure ..."

Back at the other register, the line was really starting to stack up.

"No, listen to me!" said Serge, raising his voice. "All of you, listen to me! There are more than twenty million permutations! Do the math! The government is taking all of you for a ride—"

Serge felt a tap on his shoulder and turned around. "Yeah?"

An assistant manager stood dumbstruck. "What do you think you're doing?"

"What's it look like? Teaching home economics."

The supervisor opened his mouth to say something, but stopped and sniffed the air. "Do I smell alcohol?"

"I don't drink," said Serge.

The lines of irate customers pointed in unison at the other register.

Coleman punched buttons in frustration. "Darn, wrong tickets again ..."

Two men wandered away from the grocery store with holes in their shirts where their name tags had been torn off.

"I can't believe they fired us," said Coleman. "I was starting to get pretty good at that."

"Doesn't matter," said Serge. "We were going to quit tomorrow anyway."

"But we just started working there Monday."

"That's right. We reached our time limit." Serge pulled a lottery ticket from his pocket and gently caressed the image of a loggerhead turtle. "It's the key to our new lifestyle choice, moving on to a new town every week and getting another job, just like all the classic American TV road shows: *Route 66, The Fugitive, Branded, Kung Fu,* and the all-but-overlooked *Sea Hunt,* starring Lloyd Bridges. None of them ever stayed more than a week."

"Why not?"

"The next episode had to air. Even rebels must answer to the prime-time network schedule."

"Serge, why do you have a lottery ticket?"

"Not just any ticket." He raised it over his head in triumph. "This is a special-edition Guy Harvey marine-life scratch-off."

"But you told all those people back there that the lottery was stupid."

"Only if you play," said Serge. "This is going right in my collection. That way I've already won."

Coleman reached. "Can I scratch it off?"

Serge clutched it to his chest. "And ruin a mint-condition Florida souvenir?"

Coleman shrugged and pulled another miniature bottle from his pocket. "Serge, there's a dude riding by with a bunch of iguanas hanging from rubber bands on his handlebars."

"Florida happens."

The pair strolled down the sidewalk as a commercial truck pulled up to the curb. A work crew got out to update the jackpot total on another lottery billboard. The first began climbing the ladder. "Hey, Stan, check this out."

"What is it?"

"I'm not sure."

Passing motorists had been staring curiously at the unusual sign all morning, but they just assumed it was one of those 3-D gimmick billboards, this one sending a message like *You'll really regret not buying lottery tickets.*

The first worker slowly climbed a few more rungs. "What the— ... Oh my God!"

He practically jumped off the ladder. The whole crew sprinted back to their truck and got on the radio.

High above the road stood the familiar flamingo logo with a tropical splash of colors that promoted wealth without work. In front of the sign was a man wearing a short-sleeve clerk shirt with a clip-on tie. Clasped to his breast pocket: a photo ID badge from the state department of lottery. He gently swung in the breeze from the noose around his neck.

EPISODE ONE

Chapter 1

ONE MONTH EARLIER

Yellow wildflowers and cattle fences ran along the side of the country highway traveling from the middle of nowhere to the outskirts of nowhere else. It was in the soggy armpit of the state that gently bends the peninsula west up into the Panhandle.

Here and there, separated by long stretches of trees and moss, were signs of the hand of man. A corrugated aluminum building advertising well drilling, a defunct campground on the Suwanee, an unexpected scuba shop for visitors to a local spring. It was that weird swath of backwoods, off-the-radar counties that featured wanton barrenness anchored by a monstrous granite courthouse circa 1909 that could accommodate the entire population.

Then, occasionally, a modest main street of sorts. Meme's Diner; the Boon Docks restaurant with cattle skull on the roof; Tumbleweed's Smoke House with no explanation for the apostrophe; a pizza place boasting the "best service in town" with no explanation for the quote marks; Mayo Good Home Cookin Café; Daddy's Place Bar-B-Q with a mural of Malcolm X, Elijah Muhammad and Louis Farrakhan, peacefully existing next to a mechanic's garage with no customers and large, motionless white men in overalls leaning back in the humid shade as if they'd been asked to pose for *Life* magazine in 1965.

A vintage sports car zoomed across the Aucilla River, down into the elbow of the Panhandle between Goose Creek Bay and Hog Island Sound. Coleman sat up after firing a fattie. "I know I ask this question a lot, but this time I really mean it: Where in the *heck* are we going?"

Serge made a skidding right at a wooded fork. "To possibly the most isolated oasis of funk in all the state—and the first stop on my *Route 66* tour of Florida."

"What's its name?"

"Sopchoppy."

"You mean like that biker at the No Name Pub?"

"It's Creek Indian for 'long and twisted.'"

Coleman took a deep hit. "Works for me."

"The place is so remote and tiny, yet has all kinds of bonus features as both the self-proclaimed 'music capital of North Florida' and 'earthworm-harvesting capital' of the whole state. That is a bold range of culture."

"Worms and tunes." Coleman popped a Bud. "Dig it."

Serge turned onto Rose Street. "There's the town's recording studio, converted from a clapboard rooming house, and over here on Yellow Jacket Avenue is the historic old high school gymnasium, which hosts monthly performances of the Sopchoppy Opry."

"*That's* a high school gymnasium?" said Coleman. "Looks like the Alamo."

"Good analogy," said Serge. "It alone is worth the visit: hands down the state's coolest gymnasium, or anything in the scientific family of gymnasiums. Constructed in 1939 by the Works Progress Administration, it's a Spanish-mission-style fortress of cemented-together limestones. Not bricks, the actual stones, forming an arched facade where the basketball hoops are mounted inside." Serge grabbed a lockpick set and a ball from the backseat. "I must shoot a basket."

Coleman sipped his beer in the convertible and listened to quietness. Serge ran back out.

"That was fast."

Serge vaulted over the driver's door. "Strike that from the list." He drove off, making a series of turns with his eyes in the sky. "The cool thing about small towns like this is you can navigate with just the water tower."

"I see it. And there's an old train depot ..."

"... Now a museum." Serge pulled up to the curb in the busiest section of town, a total of three buildings long. Sopchoppy Grocery was made of red bricks with a tin awning and a sign that hung over the sidewalk with 1950s artwork of a pile of vegetables next to a slice of raw meat. Smaller signs in the windows advertised Coca-Cola and Cracker Jack, then homemade notices for septic repair, a lost dog, canoe rentals, a carpet service called Dirt Doctors, and an announcement that "local squash" was now in stock.

"You need food?" asked Coleman.

"No, a job." Serge hopped out. "Our *Route 66* pilgrimage requires that we secure new employment each week in a different town. That's why I picked Sopchoppy for episode one. We can't miss!"

"But how can you be so sure the grocery store will hire us?"

"They won't," said Serge. "We're starting our own business."

"What kind of business?"

Serge pointed at another sign in the window that said $2.50 A CUP next to a crayon drawing of a smiling earthworm. "Each year, people from all over descend on the tiny hamlet for the annual worm-grunting festival."

"Grunting?"

"It's what they call their patented technique for harvesting worms." Serge entered the store and walked past a produce case with an eclectic decorative display on top of antique cash registers, lanterns and tennis rackets. "It seems hard to believe now, but back in the day this was a gold-rush town of pioneers supplying the region with earthworms and making fortunes, until people started calculating fortunes differently."

"Far out."

At the other end of the vegetable case was a dignified woman in a straw hat trying to reach a zucchini decision.

"Excuse me," said Serge. "I know this place has seen better times, but thankfully all hardship is in the rearview mirror now that we've arrived. The new *Route 66,* episode one."

"Do I know you?"

"Not yet, but soon everyone in town will. Extreme worm-grunting."

"Oh, the worm festival," she said with a laugh. "You just missed the last one by a week. The kids loved it."

"I'm sure the little tykes were joyfully spitting up ice cream and cotton candy all the way home," said Serge. "But we're deadly serious. I believe I can trust you: There could soon be an employment boom around here, except we only have a week. Shooting schedule for the next episode. Sorry, but the suits make the rules."

"What are you talking about?" The female customer was possibly late thirties. Appeared slightly older from the light sun wrinkles of an outdoor life, and acted younger because of the experience.

Serge glanced around for eavesdroppers, then leaned closer. "I can get you in on the ground floor. Just point us toward the worm fields, and the highway will soon be so full of semi trucks that they'll have to reinforce the bridges."

"Do you actually know anything about worm-grunting?"

"*Everything,*" said Serge. "Do I look like some kind of amateur? You fashion a foot-and-a-half wooden stake made of persimmon or oak that's called a 'stob' and pound it into nutrient-rich soil. Next you take an equal length of metal known as a 'rooping iron' that's often a leaf spring salvaged from the suspension of an abandoned truck. Then you rub the iron over the top of the stob to mimic the frequency of the earthworm's mortal nemesis, digging moles. Consequently, your quarry flees to the surface, and before you know it"—he snapped his fingers—"you're tits-high in earthworms. Lower property taxes for everyone!"

The woman stared a moment. "Where'd you learn all that?"

"Books, Internet."

"But have you actually done it?"

"Knowledge trumps experience," said Serge. "Einstein never built an A-bomb, but ask a certain country how that turned out."

"No, I mean it's a dead art," said the woman. "Only a few old-timers out in the forest still practice it. Really hard work for horrible pay, maybe twenty bucks a pail if you're lucky. And I mean *big* pails."

"Never thought of pails!" said Serge. "See? I knew you'd be helpful ... Coleman, make a note. Pails, ten. Make it an even dozen." He turned back to the woman. "Any other wisdom you can impart? You mentioned a forest?"

"The Apalachicola, but ... don't take this wrong ..." She eyed Serge up and down. "... You look a bit too city for this line of work. I'm not joking about how hard it is."

Serge gleamed a brilliant smile. "My fingernails may look spotless, but don't underestimate my laser focus and impish tenacity ... Coleman! To the Apalachicola!"

The woman selected a vegetable.

Coleman was already in the passenger seat chugging a fresh quart. Serge stood outside the driver's door with an ancient Gulf Oil road map. "This place called Tate's Hell looks inviting ..."

The door of the grocery store opened. "Let me give you some directions. It's easy to get lost out there in the woods if you're not from these parts."

Serge turned and recalibrated his initial impression. The woman's subdued beauty was more apparent in natural light. High cheekbones, the hair a bit wild and more strawberry, almost no makeup. And he hadn't noticed the hiking boots before. Definitely a nature mama. But the main thing: green eyes, pure jade. She walked around the car and grabbed the edge of his map.

"The problem is a lot of these back roads dead-end up at the Ochlockonee River." She leaned closer to Serge and tapped a spot on the Liberty County line. "But this one bridge west of Smith Creek ..."

"And that's where the worms are?"

"You're on your own there, but it's where I'd start."

It was the slightest of brushes. The side of his arm and the side of hers. Was it on purpose? Either way, electricity clearly jumped.

She moved her finger along the map, leaning even closer until their shoulders were in full contact. Okay, now that definitely was on purpose. Then sense of smell came into sexual play. Scientists don't precisely know why, but humans are individually hardwired to be aroused by certain specific scents. She removed her straw hat, and the aroma of her hair reminded Serge of those little hazelnut coffee creamers from 7-Eleven. He got a woody.

"Wait," she said. "It'll be much easier if I just show you myself."

"You want to come with us?"

"Sure, I hike out there all the time. That is, when I'm not riding horses."

Serge mentally dialed up that last image. Heart be still. He opened the driver's door and slipped on polarized sunglasses. "Climb on in. It's only a two-seater, so I hope you don't mind Coleman's lap."

"Heck, no!"

"Coleman, I wasn't talking to you."

They all wedged inside. "Wow," said the woman. "What a cool car!"

"Genuine 1964 Corvette Stingray, just like Martin Milner drove in the third season of *Route 66*. I have the whole series on DVD. They kept changing car models each year without explanation and it briefly caused me to retain water ... Where are my manners? I'm Serge." He extended a hand.

"Lou Ellen, nice to meet." She ran her hands over the white leather interior. "Where'd you find such an old model in this condition?"

"Actually it's not mine." Serge pulled away from the curb. "The owner is just letting me use it temporarily."

"For how long?"

"Until he gets home from vacation and calls the police."

Laughter.

"What's so funny?"

"You have a great sense of humor ... Hey, have you seen our historic gymnasium?"

"It rocked my world." Serge suddenly cut the wheel. "But I'd like to see it again."

Lou Ellen braced for balance as the Corvette fishtailed its way over to the limestone landmark, until it almost crashed into it.

Serge jumped out. "Let's go!"

Coleman opened his door.

"Not you," said Serge, extending a hand to help Lou Ellen out of the car.

She started up the steps. "But I think it's locked."

"I have a key."

They went inside.

Coleman settled back with a new bottle of malt liquor. He stared without intent at a spot in the air a foot in front of his face. His brain was a test pattern.

Meanwhile, at center court in the middle of the gym's hardwood floor ...

"Oh God! Yes! Yes! Yes! Faster! Yes! ... What are you thinking about?"

"Stobs, rooping irons, pails, the old Sopchoppy lumber mills, turpentiners, cut-rail fences, indigenous blue iris and black willows used for gunpowder, Corvettes through the ages, the *Route 66* theme song, 7-Eleven ... I'm there!"

"Don't stop! ..."

Coleman upended the brown glass bottle as the gymnasium's door crashed open.

Serge sprinted down the steps and leaped into the driver's seat.

Coleman belched. "What's going on?"

"We have to get the hell out of here!"

Serge threw the Stingray in gear as a disheveled woman staggered out in a daze and pulled up a bra strap. "Wait! Why are you leaving?"

"To protect you," Serge yelled as he hit the gas. "There are a lot of serial killers running around. Luckily it was just me this time, but you need to be more careful."

MEANWHILE ...

The afternoon sun had sizzled away the remnants of the regularly scheduled rain shower, leaving greater Miami in a mild steam bath. The bustling downtown business district, from Biscayne to Flagler and Brickell, didn't have time to regard another TV news crew as out of the ordinary. The sidewalks were thick with street crazies talking to themselves, and executives with Bluetooths talking to themselves.

A baby-faced reporter with a microphone stood in front of a steep stone building. A cameraman in earphones gave him the thumbs-up.

"Good afternoon. This is Reevis Tome coming to you live for FCN outside the Miami-Dade courthouse, where a half-dozen elected officials have been indicted in a broadening kickback scandal involving no-bid contracts awarded to top campaign contributors. As first reported here on this network, our public records search unraveled a barely concealed trail of bribery and graft leading all the way to the mayor's office, which has thus far refused comment ..."

The TV station cut to archive footage of a man with a coat over his head ducking into a black sedan. "Get away from me! ..."

Then back to the reporter. "... We'll have more for you as the story develops. This is Reevis Tome for FCN in Miami ..."

FCN. That would be Florida Cable News.

Reevis Tome. That would be a twenty-seven-year-old, fiercely ethical reporter who appeared to be maybe all of nineteen. Another dying breed: the traditionally trained journalist who purely wanted to cover serious news the old way. No blogs or tweets, and definitely no Facebook posts about the newest adorable zoo baby or "six surprising beauty finds at Costco." And because he didn't care about money, they didn't pay him much. One of his Datsun's back windows was a trash bag. He only had to shave Monday and Thursday.

Reevis never imagined he'd end up on TV. In fact, he abhorred the notion. It was the ink-stained world of newspapers or nothing. Or so he thought. Then came a sea change in the industry near the turn of the millennium. The Internet had dwindled readership to the point that vulture capitalists could acquire most papers for less than the cost of the land under the buildings. Among the hardest hit was the *Journal,* which covered the Gold Coast counties of Palm Beach, Broward and Miami-Dade. Layoffs, salary cuts, unpaid furloughs, slashed health coverage. The paper began requiring all reporters to carry cell phones that took pictures, then disbanded the photo department. They eliminated the weekend cop reporter. They eliminated Palm Beach County.

The staff didn't think it could get worse.

Reevis came to work one day, and they had eliminated news.

Too expensive, they said. We'll just use stories from the wire services. Reevis was yanked off the city hall beat to cover civic luncheons where newspaper publishers received plaques.

Then they sold the land under the building.

Enter Florida Cable News. Shoestring low-budget operation. So low, in fact, that they could scarcely compete with the well-established networks and their soup-to-nuts team coverage of the most sensational stories. FCN was forced to subsist on the leftover material that was beneath the dignity of the big outfits. Reevis was assigned to cover actual news.

A TV cameraman snapped his fingers in front of Reevis's face. "You okay?"

Reevis blinked and returned to the present. "Just another flashback."

The cameraman was named Rock. Rock Blister. He muscularly trotted back to the satellite van as if the weighty camera and battery belt were helium balloons. "We're rolling!"

Reevis jumped in the passenger side a half second after the vehicle had started to move. He grabbed a clipboard off the dash and scanned a grid of time blocks. "Where to now?"

"Convenience store on Biscayne," said Rock, his short sleeves rolled all the way up to reveal tattoos of the Chinese symbols for *love* and *hate*. Except the tattoo artist had been coming off a mulekick hangover, and the designs ended up saying *love* and *storage unit*. "The lottery jackpot rolled over again for the third time and crowds are out the door."

"Wonderful," intoned Reevis. "I have to act cheerful again interviewing poor people tragically wasting their money."

The van arrived at an ethnic bodega on the edge of Miami Gardens. A line of farmworkers ran along the front of the store, giving off a pesticide funk and waiting for air-conditioning. Inside, two automated machines burped out losing tickets at a stunning rate.

A camera light came on. Reevis raised his microphone and faked a smile. "Sir, why are you buying lottery tickets today?"

"So I can afford a divorce."

Reevis moved along the line to collect more insight: "I saw it in a dream," "I'll give it to the church," "I play my grandchildren's birthdays," "I'm wearing my lucky copper bracelet," "These are my husband's ashes" ...

Rock turned off his camera. An Asian couple behind the counter covered their mouths with the giggles. The journalists headed back to the van. The clipboard's next time block: a water-main break under a high school. Reevis's cell phone rang.

"Hello? ... Sure thing, right after we get back from the flooded cafeteria ... Well, if it's that important." He hung up.

"What's going on?" asked Rock.

"Looks like the home of the Fighting Stone Crabs won't be seen tonight."

"We're going back to the office?"

Reevis checked his phone for texts. "Apparently it's something that won't wait."

"Can I ask you a question?" said Rock. "That couple at the counter in the convenience store ..."

"What about them?"

"Why are Chinese people always laughing at me?"

The satellite truck pulled into a parking garage at the headquarters of Florida Cable News, located in beautiful downtown Coconut Creek. Reevis and Rock crossed the newsroom and stuck their heads in the office of the assignment editor.

"You wanted to see us?"

"Come inside and close the door."

They weren't alone.

"Who are these guys?" asked Reevis.

"We'll get to that," said Shug. "We're doing a major lineup overhaul, and I wanted to tell you first before the rumor mill gathered steam. You know how journalists can get."

"Right," said Reevis. "We're supposed to be aggressively curious about everything except malfeasance in our own company."

"And sarcastic," said Shug. But he was old school, too, and liked that about Reevis.

"What kind of overhaul?" asked the young reporter.

"Nothing to worry about." Shug leaned back in the leather chair and folded his arms. "Remember when CNN was all news, all the time?"

"Sure. They cast the mold."

"Then ratings began to slip, so they began filling prime time with reality shows. People working weird jobs, celebrity psychiatrists, Anthony Bourdain drunk in the Alps."

"I'm familiar," said Reevis.

"It's these crazy times," said Shug. "We're forced to evolve or perish."

"But what's all this got to do with me?"

From the side of the room: "We believe you have what it takes."

Reevis turned. "Who are you?"

A British man in a blue blazer and ascot stepped forward. "Nigel Welks."

The assignment editor cleared his throat. "Reevis, this is a production company that just flew in from Los Angeles. They're here to develop your new show."

"L.A.?" asked the reporter.

Shug's chair swiveled. "We're not remotely equipped to develop the type of shows we need to stay competitive, so corporate brought in some outside help."

Reevis's eyes moved back and forth. "Exactly what kind of show are we talking about?"

Nigel placed his palms together in front of his chest and smiled proudly. "This show will have all the elements: journalistic dilemmas, violent confrontation, betrayal, sex ..."

"Sex?" said Reevis.

"Are you allergic to latex?" asked Nigel.

"What?"

"Never mind. Just keep doing what you do best and we'll keep the cameras rolling."

"This is starting to sound like a reality show," said the reporter.

"Oh, no, no, no, no, no," said Nigel. "And we would know the difference. We specialize in reality shows. You've probably seen our latest project, *Full Boil,* about these gourmet chefs who get into adventures."

"What kind?"

"They solve crimes," said Nigel. "Then there's *Deadliest Dig,* a true-life look at the outrageously harrowing world of worm-grunters in the Apalachicola Forest."

"What are worm-grunters?"

"They trudge miles across the muck to catch earthworms for fishing-bait stores."

"Doesn't sound dangerous."

"They also solve crime."

Reevis hung his head. "Shug, I really appreciate the opportunity you gave me to do serious reporting again, but isn't there anything you can do?"

"Just hear them out," said the supervisor.

Nigel undid one of his blazer's brass buttons. "I completely understand your skepticism, so I saved the best for last. We already have a full lineup of shows where people solve crime, like the ones I already mentioned, plus Seminole blackjack dealers, retired circus people, glassblowers who don't trust outsiders, Jell-O shot waitresses, the Wives of Jiffy Lube ..."

"Where is this going?" asked Reevis.

"Don't you see? That's the beauty of it. That's the whole genius!" said Nigel. "These other people didn't know anything about detective work before we came along. But you actually have extensive experience investigating crime for a living. It's so crazy it just might work!"

"Okay," Reevis said with a sigh. "How is this show supposed to start?"

"You were fired from your last newspaper job, right?"

"What's that got to do with anything?"

Nigel held his hands apart like brackets, framing Reevis's face. "A disgraced reporter fights to clear his name in Florida's sun-scorched mean streets."

"But that's not what happened."

"How about *unfairly* disgraced?" said Nigel. "There, we're all on the same page. Kumbaya."

"Shug," said Reevis. "Some of the most important reporting isn't glamorous or made for TV. This community has already lost most of its journalistic oversight of public institutions—"

Shug held up a hand. "I've looked into this thoroughly. You won't be asked to do anything unethical or change the least little thing about your personal style ..."

Nigel nodded. "Your honesty will fool a lot of people."

"... And if you want to spend hours searching through court files, I'll back you up. The only difference is that they're going to film the whole behind-the-scenes reporting process."

"But they're bound to get in the way."

"A small price," said Shug. "You know how we're always talking about the decline of our profession? This is your big opportunity to let the public see under the hood and understand the importance of what they stand to lose."

"You really want me to do this?"

"And the timing's right," said Shug. "We're getting this production team for a bargain."

"Why?"

Nigel squinted at the reporter. "I'll put my cards on the table. We've been getting increasing blowback lately about how real our shows are."

"Like what?"

"The Gourmet Channel is about to cancel *Full Boil*," said Nigel. "Hey, they *said* they were chefs. And the minute we found out, we bought them cookbooks. We did the right thing. But no, the network kept fixating on such a small piece of finger that it will hardly be missed. We're suing the carving-saw company."

Reevis was rubbing numbness out of his hands. "Where do I come in?"

"You provide credibility," said Nigel. "The critics can vet you ten ways to Sunday, and you'll come up a bona fide investigative reporter. In fact, we've already had some of our best investigators dig deep into your past. Glassblowers."

"Excuse me," said Rock. "Do I need to make any special preparations for filming?"

"There's no easy way to say this, so I'll just say it." Nigel jerked a thumb toward the door. "You're out. We have our own cameraman."

"But I always work with Reevis."

"Nothing personal," said the producer. "You don't have the proper training."

"I have years of training," said Rock.

"Ever run?"

"What?"

Nigel turned and placed a hand on the shoulder of a narrow-eyed man standing behind him. "This is Günter Klieglyte, the eminent Bavarian videographer, world-renowned for his signature technique."

"Which is?"

"He's perfected the art of running with the camera to make it jiggle," said Nigel. "Creates a sense of peril. We do it whenever we can."

"What if there isn't peril?" said Rock.

"*Especially* when there isn't peril," said Nigel. "That's when it's needed most."

"But I'm in great shape," said Rock. "I've run with a camera many times."

"Unfortunately, we've gone over hours of your footage. You never run when you don't need to." Nigel turned to Reevis. "Doughnuts tomorrow at eight. Do you carry a weapon?"

Chapter 2

SOPCHOPPY

Serge nervously glanced over his shoulder as the sports car swerved away from the gymnasium and raced west out of town. Coleman twisted the end of a joint in his mouth. "What happened back there?"

"A close call. I had sex."

"But that's a good thing."

"It's a split decision this time," said Serge. "In most episodes of *Route 66,* besides getting a job in a new town, at least one of the guys bangs a local gal. It was required, whether they wanted to or not. Of course with TV standards back in the black-and-white days, they could only allude to it, but if you were paying attention, it was always there: a wholesome independent woman who isn't leery of the newcomers like other folk. And if she was a widow, then you definitely knew it was going down."

"You made me watch all your DVDs," said Coleman. "I never picked up on that."

"Because they were having sex during the commercials," said Serge. "If you've got a work ethic, that's more than enough time."

"You said it was a split decision?"

"That's right," said Serge. "Having sex with her was my obligation to the fidelity of the TV series. On the other hand, we're out to revolutionize worm-grunting, and intercourse always blunts your edge in a drive to the championship. Remember in *Raging Bull* how Robert De Niro shunned sex and put ice in his underpants before a prizefight? A few orgasms probably won't cost me many pails of worms, but why roll the dice?"

"So when you told her about all the serial killers running around?"

"Trying to let her down easy," said Serge. "During a breakup, you can hem and haw about 'No, it's not you; it's me,' but that can drag on for weeks. Jump right to 'serial killers' and it's a clean break."

"I admire you," said Coleman. "I could never ditch a woman that hot."

"The breakup was best for everyone," said Serge. "Otherwise, instead of becoming worm-grunting kings, you end up in a Pottery Barn picking out boysenberry candles."

"What a nightmare."

"Those places give me the willies," said Serge. "They exclusively sell shit that I didn't even know was happening. Decorative boxes and bowls and baskets full of fragrant twigs and painted wood shavings, and about half the stuff is used to hide the tissues, which is why a runny nose is sheer panic in a woman's pad. 'Dear Jesus, in which one of these fucking things is the Kleenex? Maybe inside this seashell-encrusted octagon. No, that's the monogrammed note cards. What about this faux-driftwood container? No, that's like a thousand Q-tips, which is a separate mystery. Wait, it's obvious, the antique shabby-chic metal tissue box. Crap, just jewelry' ... Until she finally catches you hiding behind a wicker birdcage full of natural sponges, which triggers another of her trick questions: 'Are you back there blowing your nose in one of my monogrammed note cards?'"

"Why not just blow your nose with toilet paper?" asked Coleman.

"Why not just *drink* out of the toilet," said Serge. "See, you have to understand how they think: Everything a man does in a bathroom is wrong, so putting toilet paper on your face probably doesn't top their Internet-profile list of turn-ons. I'll take my chances with note cards."

"That's why they're always knocking on bathroom doors and asking, 'What are you doing in there?'"

"In your case, it's a valid question," said Serge. "You chart whole new realms of forbidden territory that can piss a woman off."

"I'm just doing my thing in there, like when I was at your apartment when you were married," said Coleman. "Suddenly all this screaming."

"Coleman, even I'm dumbfounded by the unfettered spectrum of forensic fluid that you bring into play."

"It is what it is."

"You existentialist, you."

Coleman pointed toward the side of the road. "Weren't you looking for a hardware store?"

"Hardware stores are the opposite of Pottery Barns. If the two ever collided in deep space, they would explode like matter and anti-matter." He pulled into a dirt parking lot and chugged the rest of his coffee. "You always know where you stand in a Home Depot."

"They should call it the No-Bullshit Depot," said Coleman.

"You just might be onto something."

The pair went inside the cramped quarters of a family business that hadn't been inventoried since Eisenhower. Iron chains of various link sizes hung behind the counter. A skeletal man rested against a galvanized bin of roofing nails. "Can I help you fellas?"

"You already have," said Serge.

"No bullshit," said Coleman.

"A rope is a rope," said Serge. "Not something you glue in circles to make a magazine organizer. That's why I had to ditch her after the sex. No time for candles. Do you see where I'm going?"

"Not really."

"Worm-grunting! We need the works."

Ten minutes later, the old man rang them up. "Here are your stakes and irons and a dozen pails. Anything else?"

"Yes," said Serge. "My underpants. Do they sell ice nearby?"

An hour later, a silver Corvette sat on an anonymous shoulder of an unimproved road winding through the Apalachicola National Forest.

One of Florida's most diverse landscapes: hardwood hammocks, sandhills, bogs, prairies, savannahs and swamps. Bears, bats, box turtles, indigo snakes, red woodpeckers. The green, moisture-rich canopies of the lowlands seem almost luminescent, and the yellow fields of carnivorous pitcher plants digest insects and snails. In the dry season, freaky formations of cypress rise atop exposed bases of wooden legs like the walking trees in *Lord of the Rings*.

A long pole rested across Serge's shoulders, several shiny new pails on each end. He trudged on through layers of muck, decaying leaves and water beetles.

Some distance behind, labored breathing. "How many miles have we walked now?"

"Two hundred yards. Catch up!"

Pails crashed to the ground. Then a human thud. "I can't go any farther."

"Dammit." Serge dropped his own gear and helped Coleman to his feet. "This is our first day. You can't quit now! Have some ice."

"I'm not quitting," said Coleman. "I just want to try for worms here."

"But the mother lode is deep in no-man's-land!" Serge pointed onward like a conquistador. "There's no way we'll succeed unless we outlast the competition with a days-long death march into untapped terrain. We must fight the exhaustion and cramping of extremities, never giving in, drawing upon reserves of mental steel!"

"You go on," said Coleman. "I'll wait here."

"Fine, but I'm not splitting the fortune."

Coleman watched his buddy fiercely charge into the wildness. Fifty yards later, Serge set his pails down again. "That's enough marching for today." He hammered a piece of wood into the ground.

A strange vibrating sound greeted Coleman as he moseyed over. "Whatcha doin'?"

"Sliding the rooping iron over the top of my stake." Serge handed him a hammer. "Pound your own in. But not too close to mine, or we'll duplicate effort and cut into the vast quantities of worms that will soon leap into the air. I just hope the prices don't plummet when we flood the market."

After several rest breaks, Coleman finished getting a stob in place and rubbed his iron strip across the top. "How long is this supposed to take?"

Serge wickedly worked his stake like a fiddle player. "From what I've read, the results should be instantaneous and devastating."

Coleman rubbed at a less robust pace. "Serge, why does this forest look so weird?"

Rub, rub, rub. "Because you're used to dense forests, but the trees are spread out in this one, making room for a naturally occurring compost heap that harbors all the other cool stuff like newts and scorpions."

"Scorpions!"

"It's a big forest ... You've stopped rooping."

"Sorry." *Rub, rub, rub.*

An hour later, they both stopped.

"Where are all the worms?" asked Coleman. "I just see ants."

Serge scratched his head with the iron. "Something's definitely wrong. Did I skip a step?"

Coleman began crawling. "What's that thing?"

"Where?" Serge turned. "Sweet victory! It's an earthworm!"

Coleman crawled faster. "It's mine!"

"It's mine!" Serge scrambled on his knees. "It was closer to my stake!"

"It was closer to mine!"

They both dove face-first in the dirt.

"Give him to me!"

"You give him!"

"Let go of my hair!"

"Let go of my finger!"

Then a period of non-verbal yelping and growling.

It stopped. Serge stared solemnly at his hand before looking up. "You broke him."

Coleman stared, too. "Fuck it. I'm putting my half in my bucket."

They sneered at each other and resumed rubbing their respective stakes with the silence of smoldering animosity.

Afternoon passed. The sun drew down, sending long shadows across the forest floor.

A rustling sound. Coleman perked up in alarm. "What was that?"

From behind a cluster of cabbage palms, two other men appeared with overflowing pails that drooped their shoulders. Rubber boots, Levi's, bare chests with a sheen of perspiration and stuck-on dirt. Both had untrimmed beards, but only one wore a baseball cap for transmission parts.

They were personable types. "Ya fellas gruntin'?"

"Yes we are!" Serge beamed.

"Sure got a lotta pails." The one with the ball cap looked inside to see half a worm.

Serge rubbed with all his might. "They call me Clapton of the Rooping Iron."

"Well, ya fellas have a good one." They trudged off.

Coleman stared at the worm piece in the bottom of his bucket. "How the heck did those guys fill all their pails?"

"I've got an idea." Serge gathered up his implements. "Come on!"

SOUTH FLORIDA

Phones rang, copies spit out of the copy machine, people waited in a waiting room. Some had small dogs or sandwiches in their laps.

A receptionist looked up as another customer came in from the street. "She's waiting for you. Last door."

At the end of the short hall was a tight office with two things on the wall: a photo of a little girl with a firefighter, and a diploma. The diploma featured eagles that didn't take any shit.

In the middle of the room was a secondhand desk from a repossessed furniture outlet. Behind it sat a young woman in a frugal pantsuit. She looked at her watch: 12:04.

The door flew open. A livid man in a tennis shirt unleashed the dogs of profanity. The *B-* and *C*-words were the apparent theme. Then he flung a certified check at the desk. It skimmed off the edge and fell to the floor. "You're all alike!"

She picked it up casually, like she had dropped her keys. "Oh, one more thing." She reached in the top drawer. "I have something for you ..."

When people think of a law firm, they often imagine a tall building with coveted corner offices, dozens of young attorneys dreaming of "making partner," and a big imposing name like Shapiro, Heathcoate-Mendacious and Blatt.

But much more common are the modest, elbow-grease firms like this one.

The Miami Women's Legal Aid Clinic.

Yes, many of their clients were women, but more pertinent, all the attorneys were. It wasn't about women's lib, although the office definitely had a liberating current of women solely working together without all the BS frat-boy behavior. When the front doors were locked at the end of the day and the staff worked deep into the night on legal drafts and motions to quash, it was all family talk and laughter, popcorn and yogurt, T-shirts and sweat-pants, almost like a sorority dorm, but without all the BS sorority-girl behavior. Everyone immediately made partner upon joining the firm.

For example, take the woman who just picked a certified check up off the floor. Brook Campanella. She founded the clinic a year back with another young lawyer named Lopez, who had gotten her degree at night school while working in a battered-women's shelter.

At the time, Brook was front-page news. She first made headlines as a rookie lawyer for taking on a too-big-to-fail bank in a no-win case ... and winning. So she was promptly scooped up by one of the most prestigious firms in Fort Lauderdale and immediately assigned second chair in a high-profile class-action mortgage case—mainly because the jury consultant said her cute, freckled face and unassuming petiteness would play well in court. She didn't need glasses but was required to wear ones with plain glass after the consultant put her before focus groups.

Then a funny thing happened on the way to the verdict. Circumstances elevated her to lead attorney in the case, and she won again. What's more, in doing so, she uncovered massive collusion at her own firm. It was an extremely complicated legal matter that would take an entire book to explain, but one well worth buying and reading. Bottom line: A lot of people with silk handkerchiefs in their suit pockets went to prison, and television crews filmed the firm's name being taken down from the building. Brook was in demand again.

But by now, she'd had it with the kind of gilded-edge legal work handed down from skyscrapers.

She met Jacklyn Lopez at a self-defense class. Lopez was the instructor, holding up a pair of bright red training pads that Brook punched with unbridled ferocity and lean results. They got to talking. Turned out Lopez also had a law degree. Then they got to driving.

"What about that place?" asked Brook. "There's a rent sign."

Jacklyn shook her head. "Attached to a gyro shop. Once the smell gets in your clothes ..."

They turned the corner and wandered into Little Haiti. Block after block of available office space. "Is that guy carrying a chicken?" The pair navigated back to Biscayne and headed north.

More discussion as they drove slow, and honking traffic whipped around them. At each red light, people on curbs peddled roses, bottled water, redemption. "Pull over," said Brook.

They ended up in the part of town called Aventura. A dubious area with a transitional economy. It could go either way. But the neighborhood possessed the one bellwether sign that financial analysts always respect.

They just opened a Chipotle.

Brook and Jacklyn stood in the parking lot of an older two-story building. It wasn't originally designed as a strip mall, but guess what? On the bottom floor resided a nail salon and a beauty salon with just enough overlapping service on the menu that it had become the source of brooding tension between a group of Koreans and another group of Koreans.

Between the two businesses was a narrow door with a glass window leading to a warped wooden staircase. The two women looked up at a leaf-clogged rain gutter. Then they looked down again at the door—the cliché entrance of a law office. Only the gold lettering was missing. Brook grabbed the rental sign off the mailbox, and they fist-bumped ...

... That was then, this was now. The new women's law firm accepted the kind of cases that were less lucrative and more fulfilling. Like the one that began on a recent Wednesday morning.

Just after nine o'clock, the receptionist looked up. "You may go in now. Last door."

An elderly Hispanic woman was helped into Brook's office by her granddaughter. The attorney rushed around her desk to pull over an additional chair. The old woman didn't speak a word of English. Her granddaughter spoke better than most Americans, because she was one, although certain other Americans with mangled grammar weren't entirely convinced.

Brook opened a folder on her desk. "You mentioned on the phone a landlord dispute. Something about the security deposit and last month's rent?"

"That's right," said the granddaughter, named Danielle. But she answered to Danny. "They kept it all, citing cleaning and repair costs from excessive wear and tear."

"May I see what documentation they provided?"

"They didn't give my grandmother anything," said Danny. "It was all verbal. When I called to request an itemized expense statement, they just laughed and asked if I was joking."

Brook sat back. "No paperwork?"

"This is common in our area," said Danny. "They expect people who are scraping by to just move on and not challenge it because they have to make ends meet. And an eight-hundred-dollar dispute isn't worth it to most lawyers. But my grandmother cleans houses for the kind of people who are screwing her, and that money means the world. Which is why I know her apartment was immaculate when she left."

"I wish we had photos," said Brook.

Danny handed over her cell phone.

"What's this?" asked the lawyer.

"Photos," said Danny. "I took them when she moved out, just in case."

"Prudent." Brook closed the folder. "You already signed the needed paperwork, so I won't take up any more of your time." She stood. "This is straightforward. I'll be back in touch tomorrow."

They thanked her profusely and left.

Near the end of the day, Brook opened the folder again and dialed a number.

"Yeah?" Someone chewing on the other end.

"My name is Brook Campanella, and I'm an attorney representing one of your former tenants."

"Who?" A loud TV sound in the background from a sports program.

"Brook Campanella. Mrs. Dominguez retained me—"

"You a lawyer?" *Chomp, chomp, chomp.*

"Yes, and I think we can quickly clear this up. You kept her security deposit and last month's rent."

"Probably for cleaning and repairs." *Chomp, chomp.* "That's standard."

"Actually we can't be sure," said Brook. "We have no receipts for any work done."

"Christ, do you have any idea the condition these people leave their apartments in?"

"*These people?*" asked Brook.

From the other end of the line, a second voice: "Who is it?"

The first man's voice turned away from the phone. "Some ambulance chaser for one of our tenants."

"Tell him to eat shit and die."

"It's a chick."

"Hand me the nachos."

The sports sounds from the television became aggressively violent.

"Excuse me," said Brook. "I have photographs of the condition of the apartment. If we could just talk—"

"Listen, sweetie, since you sound kind of young, I'll be polite. I got *Ultimate Fighting* on pay-per-view and you're costing me money, so if you don't mind ..."

"Actually I do mind," said Brook. "I always try to avoid escalating legal action. If you could either provide me with a detailed expense sheet ..."

The man spoke away from the phone again. "She wants an expense sheet. Can you believe this broad?" Derisive laughter.

"Or a refund in full," said Brook. "In that case, I'd be willing to waive my legal fee. It's really not worth it for you to—"

Click.

Chapter 3

THE APALACHICOLA

A shiny Corvette Stingray skidded on and off the road as it raced through a section of the national forest known as Tate's Hell.

Coleman clutched the passenger-door frame with both hands. "Why are you driving so fast?"

"Because I can't wait to see if my breakthrough technique works!"

The sports car found a parking space in the dirt, and Serge raced around to the trunk. "Coleman! Get out here! I need you to carry some stuff!"

"Can I rest first? We just got here."

"Rest from what? You've just been sitting there the whole drive from Tallahassee."

"It was tiring." He reluctantly climbed out. "And why did we have to go all that way just to turn around and come back here?"

"I had to go to the nearest big city because there's no place around here that carries what I needed for my X-Treme Gruntinator," said Serge. "Because nobody's ever thought of it! ... Hold this ... and this ... and this ..."

"It's getting heavy."

Serge slammed the trunk. "Stop complaining and follow me."

They marched a few hundred yards to the same spot as the day before. Their stakes were still pounded into the dirt. Serge ignored them and went to work with a posthole digger.

Coleman sat on the ground and pulled a flask from his pocket. "Where'd you get this idea anyway?"

"I went on the Internet to study the techniques of bona fide sixth-generation grunters and found all these great video clips." Serge rammed the digger deep in the hole and dumped out another clod of dirt. "The guys were regular Mozarts. Their secret was a deft touch with the rooping iron that produced a specific-frequency metallic wheezing sound. I realized my quest now required dedication to arduous effort, until I thought: 'Bullshit on effort. I just want success. That's America!'"

Serge dumped a final lump of soil and tossed the digger aside. "Hand me that box."

"It's heavy again."

Serge ripped the container open sideways. "This is the key to the whole operation." Insulated wires dangled out the tip of a long insulated pole. At the other end was a high-tech oval bulb.

Coleman grimaced as he knocked back a slug of bottom-shelf bourbon. "What the heck is that thing?"

"Nature enthusiasts and the U.S. Navy use hydrophones to listen to majestic whales or enemy submarines, depending on which lifestyle they signed up for." Serge wrapped the bulb in thick Mylar and sank it five feet into the ground. "Most hydrophones today are passive and just listen, but this is an *active* hydrophone. It *puts* sound in the water. Like those old war movies where ships 'ping' to find subs."

"Who wants to do that?"

"Whoever just up and feels like making the water noisy. Again, another not-thought-of opportunity like gold in the streets that everyone walks by." Serge filled in the hole around the device. "Basically the same principle as those underwater speakers they use each year in the Keys for their annual scuba diver concert."

More boxes were opened. Serge pulled out a hefty battery pack and amplifier. He intricately connected them with a series of cables that led through the leaves to a lawn chair.

Coleman raised a hand. "But this isn't water."

"Precisely," said Serge. "Any scientist knows that solids conduct sound even better than liquids."

"Really?"

"Think of those old western movies where Indians put ears to the ground so they could hear the hoofbeats of horses miles away that told them the White Man was about to shit on the whole program."

"I get it," said Coleman. "Like the time when I was with you, and I was like super stoned, and you said that if I put my ear on the rail of some train tracks, I could hear the locomotive coming. So I tried it, and you were right!"

"Except you don't do it when you can also *see* the locomotive."

"Good thing those people were there to drag me off the tracks." Another slug of bourbon. Coleman's neck suddenly swung sideward. "What the hell was that noise?"

"Just more rustling in the leaves." Serge settled into his piece of patio furniture as a familiar pair of men emerged in rubber boots and crusty jeans.

The locals set down brimming pails. "You fellas havin' it another try?"

"I never heard the words 'give up,'" said Serge.

"Good for ya." Then they noticed the scientific pole sticking out of the ground, along with the rest of the equipment and all the wires. One of them tugged at the end of his beard. "Whatcha fixin' on doin'?"

"Get ready to witness history." Serge grabbed the end of the last cable, opened a laptop on his legs and plugged it in.

The locals glanced at each other and grinned—*a computer and a lawn chair?*—except it wasn't condescension, but more like amused reaction to watching a likable child do something silly. "So whatcha got cookin' there with that fancy thang?"

"Might want to stand back," said Serge.

"It gonna hurt us?"

"No." Serge tapped the keyboard. "You might damage the product."

And with that, the ground began to come alive like a deep-toned tuning fork.

Two pairs of rubber boots high-stepped it in reverse. They recognized the sound—just never heard it coming up from beneath. And at such volume. "Lord above! What in the name of creation?"

Serge continued tapping the keyboard. "I downloaded some high-end equalizer software, plus the worm-grunting Internet videos, then enhanced the audio. Behold ..."

"Jesus, Mary and all the saints!"

The entire forest floor became a living canvas of earthworms. And caterpillars and centipedes and snakes and moles and everything else unmoored from its natural bearings—like during the midday total eclipse that hit the Okeefenokee Swamp straddling the Florida-Georgia line on March 7, 1970. Serge added that last detail. "It was televised. You can look it up."

"Take your word for it, mister."

Then came the predators: swarms of birds, and smaller mammals as the food chain went into overdrive.

One of the old grunters pulled a Colt revolver and fired it in the air, scattering the wildlife that threatened Serge's harvest. "Never thought I'd see so many dad-gum earthworms if I lived to be Methuselah!"

"Your own pails are already full," said Serge. "So why don't you grab a couple of ours?"

"You brought up the worms," said Beard number one.

"They're rightly yours," said Beard two.

Serge shook his head. "We're visitors, and it's about respect. This is *your home*."

"But it's a national forest open to the public."

Serge looked over twin appearances that suggested long lives of abiding devotion to the land. He repeated himself with emphasis. "This is your home."

"Well then, let's fill 'em on up before the little buggers change their minds."

"He's Willard," said the other, bending down for worms. "I'm Jasper. Hope you fellers worked up an appetite, 'cuz you're gonna have the best meal south of the Mason when we get back to the 'stead."

"That's awfully nice," said Serge. "But it's really not necessary."

"Won't take no for an answer," said Willard. "You folks got a thirst for some mountain dew?"

"Not really," said Serge. "Soda's just empty calories."

"Naw!" Jasper laughed. "We're talkin' canned heat, John Barleycorn."

"You mean the classic album by Traffic?" asked Serge.

"Sheet, man, I'm talkin' *moonshine*."

"Hell yeah!" shouted Coleman.

"Down, boy." Willard hiked his overalls. "I say that one's got some spring in his paws."

Serge grabbed his own pail. "Wait till later."

MIAMI WOMEN'S LEGAL AID CLINIC

Brook glanced at the blank check. She thought about everything that had led to this moment, and the moments soon to come with the irate landlord standing on the other side of her desk.

He'd hung up on her during that first phone call. So a week later she'd dialed again.

"What now!" This time hockey play-offs in the background.

"Mr. Gosling, this is Brook Campanella. By the return-mail receipt I just got, I can see you received my certified letter. Do you understand it?"

"Yeah, you have mental problems. What's this thirty-five hundred dollars?"

"The price now includes mental anguish and my legal fees," said Brook.

"Over a measly eight-hundred-dollar deposit?"

"This is still bargain basement in the legal world," said Brook. "The elevator's only going north from here."

A semi-intoxicated voice in the background. "Tell her to stick it up her twat."

"Mr. Gosling," said Brook. "You can drop off a check here, or I can come to you. But it has to be this evening. Otherwise tomorrow morning I'll be forced to go to the courthouse—"

"And you'll *what*, sweetie? Damn! I can always spot one!"

"One?" asked Brook.

"Men issues. You seriously need to get laid!"

Click.

Another week went by. This time it was Brook's phone that rang. She checked the caller ID before answering. "I see I've gotten your attention."

"Fifteen thousand dollars!"

"My client's anguish—and my legal costs—grow by the hour," said Brook.

"You filed a lawsuit? You're suing *me*!"

"Don't forget the fine print," said Brook. "I intend to locate other former tenants of yours with the help of my client's granddaughter. Then during discovery, I'm going to subpoena your accounting records for the last seven years, and if we find a pattern of bad-faith refusal-to-remit deposits, we're talking about a class action with treble damages. But there's a downside for me, too. I'll have the hassle of finding a real estate agent to liquidate your apartment buildings, which the court will seize."

"Motherf— ... Do you have any idea the type of person you're dealing with?"

"Yes, but you don't," said Brook. "Now let me paint by the numbers for you. If a certified check isn't on my desk by precisely noon tomorrow, everything moves forward and you'll regret it for the rest of your life. Feel free to call any lawyer in town. I'm confident they'll all tell you not to be late." She set the receiver in its cradle.

Click.

So now we're back up to speed ...

Mr. Gosling continued fuming in front of Brook's desk, then cleared his throat for a big, hocking spit on the floor. "Happy now?"

"Not yet." She stood up and handed him a stapled set of pages.

Gosling looked in his hands. "What's this?"

"You just saved me the cost of process delivery."

"A what?"

"Consider yourself officially served," said Brook. "You voluntarily took possession of those documents."

"I'll deny I got them."

"I have a witness."

Jacklyn Lopez smiled and waved from a chair in the corner.

Gosling glanced down again. "You're *still* going to sue me? You're subpoenaing my bank statements?"

Brook tapped her wristwatch. "You came in at twelve oh four. I said twelve sharp."

"Four minutes! You can't be sane! That's—that's—that's ... just not fair!"

Brook looked over her shoulder at Jacklyn. "He said I needed to get laid."

Jacklyn shrugged. "Always works for me."

Gosling threw out his arms in panic. "Wait, wait, wait! ... You got a bird in the hand! That's a fifteen-thousand-dollar check. Don't you want the money?"

"Absolutely," said the attorney. "I intend to deposit it this afternoon."

"Well then, okay." Gosling began to uncoil. "Case over. And very funny bluffing with me like that."

"I wasn't bluffing." Brook stuck the check in her purse. "The case has only begun."

"That's where you're wrong," said the landlord, re-inflating with smugness. "I know a little about the law, too. By cashing that check, you're releasing me from all liability." He turned to leave. "I hope you choke on it. Go fuck yourself!"

"Mrs. Dominguez," said Brook.

Gosling turned back around. "What?"

"Cashing the check ends claims from Mrs. Dominguez," said Brook. "Not other new clients I'll be calling after lunch to start the class action."

"You're still actually going through with this?"

Brook looked at her watch. "It's now twelve ten."

He marched forward. "Then give me my check back."

"Sorry."

"I'll stop payment!"

"It's certified." Brook snapped her purse shut. "And after your financials arrive at my office, you'll be needing *two* lawyers."

"Why?"

"Civil and criminal," said Brook. "This kind of fraud conviction brings ten years in Raiford ... Jacklyn, isn't that right?"

"Unless they stack sentences per count."

Brook slapped herself in the forehead. "How did I miss that? He could be facing centuries."

Gosling stood in the cone of a disorienting emotional tornado. All color fled his face, then immediately flooded back with volcanic rage until he was almost purple. His eyes turned into something from a devil-possession movie.

"I'll kill you!"

He dove over the desk with outstretched hands clutching for Brook's neck.

She hadn't seen *that* coming. He was so fast his fingertips brushed her throat, and she crashed backward. But there was something even faster than his lunge.

Jacklyn.

In one fluid, blinding motion, she got a forearm around his neck, twisted one of his wrists behind his back in a restraint hold, and pinned him to the floor.

"You're hurting me! Get off!"

"As soon as the police arrive."

He struggled, and she twisted his wrist harder.

"Ahhhhhh!"

The police took statements from the women before leading the future ex-landlord away in cuffs.

Brook straightened a photo of a firefighter on the wall. Then she looked at her colleague—only slightly larger in stature than herself—and shook her head in amazement. "I still don't know how you do that."

It wasn't much of a mystery. Besides being a self-defense instructor, Jacklyn was a former NCAA wrestling All-American. She hadn't been sitting in Brook's office simply to witness the serving of papers.

Jacklyn smiled. "Want to celebrate by getting a pedicure?" She looked toward the floor. "The nail place is just downstairs."

"So is the beauty salon," said Brook. "It could be seen as taking sides."

"And?"

"It's starting to get ugly."

Chapter 4

THAT EVENING

It was not a usual sight in rural North Florida: a vintage silver Corvette pulling up to a bare-wood cracker house on the edge of Sopchoppy near the forest. It had a sagging porch roof atop four-by-fours. Two bearded men in overalls sat out front in rocking chairs they'd fashioned from cut pine.

"See you fellas made it."

"Wouldn't miss a meal like you described for the world," said Serge.

"Moonshine!" said Coleman.

They all headed inside the cabin to a single large room. Beds with chipped antique frames in back, dining table up front, and the whole space filled with a medley of aromas from the gas stove.

Jasper stirred a cast-iron pot. "Didn't know what you had a hankerin' for, so we made a little of everything. But I'm betting you'll like everything."

"How can I help?" asked Serge.

Jasper pointed with a wooden spoon the size of a boat paddle. "Venison could use a flippin' in that skillet."

"You got it," said Serge. "What's in the other pan?"

"Snapper."

"Surf and turf," said Serge.

"The kind we like up here. Willard's my brother. Probably guessed that. He's divorced. I never could take to moss ... Hey, Willard, break it out."

Willard walked over to the gun rack and reached inside one of the ammo drawers for a mason jar.

"What's that?" asked Coleman.

"The white lightnin' you been lickin' your chops about."

"Now you're talking!"

Serge flipped the meat. "Let the reindeer games begin."

"You boys just make yourself at home ..."

Behind them, Willard poured clear liquid into a pair of mismatched coffee mugs. "Easy with this stuff if ya ain't used to it."

"Don't worry about me." Coleman took a stiff pull.

"What do ya think?" asked Willard.

No answer. Coleman stood perfectly still, surprised eyes indicating an internal security breach. Then he suffered a brutal coughing fit that brought tears and drool.

"You better set yourself down."

Coleman waved him off and pounded his chest, then jiggled his coffee mug, signaling for another pour.

"You sure?"

Coleman nodded firmly.

"Damn," Willard said as he unscrewed the jar again. "Hey, Jasper, this one's got some tough bark on him."

Jasper set down his wooden spoon and turned the stove's burners to simmer. "Grab plates. We serve ourselves around here."

Soon they were all seated around the dining table with checkered place mats. The brothers tucked bibs in their bib overalls. They bowed their heads.

Coleman reached for the basket of buttermilk biscuits, but Serge slapped his hand.

"Ow. What?"

Serge gave him a hard look and pointed at the brothers.

"Oh."

They lowered their own heads.

Willard said the grace, seeing he was a volunteer at Sunday school. It was a good grace, from Ecclesiastes.

"... *A time to plant, a time to reap ...*"

Coleman whispered sideways. "Isn't this the Byrds?"

"Shhhh!"

"*Amen.*" Willard raised his head. "Dig in before someone else does."

Coleman grabbed the mason jar.

"What an incredible spread," said Serge. "There's the meat and fish, and this must be fried okra and collard greens." He cut into something else with a fork, blew on the steaming bite, and popped it in his mouth. "Mmmmmm!" He closed his eyes. "Tastes like heaven. What is it?"

"Swamp cabbage patties," Willard said with his own mouthful. "Panhandle truffles."

"Never heard of it," said Serge. "And I'm intensely comprehensive in that regard."

"Not surprisin'," said Jasper. "Even country restaurants don't have a likin' for the words 'swamp cabbage' on their menu, so they call it heart of palm, which is the tasty soft bulb you cut out of the trunk just below the base of the leaves. Cabbage palmetto, also known as—"

"Sabal palm," said Serge. "The state tree. They probably would have picked the coconut palm, but needed something that also grew in Florida's northern latitudes."

"You sure nuff know your facts."

Serge took another bite. "I'm getting a party in my mouth, but I can't place all the guests."

"Chop up the hearts with some onion, add a beaten egg, lots of pepper and bacon fat," said Jasper. "'Cept I just also add the bacon itself 'cuz life's too short. Then some flour makes the patties."

Something knocked Serge's arm, and his fork fell to the floor.

"Sorry," said Coleman, passing the mason jar to Willard.

Jasper broke off tender flakes from the snapper that still had its head. "Been meanin' to ask, and feel free to tell me it's none of my business, but how exactly did you spook all those worms with those gizmos?"

Serge wiped his mouth with his bib. "Happy to tell ..." And he slowly laid out the entire process.

Willard whistled. "That's some technique. But it doesn't make money sense if you don't mind me sayin'. We just get two sawbucks a pail, and that equipment must have broke the bank."

"It did," said Serge. "But in business, it's all about taking the long view. Yeah, it'll take years to pay off, but after that the profits just gush."

"And how long you plan on workin' these parts for worms?"

"Couple more days, till the next episode." Serge speared an okra.

A knock at the door.

"Forgot to mention," said Willard. "We might have company." He finished chewing and hollered, *"You know to come right in!"*

First they heard the screen door. Then the proper one creaked open.

Three of the men politely jumped to their feet. Serge yanked Coleman up by the arm.

"Boys," said Jasper, "I'd like you to meet our sister, Lou Ellen ... Lou Ellen, these nice fellas are Serge and Coleman, some of the best grunters we ever laid eyes on. Even let us have four pails of their haul ..."

Coleman whispered again. *"Awkward."*

Serge quickly grabbed a chair from the side of the room and brought it to the table for Lou Ellen to sit. "Listen, about the other day. I got an emergency call—"

"No need to explain."

Willard aimed a knife. "You two's acquainted?"

"Met briefly at the grocery," said their sister, lowering her voice: "And the high school."

Serge quickly slapped the table. "Say! How 'bout I fix you a plate, Lou Ellen?" He got up and the rest of the gang joined him at the stove for second helpings.

A half hour later, the guys all threw in the towel, literally. White bibs tossed on empty plates. Stomachs patted. Leaning back in chairs. "I'm stuffed." "Why'd I eat so much?" "It was good there for a while." "More moonshine, please."

Jasper broke out the toothpicks and passed the box.

"Thanks," said Serge. "All this reminds me of *Route 66*. Dinner at the house of friendly locals who take kindly to strangers."

"I remember that show," said Willard. "Every town they went to, those guys were screwing everything that wasn't nailed down, but they couldn't let on too much back then."

Coleman: *"Awwwk-ward."*

"Shut up with that."

Willard held his mason jar to unfocused eyes and poured the remnants in two mugs.

Coleman drained one. "So what do you guys do around here after drinking moonshine?"

"Only one thing *to* do," said Willard. "Shoot guns!"

"Eeee-*hah*!" said Coleman.

They stumbled back to the gun rack and crashed into it. Rifles toppled, along with Willard. Coleman got on his knees. "I'll pick up the bullets ... Here, bullet, bullet ..."

Willard reached in a drawer. "I got us another mason jar. Let's go, buddy ..."

The pair swerved out the screen door into the night.

Serge's head slowly rotated toward Jasper. "You know how sometimes when everyone is standing around in horror, and you wish you could turn back the clock to a certain point in time? This reeks of one of those points."

"They'll be fine." Jasper made a backhanded wave of assuredness. "Willard took a gun safety class."

A musical ring-tone emanated from an unseen source. Joni Mitchell's "Big Yellow Taxi." "That's mine." Lou Ellen reached in her purse. "Hello? Oh, hi, Joline ... What's the matter? You sound— ... Slow down. I can't understand a word ... Yeah, uh-huh ... Hold on a sec." She covered the phone. "I need to take this somewhere private."

She headed outside, where the evening air was filled with happy shouts, singing and gunfire.

Willard held up an empty bottle and turned to Coleman. "See if you can hit this."

"Okay."

"No, let me throw it first ..."

It became still inside the cabin as Serge and Jasper sat back in the silence of being drugged by food.

A rapid-fire burst from the Browning level-action rifles echoed across the countryside. A scream. The screen door flew open. Lou Ellen ran inside.

"What is it?" asked Serge. "Who got shot?"

"Nobody."

"Then why are you shaking?"

She grabbed a chair. "Jasper, it's Aunt Maybelline who lives in Port Saint Joe."

"What's happened to her? Is she okay?"

"We don't know," said Lou Ellen. "We can't get in touch with her."

Jasper jumped to his feet. "Call the *po*-lice! Aunt May might'n be lyin' on the bathroom floor with a busted hip!"

"It's not like that," said Lou Ellen. "The guy from the assisted-living service hasn't let Joline talk to Aunt May in nearly a month. Keeps saying she's not feeling well."

"She phone the service office?" asked Jasper.

"She did," said Lou Ellen. "The man taking care of her quit the company a few weeks ago. He told Joline he'll just be working with May now."

Outside: *Bang, bang, bang ...*

"Sounds hinky," said Jasper.

"Joline felt the same way, so she did call the cops. They talked to the guy, and all his professional certificates were up-to-date. They also talked to Aunt May and she told them she was happy ... But Joline still didn't feel right, so she went to the bank because she's joint co-signer on all of May's accounts. They said she no longer had access to them."

"Why?"

"All they could say was that new documents had been filed by my aunt, which took Joline's name off everything."

Bang, bang, bang. "Yahoo!" Bang, bang, bang ...

Serge held up a hand for permission to speak. "I hate to be indelicate, but may I inquire as to the state of your aunt's mental faculties?"

"Early stages of dementia," said Lou Ellen. "Maybe middle by now."

Serge nodded with sadness. "Unfortunately, I've seen this one too many times before."

"What are you talking about?"

"It usually starts out on the level," Serge continued. "But temptation is too great for some people. Whoever this guy is, he probably assessed her condition and started poking around her checkbook and other stuff while she was napping. Then he persuaded your aunt to replace Joline's name with his on all the accounts, giving him power of attorney, and finally cutting off all contact with her relatives."

"Then we definitely have to go back to the cops," said Jasper.

"It's a little more complicated than that," said Serge. "If this is playing out like I think, he drafted a bunch of completely legal contracts charging exorbitant fees for services rendered. I'd bet the farm that he's already cleaned her out."

"But if that's true, why is he still there?"

"Why not? If he doesn't have much drive in life, he's living there free in a spare bedroom, cashing her Social Security check each month, and propping his feet up on empty cases of Mallomars."

"And military benefits from her late husband, Homer," said Lou Ellen.

"Plus I'm sure her life insurance policy has a new beneficiary," said Serge. "No, going to the authorities isn't an option. He might end up in jail, but it won't help recover what's already been lost."

"But how can you be so sure of this just from that short phone call?" asked Lou Ellen. "How do you know all the details?"

"Wish it weren't true, but this is such a common scam in Florida that the authorities have trouble keeping up," said Serge. "Even worse, they have a harder time prosecuting the cases they do uncover because these lowlifes specifically target the elderly with health issues that make them unreliable on the witness stand. Just when you thought they couldn't drop the bar any further, this new breed of criminal comes along with no conscience at all. The old, young and weak are the first ones they go after. Call me old school, but when I pick a target ... well, it's best just to leave it at that."

"So what do we do?" asked Willard.

"*You* don't do anything," said Serge. "I've got this one."

Bang, bang, bang. "*Yippeeeee!*" *Bang, bang, bang. BOOM.* "*Oops.*"

The screen door flew open.

Willard and Coleman tumbled inside.

Jasper stood over them. "What in tarnation?"

The pair on the floor just pointed at each other in blame.

Serge walked to the window. "By any chance is there a place nearby that sells propane?"

Chapter 5

THE NEXT MORNING

Workers scaled tall ladders again to reach the catwalk along the front of a billboard. Which meant no winners had been picked in last night's lottery drawing, and the jackpot had rolled over once more. The workers pulled down old numbers and put up new. Most of their signs were in blighted neighborhoods.

Down below, predictable lines snaked out of convenience stores, and TV crews broadcast the excitement across the greater metropolitan area ...

Just over a decade ago, there were a couple of back-to-back hurricane seasons that made even lifelong Floridians go *"Damn."* For the first time ever, the weather service ran out of pre-chosen names for storms, and had to go deep into the Greek alphabet before the year was out.

Now it was lottery season, and it was the same story. Never had the state experienced such a conga line of massive jackpots. It was all about random odds. Right after one massive payout made landfall, nobody would win for several more weeks, and the next jackpot kept gathering force until it reached dizzying wind speed. Then *bam*! Another winner, and the whole mathematical process began again. Already this season there had been five jackpots with nine or ten digits after the dollar sign. And since the state had increased drawings to twice a week, the fever was constant. Billboard companies loved it.

The last winner came a month ago. The press conference featured balloons and one of those giant checks the size of a door. The Florida State Lottery gleefully introduced its latest mega-jackpot winner, an eighty-year-old woman with a poodle who chose the lump-sum payment.

Viewers at home thinking: *It's always an eighty-year-old with a poodle. What a waste.*

Lottery officials lowered the microphone for the diminutive winner: "I'm buying a speedboat."

Right after an old woman and a poodle named Bubbles set out to sea, the big numbers began ascending again. Lines spilled out of the convenience stores, and regular customers couldn't buy their Red Bull and vitamin water. TV crews forgot there was other news.

As they say, Miami is the capital of the Latin world, and local newscasts were picked up throughout Central and South America. Just below the isthmus of Panama, a satellite dish rose from the rooftop of a jungle chalet high up the side of a mountain. Inside, a group of men sat around a dining table. On the wall was a bank of video screens from a dozen security cameras. A larger screen showed a reporter interviewing hopeful people in Florida.

"It rolled over again," said one of the men at the table, sipping a glass of French wine. He looked out the window at a nearby plateau that had been cleared for a private airstrip. "When should we go?"

The man at the head of the table raised a fork with a thick chunk of prime steak from Argentina. "Wait until it rolls one more time."

Armed guards marched past the windows outside. The men resumed dining without discussion ...

... Back in Miami, billboard workers climbed down from ladders and drove up the street to their next sign. This time it was a neighborhood so bleak that even the convenience stores had cleared out.

One of those abandoned buildings sat boarded up, overgrown with weeds and loitering. The gas pumps were now just concrete oval bases. An old man with a brown paper bag sat on a citrus crate. He removed his socks, turned them inside out, and put them back on.

Surrounding the shuttered store were vacant lots of broken liquor bottles, condoms, vials and RC Cola cans. A Miami police car was parked in the middle of one such lot, pointed at the street. The car remained motionless for hours. No need to even patrol. Along this stretch of Biscayne Boulevard, crime had delivery service.

The reason for the particular placement of the police car was across the street: a feckless rectangular building of beige bricks, where the only window facing the street was a long horizontal slit filled with neon signs for beer brands.

The Sawgrass Lounge, established 1949.

Back then, it was a happening place. Sterling martini shakers, coat and ties, marble-top horseshoe bar. Today, it was still happening, just in another direction.

More people were outside the lounge than in. Mingling, exchanging esoteric handshakes, whispering in ears. It was like a casting call for *Starsky & Hutch* street villains, the kind that end up being chased by the cops and always get caught after running down a dead-end alley and tackled trying to climb a chain-link fence. The gang outside the Sawgrass was not in mint condition. More bandages than the general population. Half had just slept something off, and the rest were trying to come down. Some milled out front, and others conspired in an alley: "We have to do something about that chain-link fence." But they all had one thing in common: keeping an eye on the police car across the street.

Several miles away, a black Suburban with tinted windows cruised south on Biscayne. A man in the backseat wore headphones and adjusted dials on an expensive-looking piece of electronics with a green oscilloscope. "Raise your arms up. I need to run this under your shirt."

"What is it?" asked Reevis.

"Lapel mike. But we need to clamp it backward so it can't be seen." The sound man snapped it in place. "This tiny transmitter goes in your pants pocket, but make sure the wires aren't hanging out."

Reevis grew more skeptical by the minute. "I've been with you guys three hours now, and you still won't tell me about the story I'm supposed to be working on. You just kept filming me walking through the middle of the newsroom at the cable station. Must have been at least twenty times. Necktie on, tie off, jacket over the shoulder, sometimes running, sometimes yelling ahead to someone who wasn't there to 'hold the elevator,' which also wasn't there. It's a one-floor building."

"Trust us," Nigel said from the front seat. "Capturing reality is an art."

"Will you just tell me what I'm supposed to be investigating?"

"In due time," said Nigel. "I've found it's best to wait until the last moment to let my performers in on the key elements. That way we catch a fresh reaction from you just as you're thrown into peril."

"Peril?"

"Nothing to worry about." The sound man twisted a knob. "We've done this a million times. Taken every precaution to eliminate the peril. That gives us a safety margin to provoke peril."

Reevis sighed and stared at the ceiling.

Nigel grabbed the dashboard and leaned closer to the windshield. "Slow down. We're coming up on it now." Then he turned to Reevis. "Here's the story. Cold case. Woman went missing four years ago without a trace, body never found. We couldn't have asked for a better crime to kick off the series."

"Why's that?" asked Reevis.

"Police came up with three equal murder suspects," said Nigel. "That's essential for a classic whodunit. In this case it's the husband, a short-order cook who was seeing her on the side, and the semi-employed landscaper found driving her car after she went missing. All extremely suspicious and guilty-acting."

Reevis got out his notebook. "How were they acting guilty?"

"They haven't yet," said Nigel. "But they will when we surprise them with our camera. Their eyes always give them away."

"That's out of context," said Reevis. "You can make anyone look guilty that way."

"I told you we know what we're doing."

"No," said Reevis. "I mean it's not ethical."

"Glad you brought that up," said Nigel. "Ethics are our top priority! That's why we save the footage and only air the 'guilty eyes' shots of the people we decide are guilty."

Reevis took a deep breath. "Back up and tell me more about the missing woman's car."

Nigel flipped open a briefcase on his lap and held up a document. "Police located it at three a.m. with a Dominican behind the wheel after it was pulled over for a broken taillight. Real suspicious type. Kept changing his story. First he said he was partying with the woman and that she had lent it to him. Then after they discovered a trunk full of blood, he changed his story and said he found it abandoned outside this sketchy bar with the keys still in the ignition."

Reevis continued scribbling in his pad. "Did the police ever charge him?"

"He was the prime suspect for the first week," said Nigel. "Then suddenly the cops ruled him out and started looking at the boyfriend. Don't you find that suspicious? I think we should pump up the angle of police corruption."

"Slow down," said Reevis. "I haven't even started looking into this. Let me go through all the official files."

Nigel shook his head. "No good for TV." He handed Reevis a sheet of paper.

"What's this?"

"The script of how you're going to break the case wide open!"

The reporter handed it back. "My editor said I didn't have to change how I worked—that I could investigate cases the way they taught me in journalism school."

"And that's exactly what we were hoping you'd say!" Nigel exclaimed. "We want you to bring integrity and respect to the show. We promise to let you investigate as you see fit."

"Doesn't sound like it."

"This is a different medium." Nigel snipped the end off a large Honduran cigar. "Sometimes we have to start filming with the conclusion and do the investigating later."

"Why?"

"Lighting." Nigel puffed the cigar.

"You can't be serious."

"All we're asking is that you work with us," said Nigel. "The only hard piece of evidence is the car, so we'll start there and pick up the trail. Go into the lounge and see if you can find anyone who remembers anything. The car, the Dominican, the woman. This is a real regulars' place, same people on the same stools for years. Someone in there has answers."

"Okay, now it's finally beginning to sound like legitimate journalism." Reevis nodded. "I can do that."

"We knew you were our man." A tinted window rolled down. A large, high-def video camera pointed out the window, followed by puffs of cigar smoke.

The Suburban pulled into an empty lot at an abandoned convenience store and parked next to a police car. The loitering crowd on the opposite sidewalk stopped and stared in unison at the huge lens aimed at them. Some shouted at the SUV. Rude hand gestures.

Nigel turned around again. "Here's the deal: I called ahead to the lounge, and they said they didn't want anything to do with TV or interviews. So you're going to lead the way, and we'll come in right behind you with the camera and lights, guns a-blazing until they throw us out."

"That's not journalism," said Reevis. "What about getting answers to a cold case?"

"Later," said Nigel.

"Lighting," said the cameraman, lacing up running shoes. "We need a quick strike."

"Stop!" said Reevis. "Everyone just stop! Forget the lighting and peril. I know this turf, and that is not the kind of place you want to barge into with a TV camera."

"Sure it is," said Nigel. "The footage can't miss. Just look at the joint."

"Yes, look at it," said Reevis. "This isn't the lounge at the Hyatt, where security guards professionally ask you to leave. It's not *that* we'll be thrown out, but *how* we'll be thrown out."

"There's a police car right next to us," said Nigel. "What can go wrong?"

The police officers received a domestic disturbance call and drove away.

"I propose a wild new concept," said Reevis. "Let me go in alone without all the camera lights and see if I can talk to them politely."

"They were quite adamant on the phone, screaming in fact. 'No goddamn reporters!'" said Nigel. "But we need footage, even if it's just getting tossed out. *Especially* if it's just getting tossed out."

"I do this for a living," said Reevis. "I might even be able to persuade them to allow your camera in there. What's the harm in letting me try?"

"Except the footage won't be fresh, in the moment."

"But your camera won't get destroyed."

Nigel thought a moment and formed a cynical smile. "This could work even better. We'll stay parked here and film you going in. Then we'll film ourselves in the car—which we'll refer to as Mobile Command Central—listening while you capture salty dialogue on your hidden microphone."

"I can't do that," said Reevis.

"Sure you can," said Nigel. "Nobody will see it, especially in the dark."

"You're not understanding," said Reevis. "Florida is a two-party consent state for recording conversations. We'll be committing a felony."

Nigel quickly looked it up on his smartphone. "He's right about the statute. And we would never, ever want to break the law ... Okay, Reevis, we'll defer to your expertise. But we still need to get something on camera later."

"Great."

"Hold on," said the sound man, reaching in a bag. "Here's your gun."

"Put that stupid thing away," said Reevis. He departed the SUV.

The camera poked back out the window as the young reporter headed for the lounge's entrance. The sound man reached for a knob.

"What are you doing?" asked Nigel.

"Killing his microphone."

"No," said Nigel. "Leave it on."

THREE HUNDRED MILES NORTH

U.S. Highway 98 is the scenic route along the coast of the Florida Panhandle. You might call it the hurricane-fodder coast. But when the Gulf of Mexico isn't whipping havoc ashore, it is a pleasing panorama of gentle waves, sea oats, and sugar-white dunes rolling for miles like God's own sand trap. Stilt houses are tastefully spread out along the beach so as not to block the view. Then it's blocked: condos, mega-hotels, spring breakers and garish neon wedding-cake buildings so mammoth that it's hard to fathom they primarily sell beachwear and boogie boards.

But let's back up. There's a stretch along 98 that remains one of the state's few unpopulated coasts, from Alligator Harbor westward to Carrabelle, past St. George Sound and over the bridge and oyster boats at Apalachicola. If one has a leisurely schedule, there's a side spur called Route 30 that goes all the way through Indian Pass and down to the point at Cape San Blas. It juts out so precariously into the gulf that four lighthouses have been built over the years, and four are not there.

The last light, commissioned in 1885, was a skeletal iron structure surrounding a metal cylinder that contained a spiral staircase rising ninety-six feet to the lantern. Erosion did what it does best, and the light was deactivated in 1996. In a rare Florida success story of preservation, citizens rallied to rescue the historic landmark, and since 2014 it stands safely in retirement at a public park farther up the coast. What's left at Cape San Blas is a pristine point of beach, water all around, quiet wind, the occasional gull, all joining to create a natural retreat of sorts that nurtures spiritual peace in the undisturbed tranquillity.

A '64 Corvette skidded into the sand. "Where the fuck did the lighthouse go?"

Coleman screamed as his head bounced back from the windshield.

Serge ran up and down the beach, yelling and grabbing his temples in panic.

Coleman fell out of the car.

Serge jumped back in the Corvette and backed out, running over Coleman's big toe.

Another scream.

"Coleman! Where are you?"

"Down here."

Serge hit the brakes and stood up in the convertible. "What are you doing in the sand?"

"Lying down."

"Get back in! I miscalculated that we had a leisurely enough schedule to take the side spur!"

Coleman limped toward the passenger door.

"Why are you walking like that?"

"My toe suddenly started hurting. It can be fixed with beer."

The silver Stingray blazed northwest up the coast until reaching the modest downtown of Port St. Joe. A camera aimed out the driver's side as they passed the historic art deco Port Theatre. *Click, click, click ...*

"Oh my God! What's that on the horizon?"

Brakes squealed. A forehead met the windshield a second time. "Ahhhhhh!" Coleman wiped beer off his face. "That mysterious thing happened again."

"In your case, seat belts are mysterious." Serge chugged coffee as he whipped the sports car down Marina Drive toward a small park on the shore.

"I thought we were behind schedule," said Coleman.

"It's the San Blas lighthouse." *Click, click, click.* "What's *that* doing here? ... Something strange is going on." *Chug, chug, chug.* "I'll inquire later ... Onward ..."

The Corvette navigated worn streets in a small neighborhood before pulling up in front of a white gingerbread cottage from the 1920s. The porch railing and sturdy roofing joists suggested an expert woodworker with a name like Horatio who was banished from a whaling ship after a second mate went missing during a heated card game off Nantucket.

Serge banged on the door with a brass knocker. Coleman cracked a can of Colt 45.

Shuffling inside. A redheaded young man in a bathrobe answered the door eating a bowl of Froot Loops. "What do you want?"

Serge briefly flashed an official-looking document. "Is this the residence of Maybelline Coot?"

"She's not feeling well. Get out of here." The door began closing.

A foot stopped it.

"We're not here to see Aunt May," said Serge. "We've come to have a word with Preston Jacobs, which would be you."

Preston squeezed the door on the foot. "I'm busy."

Serge just grinned. "Right now is a very convenient time for you. Otherwise, your schedule will become amazingly busy. Actually it already has."

A delicate voice from the back of the cottage. *"Is someone here?"*

"Just a salesman," yelled Preston. "He's leaving. Watch your TV show."

"What's he want?"

"Nothing ..." A sneer through the crack in the door. "Move your foot or I'll break it!"

Serge didn't move it.

Preston put his weight into the door, which left him leaning the wrong way. He was stunned at the speed and force that Serge generated. The young man tumbled backward, and then all three of them were inside.

Coleman giggled. "He looks funny with Froot Loops in his hair."

"It's about to become a laugh riot."

Preston leaped up and wiped milk off his face. "You're both dead if you don't get out of here right now!"

"Is he selling anything I might want? ..."

"Yes!" Serge yelled toward the back bedroom.

"That's it!" said Preston. "I gave you fair warning!" He cocked his fist back ...

Three minutes later.

"Aunt May?"

"Do I know you?"

Serge grabbed a quilted chair from the vanity and pulled it to the side of the bed. "My name is Serge, and I'm a friend of Lou Ellen's. Also Willard and Jasper."

"You know my family?"

Serge held two fingers tightly together. "We're like this."

"I miss them." She made a melancholy face. "Why haven't they come to see me? Preston said he's been calling and calling them."

Serge gently placed his right hand on bony fingers. "All that's changed now. Something happened and there was, uh, a disruption in phone service."

"Is everyone okay?"

"Healthy as could be." Serge patted the hand again and stood up. "And they'll be here before you know it."

"That's nice." She strained to look out her bedroom door. "Did you see the salesman? What was he here for?"

Serge exposed gleaming teeth. "Insurance! Preston just decided he needs a lot of it."

"Preston?" said the old woman. "Where is he?"

"They called him back to the main office."

"You mean in Panama City?"

"No," said Serge. "This is the *big* main office. The one I oversee."

"But then who's going to take care of me?"

"Aunt May," said Serge. "I'd like you to meet your new assisted-living specialist, Coleman."

Coleman sipped from a large aluminum can and stared at a hand-sewn curtain featuring songbirds. His brain heard voices through the beer fog. His big round head slowly swiveled toward them. "What?"

"It's only temporary," Serge told the woman. "Until your relatives arrive. But he's one of the best in the business ... Coleman, do me a favor and grab another pillow for her head."

"But she didn't do anything to us."

"No, you idiot! *Under* her head."

"Oh, that's a relief. I didn't want to do the other." *Burp*. Coleman noticed another curtain with canaries, and he started thinking about buffalo wings.

"Coleman! The pillow!"

"Right! I'm on it ... Here you go, Aunt June."

"I'm May."

"What?"

"Who are you?"

"Coleman." *Burp*. "What's your name? April?"

Serge stood in the doorway rolling his eyes. "I'll let you two work it out." Then he was gone.

Coleman pulled up the quilted chair and looked at the TV. "What are you watching?"

"*Wheel of Fortune,*" said Aunt May. "It's boring."

"I see the remote." Coleman grabbed it off the dresser and began clicking. "Did you know you have pay-per-view?"

"What's that?"

"It's where you pay for each show—"

"No, what's that in your hand?"

"The remote."

"Your other hand."

"You mean my beer? ..."

... Meanwhile, a vintage silver Corvette raced back toward the Apalachicola National Forest. Preston was in the passenger seat. He needed propping up with a rigid piece of wood inside the back of his shirt. The paralytic agent that Serge had injected into his neck vein prevented speech or movement, but the rest of his senses remained keen.

Serge punched him playfully in the shoulder. "Glad to have you with me! It's a long drive, and good company makes it go so much faster. Coleman's fine, but he tends to zone out, and usually just when I'm zoning in. That's such a buzzkill!" He raised a travel coffee mug and chugged until it was dry, then punched Preston again. "And, man, am I zoning in right now! I know you can't talk, but I'm totally ready to, so we have a symbiotic chemistry. You're a good listener, you know that?" He accelerated to ninety and played bongos on the steering wheel. "Can you dig it? We're on a *Route 66* bender! I know what you're wondering: What's *Route 66* got to do with Florida? And that's what everyone thinks! People just assume that all the shows were filmed along the iconic 'Mother Road' highway from Chicago to Los Angeles. But the title had broader implications of unstructured life on the road during the post-Kerouac zeitgeist. I hate people who use the word 'zeitgeist' and yet I just did. That makes me a complicated, non-one-issue voter. So the *Route 66* producers roamed all over the country and—hold on to your hat—near the end they filmed a dozen shows in Florida, including the double-episode series finale in Tampa! I guess they knew the show was winding down in the winter and figured, 'Do we want to shoot in Detroit or Daytona?' Tough choice, right? And they really did go to Daytona. On February seventh, 1964, the whole country watched a Stingray just like this one drive right out onto the sand, next to pounding surf, as amazed visitors do every year along the landmark stretch of beach—and then suddenly, for no reason, they're at the City Island Library—which is a real place where they actually filmed the scene. But there's more! If your mind isn't already freaking blown, they pan to a big Airstream-like trailer sitting at the curb, attached to an ancient pickup cab. And this is what finally convinced me that Line was the smarter of the two, because Tod looks toward the street and asks what the heck that is. Line responds it's the newest thing: a mobile library that brings books to you. And Tod's brain is all overheating as he stares cross-eyed at a sign painted on the side of the trailer: 'Volusia County Bookmobile.' Well, I can tell you I almost hit the darn floor! How many people know that a Florida episode of *Route 66* introduced the nation to the concept of the bookmobile? I could go on for hours. Actually, I will. In the next episode they drive to St. Augustine across the Bridge of Lions ..."

... Back in Port St. Joe:

Aunt May was sitting straight up in bed for the first time in months. She needed both hands to clutch the cold metal can. "Preston won't let me drink this stuff."

Coleman crunched his own empty can against the side of his head Belushi-style and cracked another. "Plenty more where that came from."

"What did you say this movie was called?"

"Pulp Fiction."

"It's not boring at all."

"Hold on." Coleman pointed. "This is one of the best parts."

May leaned forward in bed. "What do you think that nice young man is going to do with that syringe?"

"Keep watching."

Travolta came down with the needle in the heart.

"Wow, that was intense!" said Aunt May. "I never knew anything before about heroin. Are there other movies like this?"

"As many as you want to watch." Coleman popped a fresh can and placed it in the old woman's hands. "There you go."

"You're a very nice young man."

Chapter 6

THE SAWGRASS LOUNGE

Reevis Tome entered the joint. It was one of those places where you could still smoke. He coughed and stopped to let his eyes adjust. All heads around the oval bar slowly turned. Bikers, barflies, suckerfish. They looked the baby-faced reporter over and returned attention to their highball drinks. Some smirked at first. That was the Reevis Effect.

He took a seat away from the others, at the end of the bar nearest the door, indicating a level of discomfort. Again, a Reevis tactic. An auburn-haired bartender strolled over.

"What can I get ya?"

"Diet Coke."

She had some mileage but she was sweet. "Coming right up." Reevis always did better with the women bartenders in knife-and-gun clubs, especially if they were moms. She came back with a soda. "That'll be a buck."

Reevis handed her two dollar bills. Another strategy. He raised the soda. "What's your name?"

"Clementine."

"That's a pretty name."

"Thank you." She left and went back to taking orders from rough trade at the other end.

Minutes passed. Laughter. Someone stuck money in the juke and punched up "Kaw-Liga." That would be a Hank Williams song, both junior and senior, but this was the original recording from 1952. More time passed. Reevis quietly finished his drink. That was his approach. Wait.

Sets of malevolent eyes occasionally gazed down the bar at Reevis, without concern of being noticed. Reevis noticed. Peripheral vision. It was the first thing he did in unfamiliar waters. Chart all points of potential confrontation. This time, an out-of-work plumber facing spousal battery, a middle-rung crack dealer bearing battle scars, and two bikers with probationary patches on their jackets. The last always carried a hammer on his belt, but he wasn't in construction.

Outside in the Suburban: "What's he doing in there?"

"He ordered a soda a few minutes ago, but since then nothing."

Nigel pounded his door panel. "Why did I let him talk me out of bursting in with the camera?"

"What are we going to do?" asked the videographer.

"Okay, I know a way to make this work," said Nigel. "Turn the camera on me."

A lens focused on Nigel's face.

An urgent, hushed tone: "Our reporter has fallen into the hands of dangerous elements. We must go in now!"

Nigel jumped out of the Suburban, followed by the cameraman. He raced toward the lounge. "Remember to make it jiggle."

"It's jiggling," said Günter.

Nigel reached the door and was just about to open it ...

"Hold up!" Günter placed a hand to the side of his head, where a small earpiece provided an audio feed from Reevis's lapel mike.

"What is it?"

"I think the kid is making some kind of progress," said Günter. "We should retreat and wait to see how it plays out."

"Okay," said Nigel. "Put the camera on me."

"You're on."

"Pull back! Pull back!" Nigel sprinted for the Suburban, and a jiggling camera followed.

Inside the bar, Reevis had raised a single finger.

The bartender strolled over with a smile. "Another Diet Coke?"

"Sure."

A refilled glass was set in front of him. "Thanks, Clementine." Two more dollars.

She began to walk away.

"Oh, excuse me?"

She turned. "Yes?"

"Well, uh, I'm a local reporter, and I'm not sure I'm in the right place," said Reevis. "Can I ask you a question?"

"What is it?"

"I'm supposed to do a feature on an old crime case that was never solved. A woman went missing about four years ago, and I heard maybe her car was abandoned behind this lounge?"

"The Dupuis case?"

"You know about it?" said Reevis.

"Shoot yeah. It was the big talk in here for months," said Clementine. "People still bring it up once in a while."

Reevis slipped out a notebook as casually as possible. "What do you remember about that night?"

"I was busy working and didn't notice much, but I do know someone who can help you. The Mouth of the South." Clementine toweled up a wet spot on the counter. "She's over there right now. I'll introduce you."

A minute later, Reevis sat at the darkest, smokiest end of the bar. Next to him was a row of stools with several older women who seemed to have history. They favored mixed drinks. Beside one glass lay a leather cigarette case with a picture of an Irish setter.

"Maddy," said Clementine. "This is a nice local reporter named— ... I didn't get your name ..."

"Reevis."

"Reevis," repeated Clementine.

Maddy laughed. "You don't look old enough to be a reporter. You don't look old enough to be in a *bar*."

Reevis grinned sheepishly. "I get that a lot."

From the corner of the reporter's eye: a plumber was nonplussed by his presence, a crack dealer incensed by his existence. The two bikers weren't currently taking account, but they would soon respectively become nonplussed and incensed.

"Maddy," said Clementine. "He was asking about the Dupuis thing."

"Holy Jesus! Don't get me started on that! I could talk all night!"

Reevis got out his notebook. "I have all night."

"What do you want to know?"

"Let's start with the missing woman's car," said Reevis. "Police had a suspect who was found driving it."

"Sanchez!" said Maddy. "He wins the putz-of-the-year award. Boy, did he step in it that night!"

"Why do you say that?"

"The guy's a regular in here ..."

"... A regular pest, if you ask me," said the woman sitting next to her.

"But nobody's asking you," said Maddy. "I'm telling the story here ... Now I lost my place."

"He was a regular," offered Reevis.

"Worked landscaping, but unsteady." Maddy slipped a new Parliament from her leather case. "By the end of the evening *always* bugging people for a dollar. Usually had mulch on him."

"There's one part that I'm trying to figure out," said Reevis. "Police pulled him over in the early hours, and he gave them two contradictory stories. First, he said the owner lent him the car, then after he found out she was missing, he told them he found it abandoned behind this place and just stole it ... You can see how that would make a big difference ruling him in or out—"

"Caprice, blue," said Maddy. "No, green, definitely green."

"You have a good memory," said Reevis.

"A *photographic* memory," clarified Maddy.

"You saw the car?"

"Of course. It was sitting right out back for hours," said Maddy. "Sanchez definitely stole it."

"How do you know?"

"Because at the end of the night, he was stomping up and down the bar, yelling, 'Yep, I'm gonna steal me that car. I'm stealing that car! Anyone dare me to steal that car?' and the rest of us are like, 'Stop getting mulch on us ...'"

Reevis could feel the heat from the eyes across the bar. The regulars became more hostile in their glares. The only thing holding them back was Clementine's de facto approval of the young reporter. You don't shit where you eat, and you don't cross bartenders in your zip code.

Reevis gathered his thoughts. "But tell me about when you actually saw the car."

"Sanchez keeps pestering me, raising his hands to heaven and saying, 'It's a sign from God!' Tells me it's brand new, driver door open, keys in the ignition, and a holy glow inside telling him the saints wanted him to have the car. I said that was the dome light, but he won't stop until I finally say, 'Okay, okay, if you'll promise to leave me alone.' So he takes me out back, and sure enough, there's this factory-spanking-new blue Caprice. I mean green; the yellow crime lights throw you off every time. And it was sitting there just like he said, door open, light on, keys, ready to roll."

Reevis was bolt upright. "What happened then?"

"I told him not to steal a car with blood all over the interior."

"You saw blood with your own eyes?" Reevis scribbled furiously. "What else?"

"Kittens."

The reporter raised his head. "Live cats were in the car?"

"No, the little stuffed ones that people make rows of in their back windows. Not me, personally, but what are you going to do?"

"Okay, and Sanchez?"

"I kept warning him about the blood, but he just jumped in the car and said, 'Screw it, I'm stealing it anyway!' And then he drove off. The next thing we knew, he was all over the news as prime suspect in a murder. Everyone in here laughing at the TV: Sanchez with that goofy, hapless expression during the perp walk. That's when police take a suspect—"

"I'm familiar with a perp walk," said Reevis. "So what happened then? I understand he was ruled out pretty quickly."

Maddy nodded as she sipped watered-down Canadian Mist through a straw. "Police came in the bar to interview me. They said Sanchez had changed his story—that at first he had been partying in the bar with the victim, and she lent him the car ... I cut them off and said Sanchez was an idiot but not a murderer, and the missing woman had never been in the bar, period. Not that night or any other. Then I told them about seeing the car abandoned with door open and the keys and the blood, and Sanchez not listening to me and speeding off in the thing."

"So that's when they ruled him out?"

"Not at first." Maddy pulled another long menthol from her cigarette case. "They said if everything I told them was true, it makes no sense for Sanchez to admit to partying with the victim the night she went missing and make himself the last person to see her alive. Well, I read a lot of mysteries, so I said, 'It makes perfect sense. When he thought he was just facing auto theft, he tried to lie his way out, but when it turned into a murder rap, he thought, 'Can I go back and take the stolen-car beef, please?'" She leaned closer and dropped her voice in secrecy. "You know who you should really look into? A guy named Larouche who works at the body shop up the street."

Reevis wrote diligently in his notepad. "Why?"

She formed tight, earnest lips. "I don't like him."

"How is he involved in the case?"

"He's not. He's dating my daughter."

Reevis removed the tip of his pen from the pad. "Maddy, you've been more than helpful, and I don't want to impose, but could I ask you a favor?"

The bottom end of her straw searched for scotch around the ice cubes. "Name it."

"My company sent a film crew because they think there's still a lot of public interest in this case. Would you possibly mind repeating what you just said on camera?"

"For you, no problem," said Maddy, signaling the bartender for a refill. "But you'll need to clear it first with Clementine ..."

... Outside, in a black Suburban. "What's going on?" asked Nigel.

The sound man cupped both hands over his earphones to hear better. "There's a lot of background noise, but it seems like he actually might get our camera into the bar after all."

"Well, I'll be," said Nigel. "Keep listening and let me know the second he gets permission ..."

Back inside, the bartender saw Reevis signal with his finger and came over with a smile.

"Another Diet Coke?"

"Thanks, Clementine. And thanks for introducing me to Maddy. She's been great—and she's agreed to an on-camera interview."

"Well, look at you!" Clementine told Maddy. "Hope you'll still remember us little people when you're a big TV star."

"If it isn't too much to ask," asked Reevis, "could we possibly bring the camera in here? I promise to be as low-key as possible and respect your other customers' privacy. We'll be completely unobtrusive and stay tightly focused on Maddy. Do you think *maybe* that might be something you could ... ?"

Clementine grinned and shook her head with amusement, like he was being silly. "Of course you can film in here. Take as long as you need."

"Really appreciate it," said Reevis. "I'll just go outside and get the crew—"

Suddenly the front door of the lounge crashed open. Blinding light filled the bar. Screaming.

Clementine spun around and shielded her eyes. "What in the living hell?"

Nigel sprinted through the bar, followed by a Bavarian with a jiggling camera. "Reevis! Thank God you're safe! ..."

Ten minutes later.

A parked black Suburban rocked to and fro on its suspension.

Günter wept and cursed in German, repeatedly slamming himself into the door.

"Easy now," said Nigel, rubbing the videographer's shoulder. "Everything will be all right."

More anguished wailing.

"There's something seriously wrong with you people," said Reevis. "I had everything under control."

"And it was an amazing thing to listen to," said the producer. "You had them eating out of your hand."

"I told you not to listen!" said the reporter. "As we sit here, that recording is evidence of a felony. You need to destroy it now."

"Can't do it," said Nigel. "It's all we've got."

"That's on you," said Reevis. "We had the interview in hand before that cowboy nonsense back there. What on earth were you thinking?"

"Priorities," said Nigel. "The interview would have been gravy—and don't think we're not thoroughly grateful for your efforts setting it up—but we needed confrontation footage."

"And where is the footage?" Reevis asked sarcastically.

"We sort of lost it when they smashed the camera," said Nigel. "How was I supposed to know that biker was carrying a hammer? What's *that* about?"

Günter sobbed louder.

"This is everything I was trying to tell you," said Reevis. "Your antics provoked an unknown variable that nobody could predict or control. That isn't crime reporting! If you're in the woods and see a gigantic bees' nest, you go around it. You don't say, 'Reevis, get a big rock and whack that thing open and we'll film whatever happens next.' We lost the camera, my interview, and your precious confrontation footage. Am I missing anything?"

"Wait," asked Nigel. "Are you saying you actually know where there's a gigantic bees' nest?"

THE APALACHICOLA

Dry leaves crunched as the tires of a silver sports car rolled slowly along the edge of a forest.

"Here we are," said Serge. "Your final *Route 66* stop of the day. We're getting near the end of this episode, and you know what that means? ... Not even a guess? I'll tell you! The climax!"

Serge grabbed some typed pages from the glove compartment. "I can't thank you enough for being so gracious back at the house and signing a few forms. Sorry, the lawyers. These are simply required to give Aunt May's relatives power of attorney over your bank accounts in the unlikely event you become incapacitated." He flipped pages to make sure every signature line was filled. "Yep, all in order. That's the last step before we begin the big contest. And who, might you ask, are the lucky contestants? Only you! Isn't that great? Significantly increases your chances. So let's get on with the show and meet today's judging panel, which is me!"

Preston remained still.

"What? Overcome with emotion? That's normal. Let me give you a hand." Serge walked around the car and opened the passenger door. Preston's head slowly turned as movement began returning to his legs.

"Perfect timing: The drug is starting to wear off." Serge helped the young man to his feet. "It has a fast taper, and you should be feeling like new in no time. The ability to speak is the last to return, so don't sweat that part."

Serge guided Preston through baby steps, then grabbed him by the shoulders and carefully leaned him against the front bumper. "Good, you didn't fall over. Now don't go anywhere."

The lid of the trunk popped and Serge unloaded his gear. He slammed it closed and looked toward the front of the car. Nobody there.

Serge scanned the forest and spotted the captive trudging away off balance like a primitive robot. He quickly caught up to Preston.

"No, no, no, the contest is over there." Preston whimpered as he was turned around and marched back.

"Now have a seat," said Serge.

Preston defied him by stiffening his legs the best he could.

"I insist." Serge kicked out his feet, and Preston fell in a bed of wet leaves.

The forest filled with the sound of a mallet pounding tent stakes. Thick braided rope went around the hostage's wrists and ankles. Serge tied the last knot in a clove hitch, leaving Preston spread-eagle on his back.

"Did you realize chicks waste this stuff by making magazine baskets?" Serge connected wires and cables. "And here's another minefield that women plant for us. You know how they're always nagging us to wash our hands? And then you comply and she screams, 'What the hell are you doing?' You tell her you're getting dirt off your hands like she wanted, and she yells, 'You're using the *decorative* soap!' And I say, 'It's *soap*.' And she grabs this starfish out of my hands. 'You ruined it!' 'What am I supposed to use?' 'Soap!' So I start reaching for other bars. 'No, not the frog! ... Not the flower! ... Not the heart! ... Not the strawberry! ... Not the cupcake!' Then I finally see an actual bar of soap. She says, 'What do you think you're doing? That's a decorative polished quartz shaped like a bar of soap.'" He grabbed the posthole digger. "Relationships are all about power."

Serge finished digging his hole and made a couple quick trips to retrieve the rest of his gear from the car. He cheerfully narrated while finishing the assembly. It was the same explanation as he had given Willard and Jasper. With one exception.

Serge held a final item in front of Preston's face. The captive thrashed with wild eyes.

"Open your mouth."

Preston shook his head and gritted his teeth.

"Don't be scared," said Serge. "Most people are freaked out by this, but that's mainly because they're already crapping their britches about having to get a root canal. This is just an oval of hard rubber that dentists use to keep a patient's jaw sufficiently wide so they have room to work and don't make costly errors that could affect your smile. It's a safety device. Now open."

Teeth clenched tighter.

"Have it your way." Serge grabbed the hammer and lightly tapped the middle of Preston's lips, drawing a trickle of blood as they cut into his teeth. "That was just a test. The next one will affect your smile ... Okay, you leave me no choice." The hammer rose in the air.

The mouth sprang open.

"I knew you were reasonable." Serge fit the jaw-spreader snugly in place. "It's a little uncomfortable at first because your mouth is propped so wide you can't open it any more to spit the thing out. But that's just another safety feature."

Large eyes stared up from the forest floor in the terror of *not knowing*.

"I'll bet you want to know!" Serge grabbed his laptop and sat cross-legged next to Preston. "But first there's something *I* want to know. How can a young, healthy person take complete advantage of an infirm senior citizen? The only conceivable conclusion is that certain people view anyone more vulnerable than them as livestock ... I know, I know, it's hard to wrap your head around that conceit, and yet the syndrome is almost an epidemic in our culture. It was impossible for me to fathom as well, until I had an epiphany! You know what made me finally figure it all out? Colonoscopies and psychopaths. It's so obvious that I feel stupid not making the connection earlier. Ever meet a psychopath?" Serge shook with the creeps as he tapped the computer's keyboard. "I never, ever want to! But I saw this documentary that said I've probably already rubbed shoulders with them many times. When you say 'psychopath,' most people think of Manson or Son of Sam, but the vast majority aren't criminals. Many are actually high-functioning success stories. For example, take a doctor who's a psychopath. It might give him a God complex and fearless, interpersonal detachment to perform world-class brain surgery with as little nervousness as if he were clipping his fingernails. Or a hedge-fund trader, corporate raider, tobacco lobbyist, or CEO who uses overseas factories so deplorable they're forced to fence in the rooftops because workers would rather jump than make another fucking game box." Serge dramatically held an index finger over the return key. "Ready for your contest?"

He pressed it. The hostage's eyes darted erratically as the ground beneath him began to hum.

"Anyway, the documentary said that one or two percent of the total population are psychopaths. Apparently the gold standard of figuring out which neighbors to keep an eye on is something called the Hare PCL-R test. I took it online, and I got a great score! Then I found out that a great score is not good. Maybe I should have studied harder. Oh well, ever heard of waterboarding? Your contest today is a kooky new variation I dreamed up that I like to call 'earthworm boarding.'" Serge clapped his hands like they do in kindergarten. "Same principle, except all my procedures have a bonus round that mercifully provides the possibility of escape. So obviously the psychopath test I took was flawed ..."

Preston turned his head to the side and watched the soil come alive with dozens of pinkish worms. Then hundreds.

"... And here's your bonus round: As I explained earlier, the sound waves drive up the worms, which will begin crawling on you and—sorry, this part is a little gross—some will fall in your mouth. But the sonic device behind it all is running on battery power, so if you can outlast the life of the power supply by eating enough earthworms, then they won't suffocate you. I know you drew one of my most distasteful contests, but on the other hand, they're an incredible source of protein. Well, that about does it. See you on the flip side ..."

Serge began walking back to the car. Preston yelped as the first worm fell in his mouth.

Serge snapped his fingers and spun around. "I totally forgot! The colonoscopy!" He ran back over and plopped down again. "I can't leave you hanging in suspense."

Preston flopped and vainly tried to spit.

"I'm trying to tell you something important. Forget about the worm and pay attention!" Serge reached in his captive's mouth and flung it aside. "Now then, as I alluded earlier, psychopaths are adept at climbing company ladders because they're easily able to make draconian decisions that would leave the rest of us sleepless for weeks. Did you know that if a colonoscopy turns up a polyp, any doctor will advise you to come back for another test within three years or risk inoperable cancer? Yet some insurance companies refuse to authorize follow-up tests for *ten* years. Know why? An executive did the harm-profit ratio and decided that at ten years, there was an acceptable fifty percent survival rate—for something that's virtually one hundred percent preventable with timely screenings. Now, if that isn't treating the customers like livestock." Serge nodded to himself with conviction. "A psychopath made that decision."

Another worm hit Preston's tongue. More squirming and gurgling.

"You're a real nervous type," said Serge. "Just relax and work the odds. Of course it all depends on the individual, but this particular contest leaves you a decent twenty to thirty percent survival rate ... Wow, I just realized something. That's less than the fifty percent used by those insurance companies." Serge stared at Preston and tapped his chin. "Give me the unvarnished truth. Do you think I should take that personality test again?"

Chapter 7

SOUTH FLORIDA

The airspace over Miami International grew crowded. An American Airlines flight from LaGuardia touched down. Then a United, Southwest, JetBlue, Delta, Virgin Atlantic, Lufthansa. Somewhere in the middle, a smaller private jet from South America landed and taxied to a separate terminal. Six serious men with mustaches got out and marched in cadence toward the customs building.

They made their way to baggage claim, where a chauffeur held a sign: MIERDA HOLDING GROUP.

The men filed into the back of the limo, and the driver climbed in up front. "Where to? ..."

It was shortly after lunch as the white stretch cruised down Brickell Avenue and double-parked outside one of the numerous downtown banks that used to launder cocaine money in the eighties, and now just laundered money. The half-dozen men entered the lobby with unwavering precision and approached a teller. One of the bank vice presidents saw them and dashed out of his office.

"Mr. Pelota," said the hurried executive, shaking hands. "Great to see you again. Mind if I call you Ocho? What brings you to town?"

Pelota silently gave him a certified check from the Caymans. The vice president raced behind the counter and practically hip-checked a female teller away from her station. "I'll take care of this personally." He looked up. "I'm assuming you want this in hundreds?"

Ten empty briefcases were passed over the counter, and ten heavy ones came back.

The limo cruised across the Miami River and north toward Aventura, passing convenience stores of varying ethnicity with numbers of customers dribbling out the doors. All along the route, billboard workers putting up new numbers. They arrived at a local office with a circular illustration on the door: an Indian maiden near a palm tree as a wooden ship approached. The sun was on the horizon, but it was ambiguous about rising or setting. The official seal of the state of Florida.

The men went inside, and the receptionist had them wait until a low-level bureaucrat in a short-sleeve dress shirt appeared in a doorway, eating a baloney-and-lettuce sandwich. "How can I help you?"

They simply pushed past him.

"Wait! You can't just go in there!"

"Which is your desk?"

"The gray one."

They pulled up a half-dozen chairs from nearby work areas. Two were being used, and people had to stand up. "What the hell do you think you're doing?"

The wordless looks they received in response convinced them that chairs suddenly were out of style.

The men gathered around the bureaucrat's desk. On the corner of the desk was a novelty plastic bird with a pointy beak that occasionally dunked down into a glass of water. The concept was to make people happier. The bureaucrat finished chewing and balled up a piece of wax paper. "Now what can I do for you?"

"We would like to buy the board," said Pelota.

The office worker had grown used to language barriers, but this wasn't a question of accents. "Buy the board?"

"Yes." Pelota leaned to read the official laminated badge clipped to the worker's shirt. "Mr. Foote."

"I'm sorry, but I don't understand."

Pelota turned and looked back at the door they had just come through. "This is the Miami office of the Florida State Lottery?"

"Yes, it is ... but if you could just explain a little more."

"We want to buy the whole board. Every number."

"Of ... *what*?"

"The lottery."

"Let me get this straight: You want to buy a ticket for every single number in the lottery?" The bird dunked in the water. "But there are over twenty million different combinations."

Pelota didn't need to say anything. Ten briefcases were promptly opened on the floor.

"Holy God! Is that what twenty million looks like? ... How can you guys carry that much cash around Miami and not feel scared?" Foote gazed into six sets of vacant eyes. "Oh."

"Sell us the board," said Pelota.

"You do realize that the lottery pays a lot less?"

"Except it's rolled over five weeks now."

"What if there are several winning tickets?" asked Foote.

"We've done the math," said Pelota. "The board, please."

"Look, I would if I could, but there just isn't any mechanism," said the employee. "The only way we sell tickets is from the machines in the stores. The lottery has a strict policy against mass sales because it would discourage individual players."

The silence lasted only seconds, but it was effective. "I am familiar with computers," said Pelota. "If one is so inclined, anything can be achieved." He pulled several packets of bills from a briefcase. "How much do you make a year?"

"Put that away!" Foote glanced around quickly and lowered his voice. "I can't take your money, and even if I did, the system is completely firewalled."

"They've hacked into the Pentagon," said Pelota.

"Our system's better. The lottery's pretty important in Florida."

Pelota's mouth firmed. "I am growing weary of you."

"Please relax," said Foote. "Here's what I would do in your shoes: Our lottery forms are good for up to ten numbers, and if you can hire enough people and hit enough stores, you just might be able to cover the board before Saturday night's drawing."

"Do you feel lucky?" asked Pelota.

"Why?"

"Because you have just placed a large bet." Pelota stood up and snapped the plastic bird's neck and left the building.

PORT ST. JOE

Serge parked in front of a gingerbread cottage.

An antique Ford pickup with three people in the cab pulled in behind him. Lou Ellen jumped out. "We got your phone call!"

"Is she okay?" asked Willard.

"What about her caretaker?" asked Jasper. "And the money?"

Serge smiled and opened his trunk. "You have nothing to worry about anymore. Everything's been taken care of." He handed them a small suitcase.

"What's this?" asked Willard.

"The money I've already recovered. You should be able to retrieve the rest with these documents." He waved a stack of pages from the glove compartment. "They give Aunt May and you power of attorney over her former caretaker's bank accounts. And if the authorities poke around, all they will see is the reversal of large transfers of money from her life savings that can only be explained by a predatory scheme on the part of her health worker. Nobody would ever suspect her."

"Suspect Aunt May of what?" asked Jasper.

Serge placed a hand on his shoulder. "The less you know, the less you can tell them." He stared off wistfully into the sky. "Whatever might come up, feel free to pin it on a pair of latter-day *Route 66*–spirited nomads traveling town to town searching for the soul of America."

"I want to see my aunt!" said Lou Ellen. "I've been worried sick!"

They all went inside and arrived as a group in the bedroom doorway.

Shock and confusion.

A ravaged pizza box sat on a nightstand. Playing cards scattered across the chenille bedspread. Dice and crumpled-up dollar bills. Aunt May tossed a Ping-Pong ball at a nearby table.

"What the hell's going on in here?" said Willard.

"Playing beer pong," said Coleman.

Aunt May pointed at the TV. "And watching *Reservoir Dogs*."

"You!" Jasper yelled at Coleman. "What kind of person gives a ninety-year-old woman beer?"

Willard walked over to the bed with a congenial smile and reached for the aluminum can she was holding. "I'll just take that from you, Aunt May."

She sneered down at his hand and growled like she would bite.

"Hold on." Lou Ellen sniffed the air. "What's that smell?"

A Ping-Pong ball flew. "Farts," said Aunt May. "We had a contest."

"No, not that," said the younger woman. "Is it ... marijuana?"

Coleman and Aunt May in unison: "No!"

The old woman picked up a game controller and switched the TV to a streaming version of *Grand Theft Auto: Vice City* ... *Tap, tap, tap.* "Die, bastards, die!" *Tap, tap, tap ...*

Serge stopped and stared curiously at a section of wall where there had been some kind of game of darts without a board. Then another direction. "Coleman, why is the vanity mirror broken?"

The old woman threw another white ball. "I did that."

Her relatives rushed bedside. "Dear God!" "Did you have an accident?" "Are you hurt?"

"No accident." May raised her beverage. "I used my cane. It was cool."

Serge's head sagged to his chest. "I thought there was no possible way to foul this up." He grabbed a meaty arm. "Don't think we're not going to discuss this later!"

Coleman looked back at the bed. "But this is the only job I've ever liked."

Aunt May sat up in alarm. "Where are you taking him?"

"Everything will be fine," Serge assured her. "The assisted-care center will be sending a properly vetted person out soon."

"But I want Coleman! He's the best caretaker ever!"

Serge tugged his colleague toward the door and turned apologetically toward the others. "Sorry it got a little messy at the end."

"No problem," said Lou Ellen. "We really appreciate all you've done."

"Oh!" Serge looked back a last time. "Almost forgot. Our next episode is about to start, so we're officially out of the grunting racket ... Willard, Jasper, I want you to have all my advanced worm equipment."

"But it cost a bundle," said Jasper.

"We can't accept that," said Willard.

Serge held up a palm. "Please, it's the least I can do for all your hospitality."

"If you insist," said Jasper. "But we're fixin' to stay here with Aunt May a spell till we're sure her new arrangements are to our likin'. Might not be able to get back there for a few moons."

"Family comes first. You do what you have to." Serge was walking toward the door when Lou Ellen ran up and gave him a hug from behind. "Will I ever see you again?"

"Anything's possible," said Serge. "But you should be looking for someone who's better suited for you."

"Where am I going to find anyone as kind, charming, intelligent, humorous, fun-loving ..."

"True, true," said Serge. "Except there's a lot you don't know about me and Coleman."

"Coleman?"

"We come as a package," said Serge. "In a way, I'm *his* caretaker. He'd never last without me."

"See?" said Lou Ellen. "You're so compassionate."

"True again. But trust me on this: There's a significant downside to getting mixed up with us. Don't be fooled if it's not apparent for a long time—"

"Hey," said Coleman. "It completely slipped my mind, but I think you need to get your aunt's toilet fixed. I didn't do anything unusual."

Serge slowly closed his eyes. "Or you may find the downside much sooner."

The relatives all gathered on the front porch to bid the out-of-towners farewell.

Serge saluted from the driver's seat. "Just remember the place where we first met. You'll find all the gear still there."

Everyone waved as the Stingray sped off.

Chapter 8

THE NEXT MORNING

Traffic stacked up on a lazy, hot stretch of Old Dixie Highway running south from Miami to Homestead. A carpet-remnant outlet just held its eighth going-out-of-business sale, but the turnout was so anemic that they had to go out of business.

Next to the store, two police cars sat side by side, facing opposite directions so the officers could talk through their open driver's windows. In prison lingo, it's called a sixty-nine.

"Two flakka arrests this morning."

"What's with these new street drugs?" said the other officer. "And why does Florida always get them first?"

"We're number one!"

"I just don't understand the drug fringe. And flakka is the worst yet. People pay good money for a substance whose primary effect is an overwhelming urge to get naked in broad daylight."

"That tends to stand out. Like the guy having sex with a tree ..."

"... Or leaping on hoods of moving cars, proclaiming he's the god Thor."

"... Or urinating in motel ice machines."

"Remember when crime had a point?"

"At least this drug makes it easy for us. Three users this month ran into police stations demanding protection from invisible enemies."

The officer facing the road stopped talking as his eyes followed a northbound vehicle. "I think we got one."

The other cop turned around. When he did, the German shepherd in the backseat also turned. The dog's name was Nixon. "Which car?"

The first officer pointed. "Rusty station wagon packed to the gills with garbage bags."

"What's our pretext?"

"The bags are blocking the view out the rear window."

"Is that an actual infraction?"

A shrug. "Courts have upheld searches as long as we *think* it's an infraction."

"I love the War on Drugs."

Both vehicles peeled out in diametric circles before regrouping on the highway. The lead patrol car radioed in the traffic stop.

Moments later ...

If traffic was backed up before, now it was a festering, motionless river of irate drivers sticking heads out windows to investigate the delay. A station wagon had been pulled over, one tire on the curb, parked at a dysfunctional angle blocking the right lane. Red and blue lights revolved atop two cruisers sitting behind it. The first officer was all business at the driver's window. "License and registration."

A brown man smiled back.

"Didn't you hear me? License and registration."

The smile got wider as the man began nodding but doing nothing else.

"Do you understand me?"

The man continued nodding. *"No hablo inglés."*

The officer spoke louder. "License-o."

The other cop held a leash, walking Nixon around the Pennzoil-dripping heap. When they reached the rear bumper, the dog sat in a perky position and barked. He received an imitation-bacon treat.

"Dougan," yelled the canine officer. "I think we got a hit."

Dougan took a step back from the driver's door and placed a hand on his holster. "Sir, get out of the car ..."

The brown man smiled and nodded.

Then a voice from the backseat: "Please, he can't speak English!"

The officer hadn't noticed the second person in the car, obscured by the pile of bags. He pulled his Glock. "Show your hands!"

Two petite sets of fingers appeared from the bags. "Don't shoot!" Thick accent, but at least the official language.

"Ma'am, don't move!" The officer glanced back at his colleague with the dog. "We have a passenger!"

The second cop quickly rounded the car and opened the door. A plump older woman raised her arms in the air and got out, tumbling garbage bags onto the pavement. "Don't shoot."

"Is that your husband?" asked the officer.

"*Sí.*"

"Tell him to step out of the car before he gets hurt."

She spoke rapidly in Spanish.

The driver complied, and they were given complimentary seats in the rear of one of the patrol cars.

"Ma'am, our dog indicated the presence of drugs in your vehicle—"

"No drugs! No drugs!"

"Then you won't mind if we search?"

"No drugs!"

More units arrived, and a tedious excavation began in the rear of the station wagon. The sidewalk was soon covered with the contents of the plastic sacks. Mostly clothes, the kind that other people leave out for Salvation Army. Then loose utensils, hot plate, doorstop, Dixie cups, plastic bowls decorated with the Flintstones, half a set of dominoes, snarled yarn, hairnet, a lamp without a shade, glow-in-the-dark Elvis, a shade without a lamp, which wouldn't fit the other lamp. It was the consumerism of hope.

Nine patrol cars later, the precinct lieutenant arrived. "Another garage sale?"

Dougan was bent over, pawing through the back of the car. "It's got to be here somewhere. Nixon definitely picked up something."

It came down to a final bag tucked low behind the spare tire. Dougan opened the top. "Well, well, well, look what we have here."

"What is it?" The lieutenant peeked inside. A fifteen-gallon plastic sack crammed with unorganized cash of all denominations.

"Malloy! Bring Nixon over!"

The dog arrived and promptly sat on the pavement, barking at the money.

They pulled the two suspects from the back of the patrol car and uncuffed them. "No drugs!"

"You're right," said Dougan. "We didn't find any illegal narcotics in your vehicle. However, our canine indicated that your cash is positive for cocaine residue, so we are required to seize it under Florida's drug forfeiture laws."

"No jail! No jail!" pleaded the wife.

"No, you're not going to jail," said the officer. "Since actual contraband wasn't uncovered during our search, we have nothing to charge you with. Consider this your lucky day. You're free to go."

She pointed at a pair of officers dumping the money into an evidence bag. *"Dinero?"*

"I told you we have to impound it."

Another officer strolled over and ripped an official page off the top of a clipboard. "Here's your receipt. Under the law, you have the right to hire an attorney and appeal."

Her eyelids rose in optimism. "You serious? We can really go?"

The patrolman gestured toward the undependable vehicle. "Stay out of trouble. And maybe have that suspension looked at."

She quickly grabbed her husband by the arm and rushed him to the car. *"Vámanos!"*

The station wagon hopped down off the curb and chugged away.

The lieutenant ambled over. "They didn't seem like drug smugglers."

"They weren't," said Dougan.

"You mean you just confiscated money from innocent people?"

"What I'm saying is that the real drug smugglers are now hiring all these poor peasants to fly under the radar for them," said the officer. "First, they were paying these unfortunate people a few hundred dollars to swallow enough condoms of drugs that it would kill everyone in our station house if they broke. Or worse: they hide drugs in a baby's diapers, because infants are the perfect camouflage. But if any leaked—" The officer looked askance. "And I thought I'd seen evil before."

"Except you didn't find any drugs in this particular vehicle?" said the lieutenant.

"That's how the pipeline works." Dougan pointed at a distant station wagon belching black smoke. "The drugs come one direction. And someone has to take the cash back the other."

"What was your probable cause to search?"

"Didn't need any. The wife gave us permission," said Dougan. "But even if she hadn't, the dog barked. Who are we to argue?"

The lieutenant looked up and down the debris-covered sidewalk, which resembled a recycling sorting station. "But why did they leave all their stuff?"

"In a hurry to get out of here," said Dougan. "More evidence of guilt."

The lieutenant briefly bit his lower lip in strained thought. "Good job. Write it up, and I might be able to put a nice word in your files."

The lieutenant departed and Officer Malloy came over. "Doesn't he know anything? How did he ever get to be lieutenant?"

"Political appointment," said Dougan. "Uncle's on the commission."

They looked farther up the road as a trail of black smoke dissipated over a bank building. "Think they'll appeal the cash forfeiture?"

"If I was a betting man ..."

MEANWHILE ...

Police cars were parked everywhere.

Because it was a police station. Coconut palms shaded a regulation handicapped ramp that led to the entrance with the city seal on the door. The seal featured a pelican because neighboring cities already had dibs on more popular birds.

The back door of a black Suburban opened. Reevis got out. "Could you please let me go in first and talk normally to these people before your blitz attack?"

"Easy enough," said Nigel. "We need to get a running start anyway."

"Whatever." Reevis strolled toward the lobby in a rumpled dress shirt that was untucked in back.

The desk sergeant looked up. "Can I help you?"

The reporter flashed his credentials. "I'm Reevis Tome with Florida Cable News. Is the public information officer available?"

"Sure, I'll get him." He picked up the phone. "Lieutenant Schott, there's a reporter here to see you ... Okay." He hung up. "The lieutenant will be out in a minute—" The sergeant suddenly jumped to his feet. "What in the hell?"

Nigel and Günter came crashing through the front doors with camera and lights.

"Turn that thing off now!" yelled the sergeant.

"Why?" asked Nigel. "Are you covering up police corruption?"

"I'm not going to ask you again!"

"You're doing great!" Nigel told the sergeant. "Do you think you could draw your gun? ..."

Fifteen minutes later, Reevis and the public information officer conferred quietly on the side of the police lobby. The lieutenant finally nodded and glanced over at the sergeant. "Uncuff 'em."

The bracelets came off, and Nigel and Günter rubbed their wrists.

"The lieutenant is going to take us back to his office now," said Reevis. "Do you think you can settle down?"

"No problem," said Nigel. "You're the journalist. You know better than anyone else how to do your job."

The police officer led the trio through the security door and down a bare white hallway.

Reevis ended up in a chair in front of the desk, reviewing detectives' files. It was still an ongoing investigation, so there was no public right to the documents. But the info officer had worked with Reevis before and knew he could be trusted—at least with the parts of the files he *wanted* the reporter to see. Another unwritten alliance in journalism: They both knew they were using each other, and everyone was content with the arrangement.

"Glad you're doing a story on the case," said the lieutenant. "When a crime goes this cold, we often get our big break when a witness we never knew existed sees something about it on TV and decides to come forward."

"That's what we're hoping for," said Reevis, flipping pages. "So you ruled out the landscaper who was found driving her car?"

"Ruled him out enough to let him go."

"What about the auto-theft charge?" asked the reporter.

"Technicality with the traffic stop," said the officer. "The dash-cam showed the turn signal actually was working, so we lost probable cause."

"But the bottom line is that all three suspects are still active?"

"We prefer you'd call them persons of interest."

"The husband?" asked Reevis.

The lieutenant shrugged. "He's the husband."

"Do you think there was motive because of his wife's affair with the short-order cook?"

"We looked into that, and it's not as suspicious as it sounds. The couple was estranged, and she had already moved into her own apartment before starting the relationship. According to all their friends, everything was out in the open, and the husband was copacetic."

"What about the cook?"

The lieutenant smiled. Officially, he could only say so much. They were entering read-between-lines territory.

"As you can see in the file, he's had some arrests, including arson about ten years ago. Did two years for torching his girlfriend's place."

"Wait," said Reevis, flipping backward through the papers. "Didn't I read where there was a small fire in the missing woman's apartment that was quickly put out? Right after she disappeared?"

The lieutenant was deliberately economical. "Officially ruled an accidental fire started by a bad electrical fuse."

Reevis scribbled notes. "I have a hard time believing that was a coincidence."

The lieutenant smiled again. "Unless someone knew how to tamper with such a fuse to cover their tracks. Some arsonists learn from their mistakes."

"And someone can pick up a lot of tips during a two-year stretch in the can."

"You said that, not me."

Reevis continued writing. "Where is the cook now?"

"Pulling another deuce. Larceny."

"Oh, I get it now." Reevis leaned back in his chair and crossed his legs. "May I theorize?"

"Be my guest."

"You think the cook did it, but you don't have a complete case. Lucky for you, he's currently being detained in prison, so there's no need to file charges and set the constitutional speedy-trial clock ticking. Your office will probably put a hold on him at the prison just before his release date."

Another grin. "That's an interesting theory."

"Any guidance you'd like to pass along?"

"Nothing really. But the Sawgrass Lounge is an interesting piece of old Florida. You might want to check it out."

"Already been there," said Reevis. "But I know where you're going with this. The missing woman never set foot in the bar, which existed a world away from her normal lifestyle. Yet her car was abandoned there. So if the cook was known to frequent the bar, it would link everything together."

"Funny thing how some places don't like to open up to the police."

"I'll see what I can do." Reevis looked back at his cameraman. "But I might have to mend some fences."

The pair stood and shook hands.

"Great seeing you again, Reevis."

"Thanks for the help, Lieutenant."

They were startled by a single, sharp clap of hands. "Exquisite!" said Nigel. "Now could you do it again from the beginning, but this time argue like you're very angry with him for questioning your lax investigation."

"Argue?" said the officer.

Nigel nodded. "Then throw him out."

"Why?" asked the lieutenant. "I don't have any reason to throw him out."

"Excuse me," said Nigel. "What's that on your desk?"

"Oh, this?" A proud smile. "It's an old cast-iron model police car with the vintage bubble-top light. They presented it to my grandfather when he retired from the force."

Nigel pulled out his keys and scratched the side of the small car with a cringe-inducing sound.

EPISODE TWO

Chapter 9

THE GULF COAST

A silver Corvette sped south on the Tamiami Trail. The sun had only been up a couple hours, but the heat felt like noon.

"This time you've got me stumped," said Serge. "We're definitely not going to do it, but curiosity is killing me: Why on earth would you want to fake that you're a scuba diver with the bends?"

"Isn't it obvious?" Coleman unwrapped an aluminum-foil package. "To get inside a decompression chamber."

Serge's eyes reflexively crossed. "I guess it's a two-part question. Why a decompression chamber?"

"Because it gets you higher." Coleman peeled back the last piece of foil. "That's why I made these brownies. Ingestion lasts longer with a delayed onset for a smooth, extended ride when there's no opportunity to blaze one. I'm really looking forward to a decompression chamber."

"But wasn't it enough for you to fake the bends last summer?"

"I didn't fake anything. They simply *assumed* I had the bends."

"Why? Just because the rescue helicopter found you floating incoherently miles off the coast, completely naked except for the scuba inflation vest that kept you from going under?"

"That's right."

"How did you even end up like that in the first place?"

"Beats me," said Coleman. "I just went out one night for a beer, and then there I was. Stuff like that keeps happening to me."

"This topic is going nowhere fast," said Serge. "I'm picking the next one."

"Which is?"

"Race relations in America."

Coleman's head snapped sideways. "Jesus, Serge! You're really going to talk about race?" He nervously glanced around the road. "I think that's a bad idea. Everyone's really angry right now."

"Screw it, I'm going there!"

"Hold on." Coleman quickly fastened his seat belt. Then he pulled something out of a duffel bag and put it on his head.

Serge looked over. "Where'd you get the football helmet?"

"I went out for a beer one night and the next thing I know I'm staring out through a face mask—"

"Never mind."

Coleman snapped the chin strap and stiffened his arms against the dashboard. "I'm ready now. Talk about race."

"Remember the movie *The Color Purple?*"

"Oprah."

"That color represents a whole subtext that defines relations in our country." Serge hit his blinker. "You know I hate trendy buzz phrases, but there's one that sums it all up: *Own it.*"

"Own what?"

"Your life. We can discuss huge racial differences as long as it comes from a position of love, like telling your aunt at a funeral that she's got toilet paper stuck to her shoe. Awkward, but you work through it as a family. The problem is the people who refuse to sit with us and break bread at the Great American Dinner Table. Why? Deep down they realize their lives suck, but they won't *own it*. 'Gee, maybe I should have done some planning and put in a little effort and not spent all my money on porn and fog lights. Could that possibly be it? Naw, someone else did this to me.'"

"That's just not being responsible," said Coleman.

"Their entire life drive is to make others as miserable as they are," said Serge. "There's no excuse for that. Everyone should be ecstatically happy every second! We're alive on earth, after all! When did *that* get taken for granted? I don't exactly know how the program works. Maybe there are a bunch of people floating around somewhere looking down on the planet and going, 'Damn, I missed the cut.' If those guys have shitty people skills, I could understand it. But the ones among us constantly taking dumps in the fun pool are just missing the point."

"How do we know who they are?"

"We don't even have to look; they readily identify themselves," said Serge. "Making comments like, 'They call each other the *N*-word all the time, then get all upset if …' Or: 'Did you know the original slave traders were other black people in Africa? … Oh, but I'm not a racist.'"

"So you're saying that we actually can criticize black people?"

"Of course," said Serge. "But only from a position of love, which brings up the title of the Oprah movie. I'll be watching some sports awards show on TV, and one of my favorite pro athletes will go up to get a trophy wearing a purple suit. And I'm sitting on the couch saying: 'Dude, I love you, man, but Christ! Purple?'"

"So purple suits are a black thing?"

"Most certainly," said Serge.

"What's an example of a white thing?"

"Laughably playing the victim card," said Serge. "'Hey, where's *my* affirmative action?' Dude, I love you, man, but in case it's not shockingly obvious, it came with your birth certificate."

"Are we done?"

"For now," said Serge. "I'll bet I'd look pretty snazzy in a purple suit."

"But I thought you just said—"

"I've evolved on that," said Serge. "Purple is the new white."

The Corvette continued on. Serge reached under his seat and passed something to his pal. "We're getting close to our destination. We need to focus on our next *Route 66* jobs."

Coleman held it up and read the yellow block lettering on the back. "Another Windbreaker?"

"Rule number one in life: Windbreakers with stuff written on the back are the key to making nosy people step back so you can have room to work. Along with clipboards and orange cones, the Windbreaker is rarely questioned."

"Like the other time when you got jackets that said 'Bail Recovery Agent'?"

"That's right." Serge placed a portable emergency scanner in his lap that squawked intermittently. "There's no rule against putting whatever you want on the back of your own jacket—just no 'Police' or 'SWAT' or 'ATF'—or you can be charged with impersonating a law enforcement officer."

"Then we've got a problem with these jackets," said Coleman. "They're bound to arrest us for impersonating."

"Not if you stop and really break it down." Serge slipped his own jacket on while driving and swerving. "Wear one of these, and most people just automatically assume you're law enforcement, but the law is all about the fine print, or in this case the large print."

"I'm confused."

"The Windbreakers or life generally?"

"Both."

"People say this is a free country so often that it's lost meaning. I'm only tapping into the possibilities that everyone else just assumes are off-limits simply because they lack the imagination to think of it themselves." Serge leaned over and tapped the back of the jacket in Coleman's hands. "Right now, only law enforcement is doing that, but what's to prevent a private citizen from taking it up as a hobby?"

Coleman looked down at his jacket again: HOSTAGE NEGOTIATION TEAM.

"But how will we find a place to use these?"

"At any particular moment in Florida, an average of fifteen standoffs are under way," said Serge. "It's only a matter of paying attention."

The other side of Serge's brain had been monitoring all the verbal traffic on the emergency radio in his lap. He set his course for an address below Sarasota. The Corvette turned a corner in a neighborhood of ranch houses where they used to cut the grass.

"Serge!" Coleman shouted. "Look at all the police cars and flashing lights!"

"It might be wise to pull around back."

He stopped in an alley as two patrol officers guarding the perimeter came running up. "You can't park there! We have a situation!"

Serge turned around to show them the back of his jacket. "Who's in charge?"

"Right this way."

They were briskly led across the front yard of the house. "Sergeant," said the first officer. "These two men—"

Serge urgently shook his hand. "Hey, boss, I'm Serge and this is Coleman. Sorry if I must be curt, but the clock is ticking. What's our status here?"

"Who *are* you?"

Serge quickly turned around to display his jacket. "Tick-tock. How many in there?"

"Just two." The sergeant pointed. "We were serving warrants when shots came through the door. He's holding his live-in girlfriend."

"Have you alerted the phone company to block all calls and redirect them to your command post?"

"Already done."

"What about electricity?"

"Cut that off, too," said the sergeant. "No air-conditioning. Figured we'd sweat him out."

"Turn it back on," said Serge. "There's a new way of thinking on that."

"Behavioral studies at Quantico? The heat might make him irritable?"

"No," said Serge. "It makes *me* irritable."

"Are you authorized?" asked the sergeant.

"We have Windbreakers."

"Who did you say you were with again?"

"Nothing personal, but I'm afraid this has already flown above your pay grade," said Serge. "The perp is on a watch list."

"So this has gone federal?" The sergeant nodded to himself. "I thought the jackets looked FBI."

"FBI, NSA, CIA, it's all the same alphabet soup since we lost our innocence. I'm not supposed to say anything, but you seem like a good man who has a right to know since this is your community. We've been a step behind this guy in six countries, and his luck finally ran out here. When this is all over, I expect a punch-bowl-ful of commendations to go around, but the ceremony will have to be classified and held at a secret location we can't tell you about. Sorry." Serge turned and walked away with Coleman.

"Hey!" yelled the sergeant. "Where are you going?"

"To negotiate."

"But you can't just walk in the house!"

"It's a free country. Hobbies are underrated." They went inside and closed the door.

A gunshot splintered back through the wood.

Serge's voice echoed out a window: "Hold your positions! Just a warning shot! ..."

ON THE OTHER SIDE OF THE STATE

Young knuckles struck polished wood.

"Come in."

Reevis opened the door.

"Have a seat," said his assignment editor at Florida Cable News.

Reevis slumped into the chair and loosened an already unkempt polyester tie. "I can't do this anymore. I'm sorry. I never want to be thought of as an unhappy camper."

"Reevis, we're all family here," said the editor. "And we know you well enough to never question your positive attitude. But you have to understand that the whole business is in transition, and we all must make adjustments."

"Adjustments?" Reevis let his neck relax over the back of the chair as he stared up at hypnotic holes in the particleboard drop ceiling. "Did you see what went on the air last night?"

"Caught a bit of it."

"Unbelievable!" said Reevis. "The confrontation with the desk officer, and later getting thrown out of the building after Nigel keyed the lieutenant's model car, not to mention all the unnecessary camera shaking. Then they spliced everything together to make the police look all suspicious like I'd uncovered Watergate."

"We received a lot of calls on that," said Shug. "Mainly positive. The people in corporate are very happy with you."

"But it's not *real!*" said Reevis. "I spent a lot of time building my relationship with that police department. And since when is my middle name 'Danger'?"

"I think most viewers understand there's a little license going on with the new emphasis on drama."

"Who says?"

"Focus groups."

"I know you," said Reevis. "I know that's not how you really feel."

A purposeful pause and then a deep exhale through the nostrils. "No, it's not. Journalism is about honesty, and I don't like this any better than you. But this comes straight from the top. Ratings and advertising revenue are way up with this crap, so until things change, we have to make the best of it. Look at it from my position, two daughters in college."

"Okay, because of all you've done for me, I'll play along," said Reevis. "But can you get them to stop piecing together footage that makes my interview subjects look ridiculous? I have to go back on the street and maintain sources."

"Say no more," replied the editor. "That's the least they can agree to. In fact, I think they may be coming around to your position. This morning I had a very productive conference call about the ethics of journalism that we take rather seriously around here."

"And they were receptive?"

The editor nodded with vigor. "They said they were eager to learn more about our moral standards, and that it would actually make for a better show. They have an appointment to meet with me right after you leave. I honestly think they're genuine about respecting your professional integrity."

The door to the assignment editor's office burst open. Günter Klieglyte led with a giant TV camera, followed by Nigel.

"Excuse me!" Shug jumped up. "We're not supposed to meet until I finish with Reevis! And nobody said anything about filming!"

Günter swiveled his camera down for a wide-angle close-up of the reporter. "What are you trying to hide?"

The reporter's hands covered the lens. "Get that thing out of my face!"

The camera swung toward the assignment editor. "Any comment?"

"I'm not finished with my reporter! Get the hell out of here!"

Günter knelt and pressed his eye hard against the rubber view-finder. Nigel crouched over his shoulder like an umpire behind a catcher. "You said on the phone that you were upholding the integrity of the fourth estate, but this stinks of a massive cover-up!"

"Get the fuck out!" yelled the assignment editor.

Another close-up of Reevis.

Hands went to the lens again. "I'll break that goddamn thing."

The editor came out from around his desk. "Do I have to call security?"

Nigel made a fist and mouthed the word *more*.

The editor grabbed his phone off the cradle. "I don't care what happens anymore! Reevis is right! This is a disgrace!"

Nigel turned to his cameraman. "We got it?"

Günter gave him the thumbs-up.

"Super." Nigel broke into a pleased expression. "You were both fabulous! Standing your high ground in the face of scandalous accusations. Priceless! ... Now, what was it that you wanted to talk to us about?"

"Out or I'll kill you!"

"Oh, right," said Nigel. "You were having a private meeting. Don't let us interrupt you." A show-business wave as he shuffled backward through the office door. "We'll just be waiting for our meeting in the chairs outside your door. Can't wait to hear what great ideas are on you mind."

Chapter 10

STANDOFF

A sweaty, sunburned man in a camouflage tank top stood in the hallway, clutching a Bushmaster .223 carbine rifle across his chest. "Get the hell out or the next shot will be on target!"

"Is that any way to start a friendly negotiation?" asked Serge.

"Are you hard of hearing? I told you to leave my house!"

"Leave?" said Serge. "Did you see all the police in your yard? The last thing I need in my life is cops."

"*You're* a cop!"

Serge and Coleman looked at each other and doubled over with laughter.

"What's so funny?"

"Us? Cops?" More laughter. "That's rich! A regular hoot!"

"But your blue Windbreakers ..."

"I've been known to pick up avocations." Serge took off his jacket and threw it on the couch.

A finger perspired on the trigger. "If you're not police, then who are you?"

"Highly wanted fugitives." Serge tapped the side of his head. "You have to admit it's pretty clever. Who would ever think of looking for a fugitive as a negotiator in a hostage standoff?"

"It's some kind of trick! This is the last time I'm going to tell you to get out!"

Serge walked over to the television. "Anything good on?"

"Are you insane?" said the man. "I have a gun here!"

"So do I." Serge briefly raised his tropical shirt, then lowered it. "See? We're off to an excellent start! Show-and-tell, gun for gun. We're bonding! That's what dudes always do the first time they visit each other's crib. 'Let me see all your coolest shit.' If you were at my place, right now we'd be looking at View-Masters and a prize collection of souvenir flattened pennies, but since it's your pad, we could be heading to the garage and an industrial cooler full of do-it-yourself shrunken heads, because America was founded on the principle of never judging a hobby. In the idiom of the times, the Founding Fathers called it 'the pursuit of happiness,' but we all really know they were worried about Franklin's big kite-flying drunk-fest coming up and wanted to give themselves some cover from the wives." He walked toward the gunman until the end of the military rifle stuck in his gut. He extended a hand. "My name's Serge."

"Jesus! You really are crazy!"

"Come on!" Serge left his hand hanging in the air. "What's your name?"

The man sighed extra hard. "Good grief." He quickly shook. "Rogelio. They call me Rog. So will you finally leave?"

"We're going backward now," said Serge. "I thought we were hitting a groove comparing our toys. Plus, I already told you, I can't leave. They've probably figured out my identity and are setting up the sniper nest as we speak." He sat down on the sofa and grabbed the remote control. Coleman plopped next to him with a joint.

"Whoa! Wait, wait, wait! What are you doing?" Rog ran over to the couch. "You can't stay! This isn't how it works!"

"You're acutely wound up." Serge clicked the remote. "Have a seat and chill ... Ooooo! The Road Runner! My favorite!"

Rog eased himself into a chair. "Okay, what is it you really want?"

"What? Oh, sorry, the coyote just put on that special helmet with the roller skate on top so he can do a headstand and zip across the canyon on that tightrope. Normally, I'm against hard drugs, but when it helps the writers create such masterpieces ..."

"Excuse me ..."

"... Like the time he painted a railroad tunnel on the side of a mountain and a locomotive comes out and runs over him. Clearly influenced by the 1903 Parisian Surrealist movement—"

"Excuse me!"

"You were saying something?"

"Yes!" said Rog. "What do you want?"

Serge leaned toward the television. "Just to continue my *Route 66* pilgrimage through Florida. In this week's episode, we've stumbled into your unassuming town and become hostage negotiators. That's the formula: new city, new gigs, sex during commercials." He suddenly pointed atop the TV. "Wow, you've got one of those cool new cable boxes that streams just about everything ever filmed. Let's binge-watch *Route 66*!"

Rog grimaced with a whimpering sound. "What can I do to make you leave?"

"I don't know," said Serge, absentmindedly examining the sleeve of his Windbreaker. "Maybe release the hostage?"

The phone rang and Rog jumped.

Serge answered it. "Hellllllloooo?"

"What's going on in there?"

"Hey, boss, I've established a rapport, but it's going to take some time."

"We need the hostage out as soon as possible, for good faith, then you can continue working on him."

"All right, boss." He hung up.

Coleman tugged his pal's arm. "Serge, why do you keep calling him 'boss'?"

"I've been studying a cultural phenomenon lately. It's another one of those little unofficial things that messes with people's social equilibrium."

"Like clipboards and orange cones?"

"Exactly," said Serge. "Those are two things that inexplicably bend people to your will. Same with calling someone 'boss.' It's like handing a little kid one of those giant swirly lollipops. The general public doesn't even realize it's happening, but on a subconscious level: 'Why yes, I guess I am kind of like the boss. And I've only known this person a few seconds, but for some reason, I really like him.' Then it completely flips the hierarchical paradigm. Once I saw these moving-company guys call their customers 'boss,' and after that they were just flinging credenzas into the truck while the homeowners happily served them cold drinks."

The phone rang again.

"Yeah, boss?"

"We're sending in the robot."

"You got a robot? Cool! I'll leave the front door open ... Hey, Coleman, they got a robot!"

"Cool!"

Serge hung up and smiled at the armed resident. "Now, where were we?"

"You mentioned a hostage," said Rog. "What hostage?"

"They told me you were holding your girlfriend."

"*Holding* her?" said Rog. "I'm not holding anyone. In fact, I can't get her to come out."

"What are you talking about?" said Serge.

"Locked herself in the bedroom," said Rog. "Totally pissed at me. Then she goes and makes a false 911 call to fuck with me."

Serge whistled. "I'll take decorative soap any day."

Coleman got up on unsteady legs. "Where's the bathroom?"

"Last door on the right," said Rog.

They heard a mechanical whirring sound as a small remote-controlled device rolled into the room on tiny tank treads. A fiber-optic antenna rotated.

"Serge, it's the robot," said Coleman. "Can I take it with me?"

"Knock yourself out." Serge stood and turned to Rog. "Let me talk to her. I have a way with the ladies."

"You don't know my girlfriend."

"You don't know me."

Rog shrugged. "Can't get any worse. Her name's Maria." He led Serge down the hall ...

... Meanwhile, outside. Officers filled the mobile command unit parked at the curb. The lighting was dim as they crowded around a flat-screen monitor.

"What am I looking at?" asked the sergeant.

"Not sure," said the officer working a joystick. "I've lost orientation control on the robot ... Hold it, what's this?" Coleman giggled on the toilet, aiming the optic antenna inside the bowl. "It looks like— ... No, it couldn't be ..."

"Something's not right," said the sergeant, picking up the phone for the local FBI office.

"Special Agent Braun here."

"Agent Braun, this is Sergeant Duffy over in Sarasota County. We've got a tactical situation here and the hostage negotiators just went in."

"How can I help you?"

"Did you send them?"

"I'm not sure I understand the question," said Braun. "Are you telling me you let people inside the box without knowing who they are?"

"Oh no, we definitely know who they are. Obviously. They had Windbreakers. Just curious, uh, if they might be yours."

"Did they say they were FBI?"

"Not in so many words. But they mentioned our guy was on a terrorist watch list."

"We always want to cooperate any way we can," said Braun. "But you know I can neither confirm nor deny any Homeland Security operation while it may still be ongoing."

"Just thought I'd ask. Thanks." The sheriff hung up.

"What did he say?" asked a nearby corporal.

"Could go either way," said Duffy. "Get the SWAT team ready ..."

... Inside the FBI office. "Someone's running an operation right under our noses," Braun told his assistant. "You know how I hate to be the last to find out. Call the other agencies ..."

... Inside the house. Knocking on a bedroom door.

A female voice from the other side. "Go screw yourself!"

"Maria, my name is Serge. I'm a hostage negotiator."

"Hostage negotiator? What are you doing here?"

"Some cops outside got this crazy idea in their heads just because you called 911," said Serge. "It would be much better for everyone if you opened the door so we could talk face-to-face."

The phone in the living room began ringing again.

"Shouldn't we answer that?" asked Rog.

Serge shook his head. "This is the most delicate part of the negotiation."

A muffled voice from the other side of the door: "Is that Rog out there?"

"Standing right next to me."

"Hey, baby," said Rog. "I can explain."

"Get away from me! I hope you rot!"

Serge tilted his head, and Rog took the cue to return to the living room.

"He just left," said Serge. "Can you please open the door? ..."

... Outside, Sergeant Duffy turned to a corporal. "Well?"

"They're not answering the phone. And we lost transmission from the robot."

"I don't like the looks of this." Duffy checked his wristwatch. "We're going in. Tell the SWAT team they have two minutes ..."

... "Please open the door," said Serge.

"Do you know what that asshole said to me in Pottery Barn?"

"Tell you what," said Serge. "You come out, and *I'll* take you to Pottery Barn."

"Promise?"

"Cross my heart."

"Okay ..." The bedroom door creaked, and she stepped into the hall just as Coleman emerged from another door with a broken robot under his arm.

Maria looked inside the bathroom. "What in the name of God happened to my guest towels!"

Coleman grinned. "Sorry ..."

... The sergeant gave the signal. "Go! Go! Go!"

Tactical officers in black gear stormed toward the house.

Serge yelled out a window: "Hostage coming out!"

"Stand down!" yelled the sergeant.

Maria stomped out the doorway and across the lawn. A SWAT member darted forward and grabbed her arm to pull her to safety, but she just jerked away. "Don't touch me!"

There was a commotion in the street as other officers attempted to detain her for debriefing. *"You men are all alike!"*

An emboldened Rog stuck his head through a crack in the door. "And don't come back, cunt!"

"What!" Serge screamed, and yanked him back inside. "Rog, a Pottery Barn can test even the strongest man's limits, which is why you always see them crying in the parking lot. But I cannot abide this level of misogyny ..."

Out in the street, Sergeant Duffy huddled with his corporal. "What do you think now?"

"That negotiator must be for real. He got the hostage released faster than I've ever seen in my life."

"I was thinking the same thing," said the sergeant. "I got nineteen years in for my pension. Can't afford to mess this up."

"The only other explanation is they simply bought Windbreakers."

"Don't be silly." Duffy was also privately thinking: *He called me "boss." For some reason I really like this guy.*

"Then what's the plan?" asked the corporal.

"We wait ..."

... Serge sat back down on the couch. "What a day! ... Rog, where are you going?"

He pointed at the front door. "Leaving. This is far too weird for me."

"Come back in here and sit down with us," said Serge. "I insist."

"But I want to give up now."

"Are you nuts?"

"No, really, I'd like to turn myself in now."

"And I need to discuss your manners with women." *Click*.

Rog raise his hands. "Why are you pointing that gun at me?"

"To negotiate."

AVENTURA

Panel trucks arrived in the parking lot of a worn two-story strip mall in Aventura. The competition between the nail and beauty salons was heating up. More and more pink neon had recently been placed in the windows to advertise new services involving wax, cucumbers and heated stones.

Men in short brown pants opened the backs of the delivery trucks. They loaded boxes on handcarts as two gangs of employees stood on the sidewalk, giving each other the hairy eyeball. The men wheeled their cartons through the doors of the salons, escorting identical shipments of the latest laser equipment to battle the heartbreak of female mustaches. The two staffs exchanged a salvo of cursing in a foreign language, then rushed back inside their establishments to play with the new stuff.

The delivery trucks left. A Honda Civic arrived. A young woman entered a door between the two businesses and went up the stairs.

A receptionist looked up from her desk and smiled. A door in the back of the waiting room opened. It was one of the founding partners, Jacklyn Lopez. "We've been expecting you."

She led the woman down the hall and opened the door to Brook's office.

"Danny, great to see you," said the lawyer, standing and giving her a hug.

"I can't thank you enough for all your work helping my grandmother with her landlord situation."

"My pleasure," said Brook. "But you didn't have to come all the way up here to tell me that."

Jacklyn had a stern expression. "It's something else. You're not going to believe her story."

"Then you better have a seat," Brook told Danny. She went back behind the desk and took her own. "Now, what is it?"

Danny sat up straight. "There are some stories going around my community. Actually they're not stories; they're true."

"So tell me a true story," said Brook.

"There's a family I want you to help," said Danny. "But they're afraid to come in, so I'd like you to help persuade them."

"Why are they afraid?"

"They're illegals," said Danny. "Migrant workers."

"I see."

"Last week the picking season ended in Homestead. They packed everything they had into a station wagon and set out for Immokalee to follow the jobs. But they were stopped by police, ostensibly because all their bags of clothes blocked the rearview mirror."

"Wait," Brook interrupted. "You said they were illegals who were stopped by the police? They weren't turned over to INS for deportation?"

Danny shook her head. "The officers just searched the vehicle and seized four thousand dollars, their whole life savings."

"On what grounds?" asked Brook.

"They claimed the money was proceeds from illicit drug trafficking," said Danny. "Except they didn't find any drugs in the car."

"Then what was their basis for impounding the money?"

"A dog barked at the cash."

Brook's expression changed. "There's got to be more."

"There isn't," said Danny.

"What were they charged with?"

"They weren't. They just let them go," said Danny. "The father didn't even have a valid driver's license or proof of insurance. That alone should have caused him to be detained. It's traffic stop one-oh-one."

"Now I'm totally baffled," said Brook.

"Don't you see? The police *wanted* them to leave," said Danny. "Word's getting around on the street about this new scheme to rob illegals under the pretext of fighting the War on Drugs. Everyone knows what's going on. Just not the people living comfortable lives."

Brook got out a fresh yellow legal pad and clicked a pen. "Okay, so what does everyone on the street know? Start at the very beginning."

"Forfeiture laws were implemented to take away the profit motive of drug dealers and prevent them from furthering their smuggling enterprise. Who isn't for that?"

"It would be a very short list."

"Except it didn't remove the profit motive; it just shifted it."

"Where?"

"To law enforcement. They get to keep a lot of the stuff," said Danny. "Sure, there's a general fund where it's supposed to go to remove the temptation, but there are ways around it. Few people realize how many top public officials are driving around in sporty luxury cars that were originally bought with cocaine money."

Brook stopped writing. "That can't be true. Where'd you hear all this?"

"From the newspapers. The ACLU wrote an editorial. Doesn't anybody read anymore?"

"Not really." Brook put pen to paper again. "And the ACLU will never win a popularity contest in this state, or any other."

"Doesn't mean it's not true," said Danny. "But I learned something else. A certain percentage of drug defendants had good lawyers who got them acquitted on the smuggling charges, then won appeals to get their seized property back. The police lost their stuff. So unscrupulous officials figured they had a better chance of keeping the forfeited goods if they just let the drug dealers go and never charged them. What criminal who just got a free walk on hard time is going to come back and appeal a forfeiture?"

"This is actually happening?" asked Brook.

Darkness descended over Aventura. Shouting down on the street outside the law office. Colored lights and screeching tires.

"You do the math," said Danny. "An incident begins with a trafficker getting pulled over, and it concludes with the criminal driving away, and the cops keeping all his money. That's like a bribe."

"Technically it's extortion," said Brook. "But I have to be honest: This is painful for me to listen to." She tilted her head toward the photo on the wall. "My dad was a firefighter, and both his brothers wore the badge, along with a bunch of other relatives and neighbors. None of them would ever conceive of this conduct."

"You're not going to help me?"

"Didn't say that," replied Brook. "Despite what you may see in movies and on TV about the Blue Wall of Silence, the one thing good cops really hate is bad cops."

"Then you'll call this family I know?"

"Except for a single detail," said Brook. "What's drug-smuggling forfeiture have to do with migrant workers?"

"Think about it," said Danny. "Besides drug dealers, who else will never come forward to appeal a seizure?"

"Illegal immigrants," said Brook, beginning to nod. "I can connect the rest of the dots. Since these workers don't have bank accounts, every time they move on to the next town, their life savings are in the car. All a crooked department has to do is look for a vehicle full of poor Latinos packed to the roof with all their possessions ... Uh, but ..."

"There a problem?" asked Danny.

"The case has a drug angle that the city's attorneys are sure to exploit, and that's way outside my field." Brook picked up the phone. "I need some expert advice on case law, and luckily I know just the attorney—"

More yelling outside. Sirens. A swirl of colored lights shone up into the law office.

Brook stared at the ceiling. "Is this a disco?"

"It doesn't look like all those colors are from emergency vehicles," said Danny.

Then the screaming became so loud it could no longer be ignored.

Brook hung up the phone and went to the window. "What on earth is going on out there?"

The others joined her, looking at a fire truck and several police cars. Curiosity got the best of them, and they trotted down the stairs into the parking lot.

"Excuse me, Officer," said Brook. "I work late hours upstairs. Is there anything I need to be concerned about?"

The officer watched as two Korean women were loaded onto stretchers. A half-dozen others sat on the curb in handcuffs. "Apparently they figured out how to use depilatory lasers as handheld weapons."

Chapter 11

NEGOTIATIONS

The TV trucks began arriving on an otherwise quiet neighborhood street in southern Sarasota County. Reporters clamored for information as officers kept them back behind the ropes.

A female correspondent held a microphone out to a sergeant. "You've got to give us something."

"All I can say at this time is that there's a standoff, but we have our best negotiating team inside."

Inside: Rog sat tensely in a straight-backed chair, staring down the barrel of a gun. "W-w-why won't you let me leave?"

"Because we haven't gotten our free pizza yet," said Serge. "Everyone knows if you take a hostage, you get free pizza. I didn't make the rules."

Coleman toked a roach. "And free drugs, too."

"That's right," said Serge. "One of the reasons they give you free pizza is to lace it with phenobarbital so you'll go to sleep."

"The key is to know your tolerance," said Coleman. "And mix it with uppers."

Serge pulled out a notepad. "Rog, what's your pleasure?"
"Huh?"
"On your pizza?"
"I really don't care."

"Okay, you can pick off the stuff you don't like ... Coleman?"

"The usual."

Serge grabbed the phone. "We're ready for our free pizza ... Two large pies, the works on one, extra phenobarbital on the other ... Crust? Let's go with garlic-butter this time ... No, we don't want to add wings or a two-liter bottle of Pepsi to make it a combo ... Okay." He hung up. "They said up to an hour because of traffic."

More whimpering. "I just want to leave."

Serge aimed the remote control at the TV. "You don't like *Route 66*? But it can be enjoyed on so many different levels. Frankly, I can just watch it with the sound off and appreciate the magnificent period black-and-white footage of our tragically lost landmarks. Let's fast-forward!" Serge hit a button on the remote. "Here's Guy Lombardo's famous Port O' Call Resort in Tierra Verde, where Tod hooks up with a female powerboat racer while showing model homes in a new development ... and that's the old Tampa Fronton in 1963. Look at what a tiny street Dale Mabry Highway was back then, and check out their rooming house on Bayshore Boulevard, where the guys befriend a jai alai player who's actually a Cuban dissident. The show really hit its intellectual stride when they got to Florida ... And here's the Nautilus Motel in Cape Coral from the episode where Linc is taken hostage. Isn't that ironic?"

"Please let me go."

"You're dwelling." Serge walked to the window and picked up the phone again. "I see you all have Dunkin' Donuts coffee out there. Bring two to the door immediately. I don't care if they already have spit on the rim. Either ask for volunteers to give theirs up or pick a couple guys who aren't carrying their weight. Later." He hung up again and snapped his fingers. "Earth to Rog? You're fading out."

"I really want to surrender now."

"Okay, okay," said Serge. "Then negotiate it."

"How?"

"Well, one of history's best negotiators for my money was former U.S. senator George Mitchell, who hammered out the breakthrough Good Friday Belfast peace accords in 1998. You know his most brilliant tactic? He'd gather everyone together, and his only ground rule for the first day was that nobody could discuss what they were there to discuss."

"I'm confused," said Rog.

"Pure genius!" said Serge. "Imagine mortal enemies meeting for the first time, and there are hundreds of dead relatives on both sides. In stand-up comedy, they call that 'a tough room.' So Mitchell said bullshit on how it's been done before: We're going to talk about our kids and sports and movies and how we suspect that all weather forecasters, regardless of race or creed, are just making the shit up. I think they also got free pizza. Then, on the second day, they're now pals: 'You know all this killing-each-other stupidness that's been going around?' 'Yeah, what's the deal with that?' ..."

"Can I kick it off?" asked Coleman.

"Rock the negotiation!"

"Rog, you know any weed guys?"

"Coleman!" said Serge. "What's it always with you and the weed guys?"

"I'm putting out feelers. Mine's become unreliable."

"Of course he's unreliable," said Serge. "He's a *weed guy.* That's his job."

"To a point," said Coleman. "But there are certain pot etiquettes, like don't show up, toke and split; or if it's offered to you free, don't bad-mouth the stash no matter how stale; or if you've made your weed guy a bundle of money, he shouldn't refuse your phone calls just because you dropped his favorite ceramic dragon bong through his glass coffee table—"

"Enough!" said Serge. "It's obvious that I need to pick the category again. Pet peeves for a hundred, Alex. I hate it when I'm watching another action movie, and for the thousandth time during the climax they cut to the gun slipping out of the hero's hand and skittering away on a catwalk. I hate that the heroes in the same movies are avenging the murder of a partner two days before his retirement. I hate the driver in front of me who thinks a right turn on red is optional. I hate complaints about first-world problems: 'The Cheesecake Factory isn't open late enough.' I hate that there's now such a thing as a 'social media butler.' I hate the perversion of the English language: *incentive-ize, pre-planning, optics, face time, at the end of the day, using up all the oxygen in the room,* saying *literally* when you mean *figuratively* ..."

Coleman raised his hand. "So I shouldn't say, 'I literally shit myself'?"

"You're the exception that proves the rule," said Serge. "But you know what I *really* hate? The public's insulting definition of 'serial killer'! ... Rog, chime in at any time."

A wild stare.

"That's why I can't just walk out of here. Who knows what they've figured out? This is my whole point. It's so unfair that there's no distinction between 'serial killer' and what I'd like to coin 'sequential killer.' ... Rog, again, feel free to buzz in."

"W-w-what's the difference?"

"Serial killers are sick, obsessive losers who will never stop until they die or get arrested. Sequential killers, on the other hand, just *happen* to be the only person around when action is required. You know how some people avoid getting involved at all costs? Not me! It's about character, Rog. A sequential killer never intends to kill again—it's just that the cosmic hand of responsibility sometimes keeps picking the same person. If I don't act, I'm selfishly leaving work for the next person. That's not how I was raised. You agree? ... A simple nod will do."

Rog's head trembled as it rose up and down.

"That's a complex nod," said Serge. "But what really muddies the water is the term 'psychopath.' People think it's synonymous with the Zodiac, the Night Stalker, Jack the Ripper, but that's more cruel injustice ... Rog, take slow, deep breaths ..."

... Meanwhile, secure phone calls began crisscrossing South Florida.

"Cargill, this is Special Agent Braun."

"What can the CIA do for you today?"

"Police have cornered an international terror suspect in Sarasota County, but his name's not on any of our watch lists."

"Give it to me."

"Rogelio Martinez."

"I'll run it through. Who's on scene besides local?"

"A pair of hostage negotiators."

"Hope you don't mind me asking, but if he's not on your watch list, how'd you know to send your negotiators instead of leaving it to the county?"

"That's the thing," said Braun. "Uh, you didn't happen to send any negotiators?"

"You mean you don't have any idea who's in the house?"

"Oh, no, no, no!" said Braun. "It's just that the situation is very fluid at the moment, and a lot of jurisdictions are involved. In case the negotiators are part of a joint task force, I wanted to give a heads-up so you didn't think we were stepping on your toes."

"Appreciate the professional courtesy," said Agent Cargill. "You'll be the first person I call as soon as I find out anything." He hung up.

An aide was standing next to him. "You're really going to call the FBI back?"

"Hell no! If that asshole Braun doesn't have a clue who's negotiating the surrender, I'll be damned if he's going to grab the headlines all for himself... Get Homeland Security on the line. I'll find out who's really inside that house..."

Inside that house: "... A psychopath could be sitting right next to you, Rog, or the person at the top of a company where you can never get a live person on the phone. Need a prime example? This one's from the file marked 'Just when you already thought corporate America couldn't stoop any lower.' Sometimes family members will suffer a sudden loss and need to fly to a funeral in a big hurry. But booking a flight at the last minute can get expensive, so in the airline industry there's something known as a 'compassion' or 'bereavement' rate designed especially for relatives of the recently deceased. But one particular airline calculated that most people wouldn't be thinking straight in their grief, and when they call to get the special fare, they're quoted a price much higher than everyone else is receiving at that very minute. A psychopath thought of that." Serge gritted his teeth. "I'm not naming names, but I could literally kill someone at that airline! ... Rog, where are you wandering off to? I meant figuratively." Serge got up and guided the sobbing man away from the front door and back to his chair. "You need to sit down. You're getting light-headed waiting for that pizza ..."

Back to the phones:

"... What can Homeland Security do for you today, Agent Cargill?"

"... We've uncovered a sleeper cell near the Sarasota-Charlotte county line, and I just wanted to keep you in the loop because our joint task force has two men inside, and I'm expecting a lot of positive press out of this. The kingpin is Rogelio 'The Scorpion' Martinez. It's such a sensitive operation that he's not on our regular watch lists."

"And how can I help?"

"Did we have some negotiators on loan to you? We're working up the press releases and wanted to make sure you receive proper credit."

"I'll check it out and get back to you, but thanks for the call."

Another aide. "But you're not calling him back?"

"Hell no!" He dialed the NSA. "Agent Cooper? This is Maxwell at Homeland ..."

Minutes later, Agent Cooper hung up.

"What is it?" asked his aide.

Cooper grabbed his coat off a rack. "Looks like a plot against the airlines, the ports and Amtrak. They have the head of the entire network cornered in Sarasota. Rogelio 'The Fighting Desert Scorpion' Martinez ... Get the chopper ready ..."

... A member of the Sarasota SWAT team walked up the front steps and knocked on the door.

Serge answered and raised eyebrows in joy. "Pizza's here! ... Which one's laced with drugs? Don't want to dose myself."

"I marked it for you," said the black-helmeted officer.

"Thanks." Serge closed the door. "Soup's on!" He opened two cardboard boxes at the counter. One of the pizzas had a toothpick with a little flag: *Phenobarbital.* Serge and Coleman dug in. "Get over here, Rog! You must be famished!"

FLORIDA CABLE NEWS

A black SUV sat on the shoulder of Highway A1A in Dania Beach. Surf crashed in the night as a stiff onshore breeze ruffled palm fronds and blew an Almond Joy wrapper through the grass. Reevis compulsively chased down the litter and stuck it in his pocket.

Günter Klieglyte strapped on his battery belt as Nigel leaned against the fender. "There it is."

"Where?" asked Reevis.

Nigel nodded toward a place across the dark street.

Reevis looked at one of the mom-and-pop motels along the beach still proudly run by the original owner. It showed. Landscaping well tended, and all the azaleas, crotons and hibiscus remained trimmed to uniform height. Even the paint job was fresh; not a flake or peeling chip anywhere in the latest coat of Creamsicle orange. All the neon letters still worked in a sign that spelled OCTOPUS ARMS.

Günter hoisted the camera to his shoulder. "All set."

Nigel faced Reevis and tightly interlaced his fingers like he was pulling for a sports team to come through on the final play. "Here's the big shot of the show! This is the quaint little motel that the victim and her husband managed at the time she went missing. The husband still operates the place, so here's what we need: Günter will walk beside you filming a tracking shot as you approach the office, saying, 'The entire cold case revolves around this unassuming tropical inn. She might have even been murdered on these very grounds. And the heartbroken husband is still keeping his wife's memory alive by keeping the place open. Or is he actually hiding something? I'm going inside to see if he'll talk and shed some light on this macabre riddle.'... Got it?"

"All but the part about 'hiding something,'" replied Reevis. "I'm not going to say that."

"Why not?"

Reevis counted off on his fingers. "Because it's not true. Because the poor guy lost a wife. Because the short-order cook probably did it."

"No time to discuss this right now." Nigel looked nervously at his Rolex. "We're on a super-tight schedule!"

"Tight?" said Reevis. "It's a four-year-old cold case."

Nigel shook his head. "There's a rival reality show on the west coast about to break a case almost identical to this one on Anna Maria Island."

"Rival?" asked Reevis.

"Total frauds. Their whole gimmick is accuracy. We've crossed paths too many times to count. And not far behind them are the Australians."

"Australians?"

"That's why speed is of the essence," said Nigel.

"I still won't do it," said Reevis.

"Okay, fine, you don't have to mention him hiding anything." Nigel turned to Günter with a pragmatic expression. "We'll B-roll it with over-dub."

"B-roll?" asked the reporter.

"That's when we shoot atmospheric footage without the talent present and voice in things they haven't said."

Günter focused the camera. "B-rolls cure a multitude of sins."

"Reevis, you ready?"

"Give me a moment." Reevis unfolded a sheet of paper with a series of questions.

"You can put that away," said Nigel.

"Why?"

"Because as soon as you enter the office, we'll come flying in behind you with the camera, demanding to know why he won't answer your questions until he throws us out."

"Maybe we could try a softer entrance?" said Reevis. "We can't be sure he won't answer my questions."

"Actually we can," said Nigel. "I called earlier to tell him we were coming over to find out what incriminating evidence he was trying to hide. He acted like a jerk."

Reevis's head fell. "Please refrain from contacting my interview subjects. I do this for a living, and first impressions are critical, especially with the reluctant ones. It takes a certain touch ..."

"And that's why you're perfect for this show!" said Nigel. "We saw your touch the other day in the Sawgrass Lounge. We called ahead there as well, but then you went inside and worked your magic. It was quite an amazing thing to watch."

"So why not let me try again with the husband?" asked Reevis.

Nigel shook his head. "Your approach worked so well at the Sawgrass that our drastic measures to get thrown out got our camera destroyed, so we need to get thrown out here. Deadline, you understand."

"You're joking with me now, right?"

Nigel formed a slightly pained countenance. "We didn't exactly capture a sense of danger at that lounge."

"I got a *tremendous* sense of danger," said Reevis. "That's why I handled it the way I did."

"Maybe if we started going to bars like that at night."

Reevis stood dazed and looked across the street at the modest motel. "One question—as I walk toward the office, you want me to say that I'd like to get some answers from the husband?"

"That's right."

"But we really don't want answers. We want to be thrown out?"

"Right again."

In the writing of novels, they call it metafiction, where someone breaks character and addresses the audience. Reevis thoughtfully paused and stared off the page of a book at the reader: "If you didn't know this conversation actually happened in Florida, you never would have believed it." ... Then, back into his role ...

"I can't go through with this," Reevis mumbled to himself as he reluctantly crossed the street toward the motel. "I have to think of something."

"Your lines?" said Nigel.

"Wait, look," said Reevis. "There's a sign in the office window." It said the manager was temporarily away and to call an emergency number if needed. Relief. Saved by the bell.

"Shoot," said Nigel. "Okay, here's what we do. Reevis, stand over here and say, 'The grounds of this motel are quite intimate, and we couldn't help but feel that we were being watched the entire time we were here, and the husband was deliberately staying away from the office to avoid our questions.'"

Reevis glanced off the book's page again at the reader—"Yep"—then faced Nigel. "Are you going to indemnify me for slander?"

"What do you mean?"

"He could be at the store getting milk."

"We don't know he's *not* avoiding us."

"That's your ethical standard?"

They continued hashing it out on the side of A1A as an ominous black SUV came up the road and parked across the street without their noticing. Meanwhile, a sign was taken down in the motel office window. "Look!" Günter pointed at the motel. "The owner's back!"

"Reevis! Hurry!" said Nigel. "Before he leaves again!"

The reporter remained still. "Are you going to behave?"

"Yes! Yes! Yes!" Nigel shoved him in the back. "Do your thing!"

"All right, but I'm calling it off the second you pull any stunts."

"Sure! Go!"

Reevis approached the office and went inside. The man behind the counter smiled warmly. "How can I help you?"

"My name is Reevis Tome, and I'm a reporter with Florida Cable News. I know this might be a sensitive subject, but would you mind at all if I spoke with you about what happened four years ago? The police believe my story might be helpful in solving—"

The owner tilted his head to see over the reporter's shoulder. "What the—?"

The door crashed open. Nigel and Günter rushed in with camera and lights.

"What are you doing?" said the manager. "Turn that thing off!"

"Reevis!" said Nigel. "Quick! Ask him why he refuses to go on camera!"

"No."

Günter advanced on the counter as the manager covered his face. "Get out!"

"Perfect!" said Nigel.

Suddenly the door crashed open again. More lights and another camera. This time they were aimed at Nigel and Günter.

"Oh no," said Nigel.

"What's going on?" asked Reevis.

"The Australians," said Nigel. "My archnemesis, the devious producer 'Cricket' Brisbane, and his inseparable videographer, Dundee."

The new camera zoomed in on Nigel's face. "What have you got to hide?"

Nigel and Günter turned their own camera around. "What have *you* got to hide?"

"I asked you first!"

"Get out of here!" shouted Nigel.

"*You* get out of here!"

"All of you leave!" yelled the owner. "Before I call the police!"

The two film crews took their disagreement outside, chasing each other in a circle in the parking lot. "Why are you running away from our camera?"

"Why are you running away from *our* camera?"

The pursuit continued until the two film units broke apart and took up defensive positions behind their respective vehicles.

"Why are you hiding behind your car?"

"Why are *you* hiding?"

The motel manager stepped outside and stood next to Reevis.

Günter popped up from behind his SUV for a quick shot with his camera. Then Dundee popped up. Then Günter ...

The owner scratched a bald spot. "What in the name of anything am I looking at?"

"A snake eating its tail," said Reevis. "Listen, I'm really sorry about all this. They weren't supposed to do that."

"That's why it seemed weird," said the owner. "I told them on the phone I'd be happy to give any interviews if it would help the case."

"You did? ..."

A news truck from the local eleven o'clock show *Action Eyewitness 7 Live* happened to be driving by and hit the brakes. A third camera began filming.

"What's going on?" asked the *Eyewitness 7* reporter, straining to make out the action in the darkness.

"Looks like some kind of shootout," said her cameraman. "Must be using silencers."

Günter popped up again before ducking back down. Then Dundee.

Nigel dropped to the ground. "Günter! Shoot under the car! You can get their feet!"

"Right." He placed the camera on the pavement.

Across the parking lot: "Where'd they go?" asked Brisbane. He looked down and saw camera lights shining off his loafers. "Oh no, they're shooting our feet."

Dundee crouched and got off a few seconds of his own low-level footage before they jumped in the front seat and took off.

"Günter! After them!" A second SUV took off down A1A, followed by the Channel 7 news truck.

Reevis pulled out his phone and called a cab.

Chapter 12

LATER THAT EVENING

Sniper rifles froze in triangulated aim at a ranch house in Sarasota County.

Rog gingerly slid his chair up to the coffee table and reached into one of the pizza boxes.

A string of hot mozzarella stretched from a slice to Serge's mouth as he chewed. "One last lesson. After you grasp the concept of a psychopath, you have to wonder, what's the opposite? An 'empath'! They feel *everything*, the suffering of people they don't even know in other countries, baby seals, the destruction of rain forests. Some of them are those former celebrities on late-night commercials with starving children who are forced to write you personal letters if you buy them rice and pencils during a drunken late-night moment of weakness, and now these letters of shame keep popping up each month like herpes. That's why I hate the terms 'bleeding heart' and 'tree hugger.' Sure, they can get so annoying you want to ram knitting needles through both your ears. But deep inside, their intentions are wonderful. Jesus was an empath. Although today I'm tempted to tweak the Sermon on the Mount: 'The meek shall inherit the earth, but only if their parents were greedy psychopaths' ..."

Tires screeched outside. A sedan with black-wall tires and tinted windows pulled up. A badge flashed. "FBI special agent Braun ... You must be Sergeant Duffy ..."

Another skidding of tires. Another sedan with lots of antennas. A different badge. "CIA special agent Cargill ..."

... Serge leaned back on the couch and patted his stomach. "I'm stuffed."

"So am I," said Coleman.

Serge slowly stood and stretched his back. "I guess that means it's time to surrender."

Rog perked up. "You mean it?"

"Sure."

"Uh, Serge," said Coleman. "I think we might have a problem."

"What's that?"

"We've gotten ourselves cornered," said Coleman. "The whole place is surrounded by cops. I don't see how we can get away."

"There's always hope." Serge walked to the front of the house and grabbed the doorknob.

"Great!" said Coleman. "I knew you'd have a plan! What is it?"

"That is the plan," said Serge.

"Hope? ... No, seriously."

"I *am* serious." Serge cracked the door a slit and waved a pizza-stained napkin. "We're coming out!"

"Everyone in position!" yelled Sergeant Duffy. "But hold your fire."

Clacking sounds as the SWAT team crouched and readied their weapons. Other officers shielded themselves behind the open doors of their squad cars. Agents Duffy and Cargill pulled Glocks from shoulder holsters inside their suits. A half block away behind the police lines, the entire press corps stopped talking. Cameras zoomed in on the front of the house.

All sound stopped. Time slowed down. Perspiration trickled on cheeks. Fingers twitched on triggers. Duffy took one last, careful look around and raised a megaphone. "Okay, we're ready!"

The door opened the rest of the way. Rog burst from the house—"Thank God! Those guys are out of their minds! They held me hostage!" One of the SWAT team tackled him in the middle of the yard, and soon there was a pile of ten. Somewhere at the bottom, handcuffs snapped closed.

Serge and Coleman strolled across the grass in Windbreakers. "Sergeant Duffy, I'm taking a wild stab that you'd like to have a word with us."

"Yes! Definitely! Don't go anywhere!"

The tactical human pile in the middle of the yard began to sort itself out. They helped Rogelio to his feet, and Duffy led him to the back of a blue-and-white police transport van.

A suit with a thin tie stepped in front of him. "Excellent work," said Agent Braun. "We'll take the prisoner now."

"No disrespect," said Duffy. "But I'd like to get him processed at the jail before anything else. This *is* my city."

"National security takes precedence," said Braun.

From behind: "Yes, it does," said Agent Cargill. "And *I'm* taking custody of the prisoner."

Serge tapped the sergeant's shoulder. "You wanted to talk to us?"

"Not now!" Duffy swatted his hand away. "I strenuously object ... Officers, take the prisoner."

"Sergeant," said Braun. "Don't force me to arrest you."

"Sergeant," said Cargill. "I authorize you to take the prisoner to my headquarters."

"Excuse me?" said Serge. "Are you guys with the FBI and CIA? You're probably curious who we are."

In unison: "Not now!"

People had Rogelio by both arms, swinging him back and forth. Another sedan pulled up. The seal on the door was Homeland Security. So was the badge. "Agent Maxwell. We'll take it from here ..."

"Now just a minute!" said Cargill.

"Let's see some paperwork!" said Braun.//
"We were here first!" said Duffy.
"My arms are starting to hurt," said Rog.
"Excuse me?" said Serge.

Leaves and litter began to swirl in the air. Everyone covered their ears and looked up as a black helicopter landed in the street. Agents with night-vision goggles jumped out. "We're asserting jurisdiction ..."

Serge shrugged at Coleman. They strolled behind the house and hopped in their silver Corvette, then drove back around front to the street. A large argument was blocking them.

Beep, beep!

Everyone scooted to the side as they continued yelling in each other's faces. The Corvette slipped by and approached the police line holding back the reporters.

Beep, beep!

The officers on the perimeter turned toward the car with the Windbreakers.

Beep, beep!

They lifted the rope to let them through.

MART-MART

A construction worker peered down into the glass case like he was looking at engagement rings. He finally came to a life decision at the checkout counter in the convenience store.

"I'll take the Monopoly scratch-off, the Florida Treasure Hunt, Cash Inferno, Bring on the Benjamins, a Lotto quick-pick for this weekend's drawing, a pack of Marlboro and the beer."

If you drive around South Florida enough, there are those new, brightly lit convenience stores the size of small supermarkets, with wide aisles, walk-in beer coolers, waxed floors, fresh deli sandwiches and sixteen touch-screen gas pumps.

This was not one of them.

It had a gray exterior with an accumulation of trash along the front. An official notice said not to loiter or consume alcoholic beverages within five hundred feet, but its view was blocked by people doing both. Inside were half-empty shelves with dusty cans of Campbell's soup and other food-like containers with Spanish names. Only one person could fit down each aisle, unless they were fat and had to turn sideways, which usually made no geometric difference. The checkout counter had a pair of revolving displays for Zippo lighters and onyx marijuana pipes. Clothespins held a row of calling cards to countries across the Lesser Antilles and most of the Greater. The sign out front said MART-MART, in case there was any doubt.

The line at the counter was fifteen deep. It would have been shorter, but the clerk was on his phone with friends. The next customer stepped up. "I'll take a Gold Rush, Flamingo Fortune, Margaritaville, one quick-pick, a pack of Kools and the beer."

The rest of the transactions were pretty much the same, except for the customers who asked to use the bathroom and were told that it was broken. The night wore into the wee hours. The clerk used the bathroom. More people pulled into the potholed parking lot. Pickups, sports cars, motorcycles and a glass replacement truck featuring giant replacement windows attached to the side with industrial suction cups. Farmworkers jumped down from flatbeds. Someone went in to return an opened pack of cigarettes. "These don't have the tax stamp. Whenever they say 'not for domestic sale,' they always taste stale." The clerk snatched them for a prompt, no-questions-asked refund. The next person also received cash: fifty bucks for a hundred in food stamps. The store made up for its appearance with extra service.

The parade of dysfunction grew on the side of U.S. 1 in Fort Lauderdale. The products that sold themselves continued to do so. Beer, smokes and tickets flowed out the door. A bearded man came in wearing jeans with a white circle on his back pocket where he carried his tin of Skoal. "I want to see if this won anything."

The clerk ran the ticket under the scanner. "You did." He handed a five to the customer, who handed it back. "Beer."

The customer left and got inside an unmarked van parked up the street.

He joined the other state agents who were gathered around a computer screen. The Florida Lottery was an efficiently humming, firewalled, hack-proof operation in all respects. Except for one minor detail. You could have a ticket scanned to see if it won, then actually cash it in later at a different location. This tiny fissure had no foreseen consequence, until certain retail outlets decided to wedge it wide open.

All lottery activity was recorded by state computers. But with hundreds of games, thousands of outlets and millions of customers—and no suspicion or real idea what to look for—the data stayed stored.

Then a few things happened. The state of Florida always understood that lotteries inevitably create a gray economy. There were many ways not to become a millionaire, but still hit a few grand. And if that winner had tax issues, or alimony, or child support, or no green card—and, say, a ticket was scanned for a jackpot above the legal reporting trip wire—it became an inconvenient time to be in a convenience store.

As the lottery grew, so did the amount of data in its computer banks. Patterns emerged, numbers crunched, statistical deviations became improbable. State auditors began to notice that tickets were initially being scanned across a reasonable geographic distribution, but when it came time to cash them in, impossible spikes appeared again and again at specific locations across South Florida, under specific names. Here's what they found: Some of the biggest repeat winners were the store owners themselves. Authorities correctly guessed that certain retailers were moonlighting as brokers, paying eighty cents or so on the dollar for the winning tickets of people who couldn't exactly come forward. The customer would originally have the ticket scanned at a legitimate store, and upon finding they had won too much, asked for the ticket back and went over to one of the brokers who had put the word out on the street. It was an awfully hard thing for officials to prove, but more on point, they subconsciously didn't *want* to prove it. Cracking down on the practice would scare away the people with issues, who were their best customers. That's why they had issues.

That's when another thing happened. More and more customers began to complain about something else. A few of these shady stores had gotten greedy. They began scanning scratch-off instant games and telling the customers that it was only worth five or ten bucks, paying them out of the register. Then, after the customer left, the store owners would cash in a several-hundred-dollar ticket for themselves. Now, *this* was a crackdown that would be popular among the betting public.

And now ... The state agents became fidgety inside their mobile command unit parked three blocks up the street from Mart-Mart.

"Anything yet?"

"Just the initial ticket scan," said the tech at the computer screen. "From when our undercover guy asked if he had a winner."

"It's been a half hour. What's that clerk waiting for?"

"Probably has customers and is on the phone."

Numbers changed on the screen. "Wait, he just claimed it. Six hundred and forty-two bucks. You want to move?"

The agent in charge shook his head. "Strictly surveillance for now. Believe it or not, that store is part of a chain of seventeen in the area. We want to see where all this is going ..."

Back inside, a migrant worker stepped up to the counter. He glanced around before clandestinely showing the clerk a Lotto ticket that he refused to let go of, so the clerk had to pull the man's arm toward the scanner. Not a complete winner, but close. Five of six numbers.

The clerk abruptly ended his personal phone call and dialed another number. "... Yes, I'm sure. I scanned it myself ... all right I'll tell him ..." He hung up. "Wait outside at the corner."

A white Audi eventually pulled up, and the back door opened. The farmhand climbed into a lifestyle he had never seen before. The car drove off. A laconic man in a tight bicycle shirt inspected the $7,931 ticket. He stuck it in his briefcase and handed the worker an envelope with five grand.

They dropped him off at a strip club.

Chapter 13

THOREAU CLUB

Traffic crawled north on U.S. 1, and the cross streets began bearing presidents' names. When you reached Roosevelt, you knew which one it was because it lay between McKinley and Taft. The last was Coolidge, a hint at the age of the planned community that opened in 1925.

Hollywood, Florida.

The 1920s were a high-water mark of optimism in the Sunshine State. People imagined everything from floating hotels to golf courses in the Everglades. The city of Hollywood, for instance, had a wishful-thinking main street called Hollywood Boulevard, and there was even a Hollywood Bowl on the shore. It was all designed to give the California movie industry a stiff run.

Didn't quite work out that way. But when the hucksters and hoopla dissipated, a tastefully quaint community accidentally emerged from the fog of failed avarice. Reevis's car reached the middle of town and entered a massive roundabout circling a green space for children called Anniversary Park. He turned east toward the sea. Along both sides of the road, stucco houses and bright splashes of color: flowers, trees, canvas awnings, Bahama shutters. Reevis approached a blue street sign for Clownfish Lane. He made a left and pulled up to a modest beach apartment building constructed during the Gulf of Tonkin incident. A single story of eight units in a row, white with orange-and-green citrus trim. The screen doors still had those sixties-era wire sculptures of herons and palm trees and swordfish. A lizard made ripples in the concrete birdbath supported by a concrete seahorse. What used to be a lush lawn had since been replaced by a yard of big, smooth white rocks, because the owner had taken up apathy. The same reason was behind a landscaping theme of sea grapes and banana trees. Try to make them *not* grow. It was one of perhaps a hundred such apartments in Florida with names like the Surfcomber, the Sands, the Tides, the Tradewinds. Except this one wasn't called anything.

Reevis got out and approached unit number three with keys in hand. He originally wanted a place in the Gables, because of his fondness for coquina and banyans, but that was not in a journalist's budget. Still, this place had personality.

"All right," said Brook Campanella, walking up behind him. "Let's see this great new pad you've been bragging about."

Reevis opened up. *Cozy* was generous. Just a bedroom and a living room, with a kitchen nook clinging in the corner.

Brook stood amid the terrazzo floor. "I like it. When does the rest of your stuff arrive?"

"This is it."

"Two wicker patio chairs? Not even a TV?"

"I've decided to minimalize," said Reevis. "Every move, so many possessions to haul around, until it was almost like they were possessing me."

"You've been reading Thoreau again."

"Actually *Fight Club*, but there's a parallel."

"I've got to see the bedroom." She strolled and stopped in the doorway. "A mattress on the floor and an alarm clock?"

"Lifestyle aesthetics," said Reevis. "I was concerned about losing my enthusiasm for all the little things."

"In other words, you got rid of distractions so you could be distracted?"

"Something like that."

She put her arms around his neck and gave him a quick kiss. "Don't change."

"Then you'll dig this." He quickly led her into the kitchen nook, reached up and opened doors. The cupboards were as unburdened as the rooms. He pulled down the only thing on the bottom shelf, a shiny device with a handle and no moving parts. "I bought a classic old-style stove-top espresso machine. I was just going through the motions flipping the switch on my Mr. Coffee. But this baby ..." He held it at eye level and began twisting. "... You unscrew the bottom half and fill it with water. Then replace the perforated little metal chamber where you tamp down the coffee grounds. Turn the burner on and wait for the water to boil up and trickle out a post in the upper chamber. It takes a lot more time, but you can't compare the taste."

"Waiting makes it taste better?"

"I'm introducing a new set of simple ablutions into my daily routine." He opened another cupboard and placed a pair of miniature cups and saucers on the counter. "Then I carefully pour it into authentic Cuban demitasse. Check out the tiny gold rims and blue-and-red diamond patterns like tile work from Ybor City."

"Demitasse ablutions?"

"It's all about the little stuff."

"Don't take this the wrong way, but you're starting to remind me of someone."

"I take it as a compliment."

She looked toward a brown paper grocery bag with the end of a loaf poking out the top. "Is that the dinner you promised me?"

"I went shopping at this funky market in Little Havana next to the dominoes park. The palm sprig they stuck in the bag is some Catholic tradition."

"There are only about five hundred closer supermarkets."

He grabbed the sack and pulled out the loaf. "*Real* Cuban bread ..." Then the bulk of the contents. "... Rice, black beans, tomato sauce, plantain chips—don't know how to cook regulars yet—green peppers, one large onion, one clove garlic, and the beef is in the fridge."

"You're making me traditional ropa vieja? That's so romantic."

"Means 'old clothes' or 'rags,' probably because of how the beef is shredded."

"I know." She opened a drawer for a knife and went to work on the onion. "I'm starting to get what you see in all this."

"Peace." There was a small boom box on top of the refrigerator, and Reevis punched up his date-night theme track. "How's the law clinic going?"

"Seriously pissed off at a landlord." Brook's eyes started to water. "Looks like a pattern of fraud—something you'd like to cover?"

"... *Take a sad song ...*"

"Right in my wheelhouse," said Reevis. "Just have to ditch these new TV producers and sneak out with my old cameraman."

"That bad?"

"They want me to use the middle name 'Danger.'"

"... *Hey Jude ...*"

Brook stopped to listen to the music. "This is the Beatles, but it's not the Beatles."

"Wilson Pickett's recording from 1968 in Muscle Shoals, Alabama."

"You're into Pickett?"

"As much as the next guy." Reevis oiled a frying pan and tossed the meat in with some garlic. "But the real reason I love this version is the big crescendo at the end when an unknown session guitarist from Florida nicknamed Skydog blew everyone away with an insane riff. Nothing like it had ever been heard on an R-and-B record. And today, that precise moment three minutes into the song is called the birth of Southern rock. Eric Clapton called it the best guitar solo he'd ever heard, so he tracked down Skydog, learned his real name was Duane Allman, and invited him to play guitar on Eric's next album that they recorded in Miami."

"Now you're definitely reminding me of our mutual friend."

"With good reason. Follow me."

They set all the stove dials to simmer, and Reevis headed back to the bedroom.

"I've already seen this," said Brook. "Mattress and clock."

"Not everything." Reevis opened the slat accordion doors to a closet.

"Good God," said Brook. "Look at the size of that bookcase. There's certainly no downsizing here."

"I'm blocking it from distraction with the closet doors," said Reevis. "But a few things I just can't get rid of."

"Few things? This is the biggest reference library on Florida I've ever seen, including music and movies."

Reevis pulled a plastic CD case off the shelf and handed it to Brook.

"*The Duane Allman Anthology*? Him again?"

"No, open it. That's how I learned the trivia I just told you in the kitchen."

"There's a letter tucked in here." Her lips moved silently as her eyes flowed down the page, then she read aloud as she reached the bottom. "... 'Shortly after the 'Hey Jude' session, Duane returned to Jacksonville and formed the Allman Brothers Band.'" Her eyes suddenly shot up to Reevis. "It's signed 'Serge'!"

"He sends a package every week," said the reporter. "Sometimes the return address is in the middle of Lake Okeechobee; sometimes the governor's mansion."

"You've been in contact with him?" Ultra-urgent now. "How is he? What's going on? Why didn't you tell me? When did—"

"Stop." Reevis shook his head. "I don't know a thing. The parcels just arrive. Sometimes there's a note but nothing specific."

"What kind of stuff is he sending you?"

Reevis looked sideways. "Pretty much that whole bookcase."

"That's it? But why?"

"I think he fancies me as some kind of protégé he's mentoring." The reporter idly pulled down a pictorial book on the Sarasota architecture of Paul Rudolph, then a spiral-bound sailing guide to the Keys with aerial photos of Adams Cut and Tavernier Creek. "It almost has a fatalistic aura, like he needs to pass this knowledge down to an heir. Do you think he's okay?"

"Serge isn't close to okay," Brook said with a smile. "I sometimes worry."

"You two used to have a thing, didn't you?"

"More like *I* had a crush, but nothing developed. Then I met you." She held one of his hands. "Don't give that history another thought."

"I don't. I considered him a good friend, too." Reevis closed the closet. "I've thought about trying to find him, but all I have is an old cell-phone number."

"Why don't you call it?"

"Come on." A knowing look. "From what we've learned about him since our ordeal in Key West, he would have been caught five times if he used anything except a series of disposables. And this number is a year old."

"It's odd, but until this very second I didn't realize the impact he had on both our lives."

"He's the reason we met, after all," said Reevis.

"The reason we're *together*," said Brook. "Like a couple that first bonds at a showing of their favorite classic movie."

"Or teaching me his favorite Latin recipes."

Their eyes suddenly locked.

"Dinner!"

Reevis ran into the kitchen and fanned the smoke. Brook opened the windows. "What's it look like?"

"Just a tiny bit burnt." He began scooping rice and beans and Cuban meat stew onto plates.

"You don't have a table," said Brook. "We eat standing up?"

"No." Reevis opened the door under the sink.

"Wicker trays?"

"Matches the patio chairs."

Moments later, they sat side by side, sopping up tomato sauce with the thick bread. Brook chewed and looked toward where a

TV normally would have been. "I didn't notice the poster before. Isn't that some kind of famous work of art?"

"Serge again. Came rolled up in a mailing tube." Reevis munched a plantain chip. "Watercolor called *A Norther,* painted in Key West in 1886 by Winslow Homer. Now it's my favorite painting of all time. I picked a spot in the apartment where I'd see it a lot."

"So instead of watching TV, you sit there each night and watch the painting?"

"Simplify." *Munch.* "My nerves need it these days."

"You need to figure out what to do with those crazy producers of yours," said Brook. "Never seen you so stressed."

"Figured I'd get out in front of this thing by advancing my own stories before they can come up with more inane ideas of their own."

"By the way," said Brook. "Thanks for your coverage of the police forfeiture case I'm handling. Public opinion isn't supposed to count, but judges are still elected around here. And you drummed up a lot of new business for the firm."

"That whole fiasco was constitutionally reprehensible," said Reevis.

"Still waiting for our day in court," said Brook.

"Working on anything else that I might be interested in?"

"You'll be the first to know."

Sunlight prematurely departed outside the apartment's jalousie windows. Floridians know the drill. Most rain will play itself out in minutes. But when the sky turns purple, and palm fronds are already flying in the wind before the first drop has fallen, hang on to your hat.

"I hope the car windows are up," said Brook.

"I love these storms," said Reevis.

The downpour crashed into the sea grapes and banana trees with a crackling roar, and the living room grew dark.

"Maybe turn on a light?" asked Brook.

"Have a better idea." Reevis grabbed something else from the cupboard and struck a wooden match. A dim glow flickered high up the walls.

"A Santería candle?" asked Brook.

"Went shopping at this colorful market in Little Haiti," said Reevis. "I was *this close* to buying a live chicken and making arroz con pollo for you tonight."

"What stopped you?"

"At first I thought it would be the ultimate gesture in simplifying my life," said Reevis. "But as I mulled the implications of the bird process, it only seemed more complex."

"You ... entertain me. That's important." Brook looked fondly into his eyes.

"Listen to what's happening out there," said Reevis. "It's really beautiful."

They returned to their final bites of Cuban cuisine. Then it was that kind of quiet and stillness of air like when the electricity goes out. The pair oddly found themselves coupled together as they silently watched the show going on in the Winslow Homer painting.

Outside the apartment windows, palm trees yielded in a dark and overbearing sky. In the painting, same thing.

The stillness in the apartment continued as a series of brilliant blue-white flashes filled the room. A delay followed the lightning, then the marching drum line of thunder.

Reevis noticed the clock was out on the stove. One of the flashes outside had actually been a transformer blowing. The power was out for real. Even more still now without the moving air of the central A/C. A smile. Reevis thought: *If you've never sat in candlelight and heard rain hit a banana leaf...*

They both quietly looked at the painting.

"It was storming that night, too," said Brook. "The trees were bending in Key West."

"Almost exactly a year ago," said Reevis. "The last time we saw Serge."

"I wonder where he could possibly be."

EPISODE THREE

Chapter 14

A NEW DAY

There are parts of greater Miami where even crime doesn't pay. These are the desolate, bombed-out sections of the metro area with few forms of life above the virus level. Deserted industrial lots and underpasses and rock pits all but abandoned to the lizards and Sterno bums and roaming dogs with visible ribs.

One such stretch sat in the small city of Hialeah near the Palmetto Expressway.

Only two businesses with the loose definition of commerce: a U-Grab-It auto-parts salvage yard and, next door, a squat concrete pillbox of an office that had been repeatedly painted over as it went from bail bonds to title loans to just painted over.

Only two sounds echoed across the steaming badlands: someone with a socket wrench cursing under the hood of a Plymouth, and Jimi Hendrix from the *Electric Ladyland* album.

The psychedelic guitar licks led back to the pillbox. All the windows had burglar bars, and steel plates covered the dead bolts. The single room inside was divided in two by a curtain of purple beads. A large clay ashtray from Tijuana brimmed with burned-down roaches.

Another roach singed the fingertips of a stubby, potbellied man in a Pink Floyd tour T-shirt featuring a prism and spectrum of light. Bald on top, with wild gray curls of hair on the side, going every which way over his ears like Allen Ginsberg. The T-shirt was too tight.

He cranked up the stereo.

"... *'Cause I'm a voodoo chile!* ..."

Time for the low-demand lawyer to rehearse opening arguments. There was a final, rapid toking on the roach as smoke rose toward an unbalanced ceiling fan. "Okay, focus yourself. I need to remember that, and then that, and the other thing. All right, I think I've got it ..." A last big hit and he stamped out the end of the joint. "Ladies and gentleman of the jury, let's get something out in the open right away because it's what we're all thinking about. Not by a long shot is this the crime of the century, and yet when you say 'sex with a goat,' you can't help but vividly picture it, and then you can't get the horrible image out of your head, and you unfairly imagine my poor client standing behind livestock ... Shit, that's way too visual. They'll just picture it even more. Okay, how about this. Ahem ... Ladies and gentlemen of the jury, society as a whole treats the goat rather badly. Can we at least agree on that point? ... No, stop. That's stupid. Maybe this: ... Ladies and gentlemen, blah-blah-blah. Did you know that in certain regions of Nepal, the goat is used in ... Fuck it." He punched numbers on his cell phone. "Yeah, it's me. Listen, dude, you really gotta plead this one out ... No, I'm sure ..."

He hung up, and the phone rang immediately.

"Ziggy Blade, attorney at law, citizen of the planet ... Oh, hi, Brook. What's up? ... I can't hear you ... I still can't hear you! ... Oh, right, that's Hendrix. I'll turn it down ... Where were we? ... I'm just in my office working on opening arguments for a jury. It's a myth that goats eat tin cans, but they do climb trees if at the proper angle ... No, no, no, no, I'm not high, no, no, okay yes, just a teensy bit, but only to center my head for the trial ... Advice? What type of case? ... Uh-huh, uh-huh, uh-huh ... What kind of drug residue on the cash? ... Cocaine? Piece of cake. And I thought this was going to be a tough quiz. *Miami Herald,* 1985 ... I realize newspaper articles can't be introduced as evidence *res ipso al fresco,* so you federally cite Ninth Circuit Appeals Los Angeles 1994. Vast majority of all big-city bills test positive, higher in Florida. Takes as little as point-zero-zero-six micrograms ... No, only a tiny percentage of the currency has been handled by traffickers. The rest is cross-contamination from ATMs and currency counters at banks. Remember how finely milled, weaponized anthrax got spread in 2001 from mail-sorting machines? ... No, I didn't take a special legal seminar. Everyone out on the street knows this stuff."

The stoned attorney listened to profuse thanks from the Women's Legal Aid Clinic.

"Just glad I could help," said Ziggy, tilting his head back and dripping Visine into road-map eyes. "And if I may say so, Brook, it's really good to hear your voice after all this time. How long has it been? Back in Key West with Serge? ... No, I don't have any idea where he is. You know that maniac—he's liable to be anywhere ..."

MEANWHILE ...

A silver Corvette drove extra slow around a quiet lake in western Volusia County.

"This is boring," said Coleman.

"Just keep your eyes peeled." Serge carefully scanned the side of the road. "I didn't spend all my time rigging the car stereo up to that bullhorn for nothing."

"Wait." Coleman pointed. "I think I see one."

Serge scooched up to the windshield. "You're right." He accelerated.

"We're almost next to him," said Coleman.

"Get ready with that bullhorn." Serge pulled closer to the grass and a narrow footpath circling the water.

Coleman giggled. "Is he going to be surprised!"

"That's the whole point," said Serge, reaching for a knob. "This is all about unlocking inner potential."

They had just about reached the jogger when Coleman aimed the bullhorn out his window, and Serge cranked the volume.

"... *Eye of the tiger!* ..."

"Man, did he jump," said Coleman.

"But notice how he's moving faster?" Serge depressed the gas pedal to remain precisely beside the runner. "Just keep that bullhorn up."

"... *Eye of the tiger!* ..."

"He keeps glancing back at us," said Coleman. "He's running even faster now."

"I have a gift for motivating people." The Corvette continued alongside the runner. "There are a lot of openings today for life coaches."

"Is that your new job for the next episode of *Route 66*?"

"This is just a vignette."

"... *Eye of the tiger!* ..."

"He just left the path and is racing down the bank," said Coleman. "Now he jumped in the lake."

"See? He was limiting himself to just running," said Serge, "when it only took me a couple minutes to show him the possibilities of triathlons."

The music cut off, and Coleman fiddled with the bullhorn in his lap. "How'd you come up with this great idea, anyway?"

"Can't take credit," said Serge. "It's a new underground Internet phenomenon. Check it out on my smartphone."

Coleman scrolled down through various video clips. "Damn, hundreds of others are all doing the same thing we just did."

"And people say America doesn't have culture." The Stingray crested a small hill leading out into the countryside.

"So what *is* your next job?"

"That will become readily apparent when we get to Cassadaga."

Coleman twisted up a fat one. "Never heard of it."

"Most people haven't," said Serge. "But it's possibly the most unique place in all the state, way off the beaten track between DeLand and Deltona. There isn't even a proper highway exit, so you have to keep jumping country roads until you reach this tiny—and I mean tiny—little town out in the woods."

"How much longer?"

"You'll know when you start seeing the signs."

They started seeing the signs: MEDICINE MAN PASTOR PETE; PSYCHIC SHOP; CRYSTALS, JEWELRY, AURA PHOTOS; MEDIUMS & HEALERS; PURPLE ROSE READINGS; NATIVE AMERICAN AND METAPHYSICAL STUFF; WE NOW DO ASTROLOGY CHARTS; TAROT CARDS; CERTIFIED MENTALIST ON DUTY; KATHY IS HERE.

"You're right," said Coleman. "This is the weirdest place I've ever seen. All these psychics."

"But that's not the strangest thing to me," said Serge. "It's the total retail hegemony, like if you drove into a town and every single business only sold yogurt."

"But how did this place happen?"

"Founded in 1894 by a New York man named George Colby, who wanted to establish a paranormal-friendly community." Serge made a right turn onto Stevens Street. "What caps it off for me is all the history, like the majestic Cassadaga Hotel over there, built in 1927. Where else can you drive deep into the sticks, and then suddenly find this time-frozen grande dame rising out of nowhere with spinning paddle fans on the sitting porch and an antique wooden phone booth in the lobby that's been converted into a 'Meditation Station,' where you go inside to make toll-free calls to your third eye?"

"What's this other place across the street?"

"Where we get our start." Serge parked in front of a century-old wooden-slat building with a new tin roof. They entered through double doors beneath a sign: BOOKSTORE AND INFORMATION CENTER.

Coleman strolled down an aisle, picking up items for sale. "This place sure is into scented oils and candles."

"Like a Pottery Barn without the strings."

They moved along a wall with shelves full of crystals in the shapes of pyramids, obelisks and opaque spheres resting atop tripods. Other crystals were raw in form, glistening green with pointy purple formations encased in rocks that had been cut in half by special saws.

"What's the deal with all the crystals?" asked Coleman.

"They're imbued with a menu of special powers by those so inclined to think," said Serge. "Healing properties, energy, spiritual connections. Some even believe they contain ancient memories."

"How do they work?"

"Many ways. Some believers put them in glasses of water to drink, or boil them with potions to produce a pleasant vapor for aromatherapy. Others rub them on their skin or just carry them around in their pockets. But I think mostly they just look at them." Serge grabbed a statue of a wizard holding a crystal. "Like this thing. Stick it in the middle of the dining room table full of believers, and everyone gets jazzed."

Coleman chuckled. "That's messed up."

"Maybe on the surface, to outsiders," said Serge. "But I'm not so quick to judge. The part where they simply stare at the things is likely a placebo effect. On the other hand, these are real chemical compounds, forming lattice structures in compliance with the laws of the periodic table. This crystal may look totally solid, but most of it is actually empty space with electrons furiously orbiting shit, so who really knows what's going on? Ironically, it's science itself that causes me to be open-minded and insatiably curious about something apparently unscientific. Now I must do further research."

Serge grabbed a large reference volume off a shelf and approached the counter.

"Anything else?" asked the cashier.

"Just the book on lucky crystals," said Serge. "Sorry, I'm guessing 'lucky' has a pejorative tone around here. I meant 'all-powerful.' It's about respect and proper manners. If you're a guest at someone else's church, you don't stand there the whole time the pastor is preaching and sarcastically say, 'Yeah, right,' or worse ..."

He turned toward the crystal display and said "Yeah, right" again, but this time he also pumped a fist up and down in a jerking-off gesture. He faced the cashier again. "That would be bad, too. How much for the book? ..."

Serge grabbed his gift bag and walked to the back of the store. A wooden sign hung high on a wall: EXPECT A MIRACLE. Below it was a door. "I must open it." He led Coleman inside an empty room that looked completely different from the front of the building. Drop ceiling, wood paneling, American flag, long folding tables with plastic cloths covered in sunflowers.

"This is like an Elks lodge," said Coleman.

"It's exactly like an Elks lodge," said Serge, staring at a podium under another sign: SOUTHERN CASSADAGA SPIRITUALIST ASSOCIATION.

From behind: "Excuse me, can I help you?"

The guys turned to see a middle-aged woman wiping her hands in the doorway of the adjacent kitchen.

"Sorry if we're not supposed to be in here," said Serge. "I see new doors and need to open them. You have to live by a code. I'm naturally curious, more so than most."

"That's all right," said the woman. "We encourage curiosity around here."

Serge's head snapped back with a puzzled look. "You *encourage* curiosity? And yet you call yourself a religion?" He quickly covered his mouth. "Oops, I think I just offended everyone in the world."

"Nobody gets offended around here. Everyone's free to be an individual."

"I'm beginning to feel that vibe," said Serge. "Not like those creepy walled compounds out west where church elders banish all the young men and force the women to wear gingham and become grandmothers before they can vote."

"Are you okay?"

"Listen, I don't want to horn in on anyone's action," said Serge, "but the episode only lasts a week and I need to fast-track my next job as a psychic. I have a gift."

"Ah, I understand now," said the woman. "You've come to develop yourself. That's absolutely wonderful. I'm not quite sure, though, about a week ..."

"Any advice would be greatly appreciated."

"May I suggest coming back here Sunday morning? We have a nice breakfast in this hall purely on a donation basis, followed by the Grove Service."

"What's that?"

"In the old days, it was held out in an orange grove, but now we have this building. You'll meet regular and apprentice mediums who go table to table for a series of three-minute readings."

"Cool. Psychic speed dating," said Serge. "But Sunday's pushing it. What about, say, right now?"

"In that case ..." She pointed back through the door. "There's a separate room at the end of the store. You'll find a telephone and a washable whiteboard with listings of everyone currently on call—"

The hall was empty before she could finish, and the door swung closed.

Serge stared up at the whiteboard and rubbed his mouth. "I didn't realize this was so involved. The listings are rigidly divided between mediums and healers. All guaranteed to be officially certified and permitted."

Coleman tapped Serge on the back. "What kind of test do you think they give to certify them?"

"Probably a blank piece of paper," said Serge. "Then they turn it back in blank because the person grading the exam is also a psychic."

A TV was on in the corner, playing a promotional. Serge walked over and turned up the volume.

"What's going on?" asked Coleman.

"A reality show is using a psychic to try to solve a missing-persons case."

A woman in a paisley silk robe sat in a darkened room and closed her eyes. She held a photograph of a teenage girl. Her hands began to tremble. *"Her body won't be found immediately ..."*

"Wow," said Coleman. "Do you think she's really going to crack the case?"

"Not a chance," said Serge. "I once watched an otherwise reputable crime program, and even the cops were taken in by the charlatan they'd hired. The key to the whole scam is making the general sound specific, like, 'The victim's body will be found near water. There is some kind of mechanical sound. I'm getting a vision of colored lights.' ... And if the police ask about a name, she says she sees the letters *E* and *T*."

"Sounds pretty specific to me," said Coleman.

"That's the whole point," said Serge. "But *E* and *T* are the most common letters in the English language. And try *getting away* from water, sounds and lights. Who's to say how near is near? In the show I saw, they later found the body in the woods. And as proof the psychic was right, the narrator said there was a river on the edge of town, jackhammers were fixing a road, and some intersection had a traffic signal."

"That's amazing!" said Coleman.

"It's amazing she earns a living," said Serge. "That's why I know it's the job for me. The whole point is to find the body, so when they finally do locate the shallow grave, that's all they care about—totally forgetting some psychic gibberish five months ago that was so vague it fit half the cold cases in the country. That's why I say screw generalizing and give them a real show: 'The body will be found strangled with a Siberian weasel and buried in a calliope beneath a time-share sweat lodge.' And if they ask me about a name, I'll respond with African clicking sounds."

The TV continued in the background. "*... I see colored lights and the letters* E *and* T *...*"

Coleman followed Serge back to the whiteboard. "Which one are you going to call?"

"This one looks interesting." Serge picked up the phone. "Madam Bovary ..."

BACK AT THE OFFICE

The fluorescent newsroom hummed the hum of a major breaking story. Phones rang, keyboards clattered, people rushed past each other with documents. Reason: City work crews had just discovered sixty-five bodies buried along Interstate 95. The grisly remains turned out to be a forgotten cemetery, but TV is a visual medium, and bulldozers and bones are always welcome.

More reporters ran across the newsroom. At the end of the open floor plan sat a row of glassed-in executive offices. Through the window of one such office, the staff could see silent gestures and emotional body language. An important person sat behind the desk, and someone less so sat in front.

Reevis rubbed both hands down his face in frustration.

"Are you all right?" asked his assignment editor.

"I can't work with these guys anymore," said Reevis. "They stand for everything I'm against."

"I know this has been a rough transition—"

"Rough? Did you see my ridiculous noon segment at the graveyard by the highway?" asked Reevis. "After I refused to drive a bulldozer, Nigel actually dug up a skull and tossed it to me while I was live on the air."

The editor winced. "That part could have been handled with more sensitivity."

"Not to mention what happened yesterday," said Reevis. "I had a key person ready to be interviewed, and they wrecked it again."

"That also was unfortunate," the editor said evenly. "And I passed your objections up through proper channels."

"Obviously it didn't help," said Reevis. "They put it on the air last night anyway. The chaos with the motel owner, and then two camera crews chasing each other around the parking lot. Not to mention the day before, when they charged into our meeting and jammed a lens in my face, making me look like a clown."

The editor took a slow, diplomatic breath. "We discussed that at the marketing breakfast this morning. It seems we received very favorable feedback on that last segment."

"What segment?" asked Reevis. "They just manufactured a meaningless confrontation by rudely barging into your office for no reason."

"Exactly," said Shug. "The focus group loved the idea of us ruthlessly investigating ourselves. Our confidence and trust ratings went through the roof."

"But we *weren't* investigating ourselves."

"And our parent company insists we continue."

"Continue doing something we're not doing?"

"They said it boosts the audience's faith."

"Let me see if I have this straight," said Reevis. "We fake stuff to show we have principles?"

"And integrity."

Reevis rolled his eyes. "Anything else?"

"Corporate wants us to follow up by allowing Nigel and Günter to film us as we clean house."

"What for?"

"Weed out all the journalistic corruption that's led to an epidemic of fabricated stories."

"Who's fabricating stories?"

"Just Nigel and Günter," said the editor. "There are going to be a number of firings. It could get ugly."

The pair were interrupted by screaming outside in the general newsroom. A woman wept hysterically at her desk as a film crew bore down on her with their camera. Then she fled for the exit, and Günter ran jiggling after her.

Reevis turned back around. "And you're okay with this?"

"I've got kids in college." Shug looked out his office window. "Uh-oh."

"They're heading over here."

The editor got up and locked the door.

Nigel rattled the knob and knocked. *"Come on guys, let us in."*

"Where were we?" asked Shug.

"It could get ugly." Reevis pointed. "Now they're filming us through the window."

The editor walked over and closed the blinds. "We're entering a period that's going to become a little turbulent, but it's only temporary."

Knocking on the glass. *"Open the blinds."*

"So you're going to force me to keep working with them?" said Reevis.

"I've got kids—"

"I know, college," said Reevis. "Okay, if it's only temporary, I'll play ball. You gave me my big break at this station, so it's only right that I return the favor."

"I'm glad to hear you feel that way," said the editor. "Then you'll completely understand ..."

The assignment editor got up and opened the door to his office. Nigel and Günter stormed in and stuck the camera in the young reporter's face.

"Reevis!" yelled his editor. "You're fired!"

"What?"

"I'm shocked and saddened!" said Shug. "Of all people, I never thought you would falsify material to sensationalize a story!"

"You're actually firing me?"

"It's only temporary. We'll rehire you right after they film the security guys ejecting you from the building. Nigel already has your new employment application."

Nigel waved the document. "Viewers love a comeback story."

The guards came in and grabbed Reevis.

"But we have to hurry," said Nigel. "Your next assignment is a long drive up north."

Chapter 15

LAST CASE OF THE DAY

The flags of the United States and the state of Florida stood against the wall. A clock ticked. A bailiff stood and tried not to yawn. The court stenographer sat with fingers at the ready.

Between the flags, a man in a black robe set some papers down and looked out over his reading glasses. "Let me see if I have this straight, counsel. You are asking me to return seized property to a client you refuse to identify?"

"That's correct," said Brook.

Another attorney jumped to his feet. "Your Honor, I move that you immediately dismiss this specious appeal against the upstanding municipality of Coral Cove!"

"Calm down," said the judge. "You're already winning, so can we just wrap this up and get to dinner?"

"Of course, Your Honor."

"Now then," said the judge. "Unlike regular criminal cases, seizure appeals require a certain burden of proof upon the person seeking to retrieve their property." He turned to Brook. "If your clients won't come forward to testify, I find it insurmountably problematic for your case."

"Your Honor," said Brook. "The fact that I won't identify my client *is* our case."

The judge took off his glasses and searched for words. Finally, "What?"

"Why don't you ask opposing counsel?"

The other attorney just gave a clueless shrug.

The judge sat back and gazed at the plaintiff's table. "Why don't you simply come out and say what's on your mind in plain terms."

"Your Honor," said Brook. "It's so hugely obvious that everyone is missing it. The city of Coral Cove is claiming that the appeal should be denied because my client won't come forward."

The other lawyer was back on his feet. "That's right, Your Honor. This was a justified drug-trafficking forfeiture designed to undercut the scourge of narcotics, exactly as the legislature intended." He swelled with cockiness and gave Brook an accusing glare. "If her clients won't present themselves, I think we all have a pretty good idea why."

The judge raised his eyebrows in her direction.

"If I may continue," said Brook. "The city is making an issue of me not identifying my clients. But it was *their* police department that made the traffic stop and took property. Why don't *they* have the ID?"

The judge's head swung. "Is that true?"

The municipal attorney nervously flipped through papers in his briefcase. "I'm sure it's in here somewhere."

"That's not even close to good enough," said the judge. "But we'll get back to that. What was your basis to seize the money?"

"Our canine alerted to drugs."

"Did you find any?"

"No, but there was a large, unexplained amount of currency, and our experience has found that such cash often has trace amounts of drugs that our dogs detect."

Brook held up a newspaper. "According to an investigation by the *Miami Herald,* most twenty-dollar bills in the Metro-Dade area have at least some drug residue. The newspaper collected sample money to be tested from prominent businesspeople, politicians, even clergy. This article has been accepted as evidence in other jurisdictions."

"I object," said her adversary. "Unless she's prepared to swear in these reporters—"

"Won't be necessary," said Brook. "My main point is they never intended to charge my client with any offense. In fact, they didn't even issue a ticket for the ostensible traffic offense, and neither of the vehicle's occupants had a valid driver's license between them. Yet they were still let go."

The judge looked the other way for an answer. The city attorney brimmed with a smile. "Your Honor, she just made my argument. Smugglers often use undocumented aliens as couriers. That's the real reason her clients didn't have a driver's license and aren't present today. They're here illegally!"

"What do you have to say?" asked the judge.

"He's absolutely right," said Brook. "They are here illegally."

"Wait, you're admitting this in open court?"

"If I could call a witness."

The judge shook his head to clear the legal haze. "Go ahead."

A police officer put one hand on the Bible and raised the other. Brook approached.

"Officer Malloy," said Brook. "You handle the police canine named Nixon?"

"He's more like a partner."

"How does he rate as a drug sniffer?"

"In a controlled test, he correctly identified all twenty-three sources."

"Is he obedient and easily trained?"

"Completely."

"Could you make him bark at will?"

"I guess I could."

"I'll take that as a yes," said Brook. "Does he bark for any other reason?"

"Well ..." Malloy broke into a grin. "For some reason, squirrels."

"And do you detain these squirrels?"

The bailiff snickered and quickly covered his mouth.

"Counsel!" said the judge. "I will not indulge such sarcasm, especially in disrespect for a law enforcement officer."

"My apologies. That was out of line," said Brook. "And I can't do this anymore. I'm just going to tell you how I feel. Yes, I represent illegal aliens, and what they're doing is wrong. But there's a bigger wrong. On a personal level, I come from a family tree full of officers, and have nothing but respect for the vast majority of police in our state who don't pull these shenanigans, and don't deserve to have their integrity tainted. Forfeiture started out well intentioned enough, except there's so much temptation that it's gotten completely out of hand. There's a sheriff on the west coast driving a confiscated Hummer, for heaven's sake—"

The judge held up a hand for her to stop. "And everyone knows that migrant workers don't have bank accounts ... I'm way ahead of you. My dad and both brothers were on the force." He turned and glared at the city attorney. "Appeal is granted."

The lawyer sighed. "I understand, Your Honor." He began putting files back in his briefcase.

"Go get it."

The attorney looked up quickly. "Get what?"

"The money."

"Now?"

"You don't want to test my patience because you're going to be spending a lot of time in this courtroom. I'm requesting that the state attorney convene a grand jury to investigate your seizure practices ..." Then toward Brook: "Hope you have calendar space for a few more clients."

CASSADAGA

The silver Corvette rolled through the tiny paranormal community, passing a number of pastel wooden cottages that composed psychic row.

"Look," said Coleman. "The first regular sign. 'Warning: Neighborhood Watch.'"

"Perhaps the most ominous of all," said Serge. "What idiot would pull a burglary in this town? You're definitely going to get caught, possibly even before you enter the property."

"There's Madam Bovary's," said Coleman. "That last pink house with all the painted boards nailed to a post by the door: 'Palm Reading,' 'Numerology,' 'Past-Life Regression,' 'The Psychic Is In.'"

Serge walked up the porch steps and glanced at a cheerful silk flag of flowers and rainbows and three words: LAUGH, LIVE, LOVE.

Knock, knock, knock.

The door opened. "Please come in."

A thirty-something woman with a wreath of daisies in her hair led them into the parlor, lit only by the orange flame of a kerosene lamp. They all took seats around a circular oak table usually used for séances. A crystal ball sat in the middle.

Serge brought out his own ball. He set it next to the glass one.

Madam Bovary looked up in confusion. "You brought a toy?"

"The Eight Ball is my quality-control element," said Serge. "Like a double-blind test. I *want* to believe all this mumbo jumbo, but questions have arisen. For instance, since Cassadaga calls itself 'The Psychic Capital of the World,' then it should also be 'The Lottery-Winning Capital.' But where are all the mansions?"

A theatrical smile. "Skepticism is healthy."

Serge checked the message window in his Eight Ball. "So far so good."

"Let me have your hands ..." She took them in hers. "Now close your eyes ..."

"They're closed," said Serge. "But this better not be a ruse to silence the Eight Ball."

"Shhhh, relax ... Focus on a point in the center of your mind ... Do you see anything? ..."

"It's just dark with barely visible little blobs floating around, except when I try to look at one, it just floats off to the side. What is that fuckery?"

"You're still too tense," said Bovary. "Take a deep breath. Let go and float ..."

"I'm floating ..."

A loud thud.

"Holy Jesus!" Serge jumped up. "What was that? Some dead relative trying to contact me? If they've been able to watch me all these years, I'm going to be *sooooooo* embarrassed ... Who was it? My grandfather?"

The woman sighed and pointed at the floor.

Coleman lay sprawled on a Tibetan rug. "Time for my nap."

Serge checked the Eight Ball. "He's right ... Proceed."

"Uh ..." Bovary looked dubiously at the unconscious guest beginning to snore. "... This is highly unusual."

"You're the one with the weird town."

This time it was the psychic who needed a deep breath. "Now then, you mentioned when you called from the spiritual center that you had an interest in past-life regression?"

"That's right. I'm all about history," said Serge. "If I've had any past lives, I'd like to know of any pivotal roles I might have played, like inventing the cotton gin. Did anyone actually *see* Eli Whitney tighten that last screw? We need to tease out the bullshit."

Serge's eyesight had finished adjusting in the dim light. He reassessed the woman across from him. Not too hard on the eyes. And the daisies in her raven hair brought out a certain wild-child allure.

Likewise, she was noticing him. The eyes, smile, confidence. "... Oh, sorry, I lost my place there for a second."

"It happens ... Past lives?"

"Clear your consciousness and tell me if anything comes to you."

Serge began to nod. "A pirate."

"Pirate?"

"Yeah, I don't know why, but just now I got the odd sensation that I used to be a buccaneer. Think it means anything?"

"A buccaneer?"

Serge noticed her voice had become throatier. She slowly ran a hand across her stomach, the top finger furtively tracing the underside of her breasts.

Serge winked. "You like pirates?"

A gulp. "Keep talking ..."

He looked around. "You think this is the best place?"

"I know a better one."

She took him by the hand, and they had torn off each other's clothes before they got to the back room. Serge picked her up and tossed her onto a plush Elizabethan bed.

She sat up. "Wait, where are you going?"

"To get my Eight Ball. Just be a sec."

He quickly returned and dove on top of her.

"Yes! Yes! Yes! ... You're a pirate! ... Faster, faster ... Close your eyes and keep regressing! ... But whatever you do, don't stop! ..."

"I believe I can speak for the Eight Ball that you have nothing to worry about."

Serge closed his eyes and the darkness with drifting blotches soon gave way to a sparkling light ...

A skull and crossbones flapped over the schooner as it crashed through waves in the Gulf of Mexico.

The water was a deep cerulean blue, dotted with enormous loggerhead turtles. A peg-legged sailor in the crow's nest sighted something in his telescope.

"Land ahoy!"

The creaking ship tacked starboard on a new course roughly seventy nautical miles west of Key West.

The land took shape in the telescope. Eight small islands scattered across the top of an atoll that rose abruptly from the fathoms.

The Dry Tortugas.

The ship's crew knew the islands well, as did most sailors who charted these waters. The land was low with sparse vegetation and generally of little value in restocking provisions. With a single exception.

Bird Key.

It isn't there anymore, washed away by the No-Name hurricane of 1935, but this was still 1788, and any seasoned mariner in the gulf knew that during the summer months, thousands of sooty and noddy terns migrated down from the Carolinas and converted the island into a rookery.

The schooner got as close to the key as its draft allowed and dropped anchor. The rowboats were lowered and two dozen swashbucklers made their way ashore. What they did next would seem baffling today, even mean-spirited, but there was a method. They began stomping every last one of the eggs the birds had laid in the low brush. Then they went back to the ship and slept fitfully on empty stomachs.

The next afternoon, the rowboats returned. Somehow, the crews had learned that destroying the eggs triggered a procreation instinct in the birds, and they immediately laid fresh ones that were suitable for human consumption. This time the pirates were more careful as they harvested.

They didn't call them the Dry Tortugas for nothing, because there was no fresh water to be had. The eggs were about all the islands were good for. That's why they were also perfect for a trademark seafaring practice of the eighteenth century.

Marooning.

The word conjures all kinds of romantic images of a shipwrecked Robinson Crusoe, or Tom Hanks going down in a FedEx plane.

In actual practice, marooning wasn't intended to strand someone to live out their years in isolation wearing palm-frond pants. It was a highly sadistic ritual involving the selection of an island with nothing to offer, not even protection from the sun. A sandbar worked perfectly, and death was excruciating, from dehydration, exposure and wholesale organ failure. If the crew was Catholic, as many were, then there was a final, ultimate cruelty.

The condemned man was rowed ashore and given a flintlock pistol with a single lead ball and enough powder for one shot. The end was so horrible that the temptation to take one's own life would become overwhelming. But under Catholic doctrine, suicide would damn the soul for eternity: And there you were: death with a dilemma garnish.

This particular crew had grown frighteningly low on their stocks. Fruit and meat were long gone, leaving stale, insect-ridden bread that was even less appetizing than hardtack during the Civil War. Bird Key just changed all that, and now it was time to crack the casks. Rum and eggs for everyone!

It carried on late into the starry night. Orion, Taurus, Ursa Major. The captain—a full-bearded man with a fuller frame—became surly with drink. His eyes locked on one of his more popular crew members, "Calico Kid" Serge. There had been a woman a fortnight ago in Trinidad. One of the captain's regular wenches. As the rum fermented his brain, the captain lavishly entertained the suspicion that back in port, Serge had left him sloppy seconds. Because he had.

And now here was Serge, the center of the crew's merry attention again, spazzing out with hyperactivity, walking around the deck on his hands, spinning yarns and floating grandiose concepts that wouldn't find traction for years. "No, really, I call it the cotton gin ..."

It was already in the captain's eyes. A decision had been made.

They pulled anchor at first light. Then the captain summarily ordered it dropped again before they had fully cleared the atoll.

Bird Key behind the ship—even with its unsustainably low covering of plants—was too good for Serge. The captain had his mind set on another of the islands, the one now called Hospital Key. It got the name because an epidemic of yellow fever hit Fort Jefferson on nearby Garden Key, and that's where they quarantined the stricken soldiers. But the fort and the disease hadn't arrived yet, and the island was still nameless. It was just called a sandbar.

The rowboats reached the shallows and Serge was tossed over the side. He stumbled ashore as the captain roared his amusement. Serge fell to his knees weeping as the captain hurled insults in an archaic construct that today would roughly translate: "Who's the big man now?"

Just before shoving off, the first officer tossed Serge the suicide weapon, which he quickly loaded, and shot the captain.

Splash.

"What a beautiful day!" said Serge. "Let's go have some fun!"

They helped him back into the small boat and returned to the ship ...

Chapter 16

CENTRAL FLORIDA

A black SUV left Interstate 4 behind in the late afternoon and began a meandering country drive that seemed to lead nowhere. Reevis's Datsun was right behind.

The vehicles eventually rolled up a quiet street and parked in front of a tidy cottage.

"Here's the plan," said Nigel, laying out the details.

"It's a stupid plan," said Reevis. "And just when I thought my profession couldn't sink any lower. Since when do journalists use psychics?"

"Cops hire them all the time," said Nigel. "And the viewing public loves them! You'll be a pioneer!"

"I'll be a laughingstock!"

"You heard what your editor told you back at the office," said the producer. "Just give it a try."

"But whatever happened to the missing-woman case we were supposed to be working on?" said Reevis.

"That's over," Nigel said bitterly. "It got solved."

"It did?"

"Tragically, she's alive. Mid-life crisis. Been backpacking in Europe." Nigel looked toward the front porch. "Ready?"

Reevis noticed the happy silk flag. "You sure we have the right address?"

Nigel nodded. "Been here before."

"You have?"

"I was waiting until we arrived to surprise you." Nigel eagerly rubbed his palms together. "There's a second element that will put this segment over the top, television's version of a daily double, combining two things audiences love the most. Not only are we consulting a psychic about a crime, but we'll also have a *confrontation* with a psychic!"

"Please stop," Reevis said weakly.

"No, seriously," said Nigel, leading the way up the porch steps. "We paid her to work on a show before we met you, and you'll never guess! The psychic was wrong!"

"I'm shaken."

"So was I," said the producer. "Last time she predicted the body would be found near water with sounds and lights. Just my bad luck that the victim in that case wasn't dead, either. Turns out the girl ran away with her boyfriend for a few days. So here's the deal: We start out like everything's on the level; then, when she's lulled into false confidence, you pepper her with accusations about the last case. It can't miss! The scrupulous reporter uncovering a scandalous psychic hoax."

"I feel ill."

Nigel pounded and pounded on the front door.

"I don't think anyone's home," said Reevis.

"There a car in the drive." Nigel tried the doorknob. "Günter, it's unlocked."

"I draw the line here," said the reporter. "I'm not a burglar."

"Reevis, where are you going?"

"Back to the office."

"Reevis? Reevis! ..."

The door to the Datsun slammed, and the reporter drove off.

Nigel looked at his cameraman. "He'll come around later for the voice-over. Let's go inside and get some B-roll."

Günter Klieglyte ran jiggling up the steps and barged through the door without knocking. They stood in an empty parlor.

"I know you're back there!" yelled Nigel. "Come out now! We want our money back! ..."

The cameraman ran forward in the dark room and tripped over something on the floor.

"Good God!" said Nigel. "It's a body! Get a close-up!"

DOWN THE HALL

Madam Bovary arched her back high in a prolonged tremor of ecstasy. Then she collapsed onto the mattress and hugged Serge hard around the neck. "My pirate!"

"You're welcome."

"But how was it for you?"

"Great." Serge rolled off her and caught his breath. "I usually try to think of historic stuff to heighten the experience, but this time it was so vivid."

"So you now believe in my skills at past-life regression?"

"The Eight Ball says definitely."

"By the way, my real name's Trish."

"Pleasure to meet you— ... Wait, did you hear that?"

"Hear what?"

"From the other room. Listen ..."

They both stared at the closed bedroom door.

"... *We know you're back there! Give us our money! ...*"

"Oh no," said the psychic. "Not another."

"Unhappy customer?" said Serge. "This happen often?"

"Only occasionally, but it's never pleasant."

Serge hopped out of bed. "This one's on me."

"What are you going to do?"

"Let you relax and enjoy the afterglow." Serge kissed her forehead and trotted toward the parlor. "*Just a minute!*"

Günter had the camera rolling on a close-up of a prostrate Coleman when Serge came skipping into the room wearing only black Miami Heat boxers. "How can I help you crazy kids? You've caught me in a great mood. Out of the blue, I just got fucked stupid by a smoking-hot babe that I only met a few minutes ago. So how's your own day going?"

"Are you getting all this?" whispered Nigel.

Günter nodded as he kept his face against the rubber eyepiece and panned down to the underwear.

Nigel pointed at the floor. "Why did you kill this man?"

"Coleman?" Serge kicked him in the thigh.

The body sat up with a groan, then conked out again.

"He just has a different day planner," said Serge. "Anything else?"

"Yes! I'm here to demand the return of two hundred dollars from a fraudulent session that hoaxed a respected media outlet and traumatized the parents of a missing girl."

"That's terrible!" said Serge. "I have to make this right!"

"Where's Madam Bovary? We want to talk to her this very second!"

"I'm afraid that's impossible." Serge sat down at the table and grabbed his Eight Ball. "She's been recalled to the Mother Ship."

"Do we look like saps to you? A UFO?"

"No, Parliament Funkadelic," said Serge. "Backup singer, great pipes ... It's almost supernatural how that band keeps cropping up in my work."

Nigel pounded the séance table, sloshing fluid in the Eight Ball. "I want to see some hard cash immediately!"

"Tell you what," said Serge. "I'll give you a top-shelf session at no charge, and if you aren't satisfied, money back, no questions asked."

"Who exactly are you?"

"Madam Bovary's mentor, the Calico Kid," said Serge. "Ready for my cosmic report?"

Nigel and Günter gave each other hopeful looks.

"Okay," said Nigel. "But no funny stuff!"

"You mean like this?" Serge held his hands toward the kerosene lamp, casting a shadow puppet on the wall of a tap-dancing penis.

Nigel elbowed Günter.

"I'm getting it," whispered the Bavarian.

"Now then," said Nigel. "We're working a four-year-old missing-persons case, probably a murder. Owned a motel with her husband and—"

"That's a trick question," said Serge. "She's probably still alive."

Nigel recoiled. "How'd you know?"

"I'll do you one better," said Serge. "A murder that hasn't even been reported yet."

"Really?"

Serge gazed strenuously into his Eight Ball. "I see a body in pine needles on the floor of the Apalachicola National Forest. Drive precisely five-point-seven miles from the Sopchoppy spur into Tate's Hell, and walk two hundred yards east-southeast until you come to a log with a big mushroom-looking fungus. Despite being discovered far from open water, the body will be near a deep-sea transmitter, with a jaw-spreader in the mouth and stomach contents including earthworms and possibly Mallomars. He has a history of working in the health care field, but never fulfilled early aspirations of founding a network of pick-your-own catfish farms in an attempt to woo the affections of the second-chair bassoon at the Met. That Eight Ball is shaky on whether that last part is prescience or coffee, so no money back there."

Nigel and Günter just stared with open mouths.

"What? Cat got your tongue?"

"H-h-how do you know such specific details about an unreported homicide?"

"Let you in on a little secret if you promise not to put it on the air." Serge leaned in like they were old pals. "It's the art of making the general seem specific. Earthworms, sonar equipment, jaw-spreaders? I mean, come on, when *haven't* you seen that?" He sat back and grinned.

"Uh, so ..." Nigel muttered nervously. "You wouldn't have a name for this murder victim, would you?"

African clicking sounds.

Chapter 17

A FEW MINUTES LATER

Serge shook his Eight Ball and called to the bedroom. "Coast is clear!"

The psychic came out and took a seat at the table. "How'd you get rid of them?"

"Gave 'em what they wanted. I'm a student of character that way." He set the black ball down and opened the new book he had purchased at the gift shop. "What do you think of this stuff?"

"Crystals?" She grabbed her own clear ball from the middle of the table. "I'm on the fence, but some people swear by them. There are hundreds of varieties with their own vibration levels and energy fields, giving each one specific gifts similar to patron saints: peace, love, creativity, decision making."

Serge flipped pages. "I loved crystals when I was a kid, but I was looking at little bitty ones with the microscope I got for Christmas. In fact, I used it to examine the whole house. That microscope opened a whole new world for me! I was so excited: 'Mom! Come quick! You have to see this stuff magnified! All kinds of crazy little creatures are running around!' Then she'd take a peek and ask what she was looking at. 'Mom, it's what you made for dinner.' That was the end of my microscope period."

A cell phone rang. Trish checked the caller ID. "It's the spiritual center's referral line." She got up to take it. "Hello? ... No, I'm sorry, but I'm not taking any more customers today ... No, I'm sure ... Well, if it's an emergency, there are plenty of others on the board who would be happy to see you ... What? ... Wait, your voice. Who *is* this? ..."

"... Then I got a telescope," said Serge, "and I could literally read a newspaper through our neighbor's living room window, but I was still too young to process the bedroom scenes ..."

Madam Bovary hung up and walked to the table.

"What is it?" asked Serge. "Another unsatisfied customer?"

She steadied herself as she sat back down.

"Good God, what's wrong? You look terrible, and I'm not even psychic."

"He found me again."

"Who?"

"My ex. He just called from the spiritual center and is on his way over."

"Then we only have a few minutes." Serge noticed her shaking uncontrollably. "I've seen the previews to this movie before, so give me the quick version."

"I've called the police, got restraining orders, moved ten times, legally changed my name, but it's never enough. Once, he even found me through public records when I hooked up to the city water. Except this time I thought I was so far off the grid he wouldn't stand a chance. But just now he said he saw me on TV when I did that cold-case segment."

"TV!" said Serge. "That's the opposite of off the grid."

"I know, I know, but I've never been east of Colorado before. Who would have thought he'd see that show—"

"Has he ever hit you?"

"Hit me, choked me, thrown me down stairs, burned me." She turned her arm over, and Serge cringed. "Swears he's going to kill me."

"If you don't go back with him?"

"No, says he'll do it someday anyway, just doesn't feel like it yet. When we were out west, detectives came around one day asking about his missing first wife, and that's when I finally split for Florida."

"I've heard enough." Serge ran to the window and checked out the curtains. "Shit, he's here. Do you have a car?"

"It's around back."

"Hopefully he'll think the Corvette's yours. Lock yourself in the bathroom and don't come out! Now! ... Oh, and what's his name? ..."

Feet ran down the back hallway. Others came up the front steps. Serge ran to the kerosene lamp and turned down the flame. Then he quietly unlocked the front door. "What an episode."

Outside: "*I'll huff, and I'll puff, and I'll blow your house in!*"

Quiet.

"*What? No answer? Is that any way to treat the love of your life?*"

The ex tried the knob. "You've got to be kidding. This is too easy." He slowly opened the door and poked his head inside with a bad Jack Nicholson impersonation. "*Heeeeeeeere's Johnnnnnnny!*"

The parlor was ultra-dark as he crept inside. "*Come out, come out, wherever you are!*"

More svelte steps across the Tibetan carpet. Trip. *Thud.* "What the hell?"

"Ow!" said Coleman. "I'm trying to sleep."

The kerosene flame came back to life.

The ex looked up from the floor. "Who the hell are you?"

"Calico Kid Serge. And you must be Gil."

Gil stood back up and aimed a pistol. "Are you the current loser fucking my wife?"

"No," said Serge. "Well, not for the last half hour."

"Son of a bitch!" Gil stormed across the room and pointed the gun between Serge's eyes. "You're a dead man!"

Serge put a hand to his mouth and yawned.

"What's the matter with you? I have a gun!"

"But I have the Eight Ball!"

"What?"

Serge shook the water in the novelty item. "Its power is much greater." He held the ball's fortune-telling window toward Gil's face. "See?"

"Where?"

"There." *Bam*. Right in the nose.

It's not the injury as much as disorientation. A pain source so close to the brain is magnified. Involuntary blinking. Whatever else your hands were doing, they can't help but drop everything and fly to the center of your face ...

Ten minutes later ...

Serge tugged hard on a stretch of rope and yelled down the hall. "You can come out now."

A wedge of light appeared as a door cautiously opened. "Is it safe?"

"Completely."

It was indeed safe, but Trish grabbed her heart anyway at the sight of Gil. He was fit to be tied—and he was. The work with the rope defined overkill. Dozens and dozens of loops like a woman left on the railroad tracks in a silent movie. A tube sock duct-taped in his mouth.

"Forget you ever saw this," said Serge. "I just have to wait for nightfall, and you'll never have to worry about him again."

SEVERAL HOURS LATER

A '62 Ford pickup sat on the shoulder of a rocky road in the Apalachicola National Forest. Two men in overalls began hiking into the woods as the sun went down.

"I sure likes that Serge," said Willard.

"Mm-hmm," said Jasper. "Leavin' us all his expensive gizmos like he did."

"We's gonna corner the worm-grunting market fer sure!"

"Where is that stuff, anyway?"

"Claimed it was in the same spot where we laid eyes."

"I think it's just behind those trees over there."

More walking. Moss and peat and toadstools. As they rounded a cluster of pines, the top of the sonar pole came into view.

"Yep, this is the place," said Willard. "Right where he told us."

A few more steps.

Willard froze and Jasper bumped into him from behind. "Why'd you stop?"

"Holy infant Jesus! Is that what I think?"

"Looks like a body," said Jasper.

City folk would have hightailed it out of there, but the brothers had seen a lot of dead stuff in the woods over the years. They crept forward.

"Gross. Look at his mouth."

"Who you think it is?"

"He's got a name tag," said Willard.

"Looks like it's from an assisted-living center. Says 'Preston.'"

"Ain't that the name of the guy who was taking care of Aunt May?"

They paused and looked at each other: "Serge."

And this is where city folk definitely would have called the police. But back in the hills, you learn early not to wait for someone else to supply the justice. They thought the deed was extreme, but they understood.

"We best get rid of this fella before Serge finds his pecker in a wringer."

"Least we can do for him."

They fetched the shovels from the pickup and went to work. Breaking through the forest floor demanded serious back work, but beneath that, the soil was rich, moist and cooperative. They knew they had to go deep because scavenger animals would follow the scent and undo their efforts.

Digging went on into the early night, and a lot of earthworms were flung aside in flying spadefuls of dirt. Finally Willard rested one arm on the end of a shovel and wiped his grimy brow with the other. "Think it's good enough?"

They were both standing in the rectangular hole, and Jasper stared eye level at the ground all around. "Nothin' can burrow this far. Give me a boost."

They got out of the pit and caught their breath. Then they stood at opposite ends of the body, grabbing wrists and ankles, and shuffled back over to the hole. They began swinging Preston.

"On three," said Willard. "One, two ..."

Suddenly running footsteps crackled through the leaves, and they were blinded by bright lights.

"Why'd you kill him?" yelled Nigel.

The wide-eyed brothers froze with the body in their hands.

CASSADAGA

A psychic peeked out the curtains. "Sure looks dark enough."

"It's not just darkness." Serge shook the Eight Ball. "It's also waiting for all the nosy people to go to bed."

Trish jumped as her cell phone rang again.

"Who's calling now?" asked Serge.

She checked the display as it continued to ring. "I don't recognize the number."

"Aren't you going to answer it?"

"Hell no!"

"You better." He checked the advice of the Eight Ball. "You don't want to vary your routine and have some idiot wandering over here."

"Okay." She held it to her head. "Hello? ... Let me check ..." She covered the phone and whispered. "It's for you."

"*Me?*" said Serge. "Who is it?"

Shrug.

Serge snatched the phone. "Talk ... Oh, it's you ... But how'd you get this number? ... You found a business card for Madam Bovary? ... Where'd you find it? ... Could you repeat that last part again? ..." He slowly closed his eyes. "No, I think I've pretty much got the full picture. I'll be there as fast as I can ..."

Smooth hands grabbed his arm. "You can't go anywhere. Don't leave me with him!"

Serge glanced around the room in thought. "Okay, you've had enough trauma already ... Coleman?"

"I'm up for the day!"

"Coleman, stay here and watch the ex-husband," said Serge. "Even Houdini couldn't escape from all those ropes and knots, but just in case, here's a gun."

"Where are you going?"

"Back soon." Serge took Trish by the hand. "Plus, I need to do some psychic shopping for Gil anyway ..."

... After a two-hour stretch of high-speed back-road driving, a silver Corvette pulled up to a handmade cabin on the outskirts of Sopchoppy.

Lightning bugs led the way as Serge and Trish headed for the porch.

Jasper flung open the door in advance. "Thank God you came! We're in a real mess! They say they're going to the police and pin a murder on us with their TV film!"

"What's the status?" asked Serge.

Willard gestured inside. "Take a gander for yourself."

They entered the homestead to find a reality-show producer and his cameraman in captivity.

Trish leaned to Serge. "Does every room in your life contain people tied to chairs?"

"Pretty much."

"We didn't know what to do," said Jasper. "We were trying to bury the body so you wouldn't get in trouble ..."

"And they snuck up on us with their camera," said Willard.

"Everything will be fine now." Serge paced across the cabin floor. "I just need some time to think ... Explain again exactly how you were able to track me down."

"These two fellas were talking a blue streak when we were tying them up," said Jasper. "I asked how they'd come to be in our neck of the woods, and with such frightful timing. They said they were working with a psychic on a murder, and he led them right to the spot."

Serge smacked himself in the forehead. "My bad. I'd completely forgotten about you guys ... These *Route 66* episodes have so many moving parts that I probably need to buy some Post-it notes."

"We watched the tape in their camera and saw that the psychic was actually you," said Willard. "Then I was searching them and found the business card for Madam Bovary in one of their pockets. Figured I'd give it a try."

"First, the most important thing," said Serge. "Do they know where this place is?"

"Doubt it," said Jasper. "We blindfolded them."

They heard a car screech up. Fast steps on the porch. Lou Ellen burst through the door. "I came as fast as I could—"

She cut herself off. There was a dramatic pause in the room as Lou Ellen stepped forward. Her alarm would have been the normal reaction to the presence of a pair of bound prisoners ... Normally ...

Lou Ellen and Trish pointed at each other. Almost an echo as they spoke at the same time: "Who the hell is *she*?"

Serge smacked himself again. "I'm definitely buying Post-it notes."

The women sneered and began to circle each other around the hostage chairs. The men actually thought they heard hissing sounds.

"Stop!" yelled Serge. "This is way too many moving parts! We've got some major untangling to do here, so right now it's time to prioritize and not fixate on itty-bitty misunderstandings that can easily be fixed with candles and soap."

"He's right," said Jasper, stepping in front of his sister. "Let's you and me go and waits by the cars and give'n him some elbow room."

They went outside to a chorus of cicadas.

"Now then ..." Serge faced the captives. There hadn't been any need to gag the pair. Once tied up inside the cabin, they became oddly quiet. "Let's take a look at this film you shot."

He picked up the camera and watched the preview screen. "Nice composition, good jiggling, and I see you subscribe to the visual rule of thirds. Unfortunately all this grave digging must hit the cutting room floor. Steals too much from the denouement." Serge pressed delete. "If you have an opening for an editor, my hours are flexible. What do you say?"

Nothing.

"Come on!" said Serge. "Where's all that spunky pushiness I saw back at Madam Bovary's?"

The producer and his cameraman just stared into headlights.

"Serge," said Jasper. "First they was yappin' like their regular nature, then around the time we broke out the rope and they seen my banjo in the corner, they started whispering somethin' 'bout *Deliverance* till they was a-trembling and quiet as church mice."

"I understand," said Serge. *"Deliverance* is a classic—"

"Seventies movie ..." Jasper reached for a book on the fireplace mantel. "Based on this here novel by James Dickey."

"Wait," said Serge. "You mention *Deliverance* and most people default to *Smokey and the Bandit* and hillbilly sex, because Burt Reynolds starred in that movie, along with Ned Beatty, who ... well, what's done is done ... But you know Dickey? You even *have* the novel?"

"Dad-gum right I know Dickey, Southern literary lion and poet loreeee-*ate*."

Serge regretted the off-guard surprise in his voice. "But that's high literature."

"Not quite uppin' to Faulkner, but good nuff."

Serge shook his head like a cartoon character. "You can read Faulkner?"

"'Course I can read. Thinks I'm 'literate?"

"Didn't mean it that way at all," said Serge. "I mean, Faulkner ... He's impenetrable. I *could* read him, but there's so little time in my nutty schedule and then there's the attention issue. Faulkner's like *Finnegan's Wake* in Mississippi."

"Joyce did have one powerful spell on Billy. Found scribblin' in the books on his shelves in Oxford."

"You also know James Joyce?"

"No, Dr. Joyce Brothers." A laugh. "'*Course* I'm talkin' 'bout that lace-curtain Irish mick. Here I was thinking you was smart."

"How embarrassing," said Serge. "And I'm the one who keeps telling others not to stereotype."

"No need," said Jasper. "Wants to hear my banjo?"

Musical twanging began, and the captives thrashed.

"Finally." Serge turned toward them and snarled. "Ready to talk?"

They froze again.

"Good grief." Serge pulled a pistol from under his tropical shirt. "I usually have to get this out when people won't *stop* talking." He jammed the barrel to Nigel's forehead. "I'm trying to be friendly and start a dialogue here. Work with me."

"... I have to pee ..."

"Don't we all," said Serge. "File that thought. Now, what exactly do you think is going on here? ... I'll know if you're lying and there won't be a second chance. Ask the others, except you can't."

The words came haltingly. "You're no psychic."

"Ouch, that hurts," said Serge. "What makes you think that?"

"The directions you gave were too specific, and the murder hadn't been reported yet," said Nigel. "So the only logical conclusion is that you did it."

"Give the man a cigar!" Serge tucked the gun away.

"Please don't kill us."

"That hadn't occurred to me," said Serge. "But it would eliminate some moving parts and bring a clean end to this episode."

"We'll do anything!" pleaded Nigel. "Name it!"

"Okay, if we let you go, what are your plans? Broad strokes will do."

"I swear we won't tell anyone," said Nigel. "We'll destroy all the rest of the tapes from Cassadaga and forget we were ever here ... Isn't that right, Günter?"

Emphatic nodding.

"Really?" said Serge. "I can trust you?"

"Totally!" said Nigel. "You have my word!"

Serge thought a moment, then shook his head. "No good. You'll say anything right now to get out of this."

Nigel crunched his lips and whined desperately. A puddle formed under his chair.

"Ewwww," said Serge. "All right, all right, I'll make you a deal. I know I can't trust you, so after I release you, go ahead and air what you filmed of me in Cassadaga. Or at least what I haven't deleted yet. I know you're just itching to."

"What? I don't understand."

"The number one rule in life is to promise everyone they can have everything they want at all times. Our whole presidential cycle depends on it," said Serge. "Of course you can't actually deliver on most of the stuff you promised, but in the short term, people you lie to are less douchey."

"Uh, there isn't any catch?" asked the producer.

"Oh, there's definitely a catch." Serge grinned big. "The TV segment will put the cops on my trail, but I can take care of myself. The catch is you have to leave all of my friends here out of this. Not a peep."

"You got it."

A cell phone rang. "That's mine." Serge put it to his ear. "Oh, hi, Reevis. I was just thinking about you."

"Serge, thank God I was able to find you. I would've sworn this number wouldn't work, but this is an emergency!"

"Are you okay?"

"Fine. My station just finished downloading some digital footage, but luckily I was able to intercept it."

"What's it of?"

Reevis was whispering now: "You're in some fortune-teller's place describing the location of a body."

"Is that all?" Serge laughed.

"How is this funny? These new reality guys are a nightmare!"

"How so?"

"They're ruining my life! They keep putting me in danger!"

"What! They've threatened you?" Serge exclaimed. "Say no more. And put a hold on that tape."

"No, not threatened—"

Serge hung up and stared at the pair.

"We're ready," said Nigel. "Let's go."

Serge shook his head. "On second thought, change of plans ... Willard, blindfold them."

Chapter 18

MEANWHILE IN MIAMI

The clattering noise was loud and machinelike and nonstop. All across the city, it was the same, a mesmerizing rat-a-tat at thousands of locations.

Lottery machines spit out tickets at a feverish pace to feverish people. News stations kept breaking in to update the record number of sales. Lines wrapped around 7-Eleven.

A group of serious men from South America fanned out across the metropolitan area and beyond, in an equal division of land, like precinct captains. It was a process that had begun a couple of days earlier. It involved school buses. Now it was Saturday night, and the official Ping-Pong ball drawing was precariously near.

The biggest crowds of all came at the last minute because people bad at math also weren't on time. One particular line wound down a sidewalk on Biscayne Boulevard. A school bus arrived. An intimidating Latino with a thick mustache waited on the sidewalk as the migrant workers filed off. He gave each of them a five-dollar bill as promised, plus an envelope with more cash and pre-filled lottery forms.

Once the bus was empty, he led his assemblage inside the store, passing the rest of the customers who had been waiting forever. He cut to the very front of the line with predictable reaction. Shouts, a polyglot of cursing, and overt threats of physical harm.

All the man had to do was turn and look with those dark, bottomless eyes. The reaction changed: By all means, be my guest.

Identical scenes played out at various other locations as buses drove into Fort Lauderdale and West Palm Beach.

At 11:01 p.m., the gang of five collected the last of their tickets and regrouped in the luxury suite of an extended-stay hotel near the airport. Mr. Pelota was waiting. He never had to speak loud. "How much?"

They compared tallies. "Half the board. We hit every store we could within the time possible."

"That's ten million dollars, fifty-fifty shot," said Pelota, his pulse predictably steady according to the Hare PCL-R psychopathy index for low reaction to high risk. Response to negative outcomes was another matter.

The TV neared the end of the local news. The room went silent as a pink flamingo logo appeared, followed by a game-show host in a sports coat. The night skyline of Miami was projected in the back of the studio as Ping-Pong balls frolicked deliriously in some kind of clear-plastic vortex bin before being suctioned up six tubes and read off: 48, 39, 53, 51, 43, 46.

"What's with all the high numbers?" asked one of the lower-ranking men, prompting a sharp poke to his ribs.

The suite had floor-to-ceiling plate-glass windows with a view of the skyline that matched the one on television. It efficiently shattered, left to right, and the shards rained down into the storm-water retention pond behind the hotel. Mr. Pelota calmly re-holstered his TEC-9 machine gun under a white jacket. He headed for the mini-bar, hair whipped up in a crisp new open-air breeze off Biscayne Bay. He uncapped a nine-dollar miniature of Patrón and picked a sliver of glass off his shoulder. "Juan, go down and pay the man at the front desk."

THE APALACHICOLA

There's a good reason that horror movies often choose remote, dark forests at night. They have their own creepy soundtracks. A sizzling buzz of insects with a bullfrog backbeat.

The moon was full, and wind through the thick tree canopy produced a weird effect of scattered white circles dancing in the dead leaves.

Nigel and Günter wept like colicky babies as they were prodded forward into the woods. *"I don't want to die!"*

A rifle poked Nigel between the shoulder blades. "Keep movin'!"

The trail of tears led into a mossy cluster of hardwoods. *"Where are we going?"*

"That's far nuff," said Willard.

"Don't be turnin' 'round," said Jasper.

Then Nigel saw it. *"Ahhhhhhhhh!"*

Dirt tumbled from under the toes of his shoes and into the freshly dug grave they had seen earlier. *"No! No! No! ..."*

"Shee-it," said Willard. "You fellas is more nervous than long-tailed cats in a room full of rockin' chairs."

"Don't kill us!"

"Stop pissin' and moanin'," said Willard. "We're letting you go."

"Wait, what? You're not going to bury us alive?"

"You ain't worth the trouble," said Jasper. "No way you can find us or our cabin."

"That's right," said Nigel. "We're horrible with directions."

"This here's the part where we skee-daddle," said Willard. "You know how you always see on TV where they make folks count to a thousand or some such?"

Nigel nodded with vigor. "We can count."

"Heck with countin'," said Willard. "We want you to work."

"And ... do what exactly?"

"Bury that stupid body!" said Jasper. "You interrupted us before."

Nigel gazed across the grave. Yep, the dead guy was still there.

"Two birds with one stone," said Willard. "We're getting rid of you *and* we don't need to bust our butts filling that damn hole back up."

Jasper aimed his own rifle. "Now throw him in and start a-shovelin'. And don't even think of running out of here before the job's done. We might be watchin' or comin' back ..."

The body was in the hole so fast that it startled the brothers. Soil began flying.

"Y'all behave now, ya hear?" The brothers propped rifles over their shoulders and marched off into the darkness until they seemed to dematerialize like a nightmare that had never existed.

"What are you doing?" Günter asked Nigel. "Keep shoveling!"

"They're gone.

"So what?"

"So right now we're free," said Nigel. "We can make a run for it. Every second we spend here, they could be changing their minds."

"And if we don't finish the hole, they *will* change their minds!"

"I really think they're gone." Nigel strained his eyes into the forest. "Look for yourself."

"I don't see anything."

"That's my point."

"Okay, let's get out of here."

Click, click.

They spun around at the sound of the rifles. "*Ahhhh!* How'd you get behind us?"

"Finish the damn hole."

Soil flew as if there was a soil-spraying machine.

A half hour later, they tamped down the top of the not-so-shallow grave.

"There," said Nigel. "No way they can say we didn't finish the job. Let's get out of here!"

They prepared to fling the shovels aside.

Bright lights blinded them. Shouting. A camera in their faces.

"What are you hiding? Who are you burying out here?"

"Nothing! Nobody!" Nigel held a hand up to shield squinting eyes. "It was these other people. They made us fill the hole. You have to believe us!"

"Cut! That's a wrap." The lights went out.

Nigel uncovered his eyes. "You?"

"Who else?" said Serge.

"I don't get it."

"Leverage," said Serge. "Usually my brand of leverage is permanent, but the punishment has to fit the crime, and you're just buffoons. I wouldn't want to be accused of going overboard." He tossed Nigel some car keys. "Your SUV is still parked back at the road where you left it earlier. But remember: Not a word about my friends, or I'll send this tape to the police. Then it's prison for life, and your next reality show will have an adult rating."

"My lips are sealed," said Nigel. "We'll only air the footage we shot in Cassadaga."

"Like hell you will."

"But you even said you *wanted* us to show it."

"No, I didn't. Why are you speaking such nonsense?"

"Because I heard you," said the producer. "Back at the cabin, remember?"

"The number one rule in life is when people point out that you lied, just flatly deny it. Of course *The Daily Show* will run clips of you saying it, but nobody's paying attention. Don't you follow elections in this country?"

Chapter 19

THE NEXT DAY

Another sunny morning in Miami.

Nothing out of place. Drivers sipping coffee, pedestrians reading newspapers, drifters with rolling Samsonite. People on cell phones reported credit-card issues. Some checked their wrists to see how many steps they had taken.

A decade-old Hyundai sat at a red light with a dripping brake drum and a bumper sticker from the driver's alma mater: GO TERRIBLE SWEDES (Bethany College, Lindsborg, Kansas). The employee badge clipped to his pocket said DAGWOOD FOOTE, named for some great-great-grand-uncle, but he preferred Darren. His mind wandered without attention, as did the traffic around him: His namesake relative was said to have perished a hero in Teddy Roosevelt's Rough Riders. Were the Swedish even aware of the nickname? His family lied more than most. Maybe the first Dagwood actually died in a tragic stevedore accident in Spokane, leaving behind a modest collection of vice-presidential autographs. What was the deal with Norway? He decided that life was immeasurably complex and required another bumper sticker about his son making straight B's. He took a bite of a Hot Pocket.

The radio was tuned to a Spanish news station for the English: Someone was found at sea. Someone else wasn't. Raúl Castro is still a jerk. Don't buy ranch salad dressing dated February 17 or else.

The driver leaned forward as a Marilyn Monroe drag queen sprinted through the crosswalk—"Get away from me!"—followed closely by a JFK look-alike—"But I love you! ..."

The red light turned green. The Hyundai had just started to move when it was cut off by a flying-V formation of Mercedes sedans.

Tires screeched to a stop. Hands seized through the driver's window.

"Excuse me," said Foote. "I'm having breakfast."

A sausage Hot Pocket flew as a coat was thrown over his head. Another man shoved him in the backseat of the getaway vehicle and fired gunshots in the air to intimidate bystanders, who weren't interested anyway because the same thing was happening for unrelated reasons at the other intersections.

ELSEWHERE

Mid-morning settled over the sleepy wooded settlement. Residents with gardening gloves pulled weeds from the yards of pastel cottages, and guests sipped sweetened tea on the veranda of the old Cassadaga Hotel. A silver Corvette arrived at a pink house with a silk flag. The TV could be heard from the street.

"Looks like Coleman is still awake," said Serge. "That's a good sign."

"I don't know if it was the best idea to leave your friend guarding my ex," said Trish. "He was unconscious on my rug most of the time I saw him."

"Coleman may be a fool, but he's also fool-*proof*." Serge walked up the steps with her key. "My knots were so intricate that the two of them together couldn't untie Gil."

They opened the front door, and Serge's face drooped. A human form lay sprawled again on the Tibetan carpet, gun still in hand.

The hostage had managed to tediously inch his chair across the parlor until its back rested against an antique writing desk. Then the ex-husband had blindly worked his fingertips into various drawers and nooks until he felt a knife, which he was now using to saw through the ropes around his wrists.

"Thanks a lot, Coleman." Serge walked over and glared disapprovingly at the captive. "You're not being safety-conscious. Haven't you ever heard to cut *away* from yourself?" He reached for the blade. "Let me take that before you hurt yourself."

Coleman arose from the dead. "Hey, Serge, when did you get back?"

"Apparently just in time." Serge dragged the whimpering hostage and his chair back to the center of the room. "I thought you already took a nap."

"Just resting my eyelids," said Coleman, gesturing with the gun. "But the rest of the time I kept him covered just like you asked."

Bang.

Ker-sploosh.

Serge shrieked. "My Eight Ball!"

"Sorry."

Serge snatched the pistol away. "What's wrong with you?"

"It just went off like the other times." He lay back on the floor. "Closing my eyes again."

Serge turned to the ex. "You're a neutral party. Who's in the right here? Am I crazy?"

"Serge." Trish tapped him on the shoulder. "I hate to mention it, but we have a situation here. I'm starting to get really scared. What if the police—?"

Serge wrapped his arms around her in a gentle embrace. "Don't you worry about a thing. Just go in the bedroom and catch up on sleep. When you wake up, all this aggravation will be a fading memory."

"I thought you needed cover of darkness,"

"Plans have accelerated due to last night's events. Plus, it fits nicely into my new master plan. Go take a nap."

"But you're ... I mean, you wouldn't, uh ..."

"Kill him?" said Serge. "Oh, no, no, no, no. But I have terrific powers of persuasion. I'll make him an offer he can't refuse."

It was almost as if she had been holding her breath ever since her ex arrived. Now a huge exhale of relief. "Thanks, I owe you big-time."

"No, you don't."

She padded down the hallway in exhaustion and was practically out before she hit the mattress.

"Now then ..." Serge grinned at the ex. "It's just you and me. What can we possibly do for fun? I got it!"

Serge disappeared behind him, and the captive's neck jerked back and forth. Then he felt his whole body tipping backward as the chair was dragged toward the rear door.

"Mmmmm! Mmmmm! ..."

NORTH FLORIDA

Two ghostly-white fingers carefully parted dusty blinds. A bloodshot eyeball slowly rotated.

Outside on the highway, occasional vehicles drove by at relaxed intervals. Otherwise, still air.

It was an empty stretch of U.S. 98 running through the Panhandle somewhere below Tallahassee, and it was getting late into the afternoon. A warm orange light traced the tops of the pines across the road. The trees were about all there was, except for the motel with the eyeball in the window. It was at least a mile of thick woods east or west to the next nearest anything, which was a Primitive Baptist church or an abandoned grain elevator, depending on the direction. The motel was a single-story row of rooms that was built with a hometown bank loan and the post-war optimism of a roustabout oil hand from Lubbock named Earl, who erected a sign with a giant cowboy that said RANCHO DELUXE. The parking lot was always full back before the interstate came through. Now the motel office was cluttered with the crayons and toys of a deferential family from India. There was only one car in the lot. Earl was buried nearby.

The eyeball backed away from the window and the blinds snapped shut. Trembling hands opened a childproof bottle for another tranquilizer. A cameraman balled himself up in the corner and wept.

"What are we going to do?" asked Günter. "There's video of us burying the body!"

"I don't know." Nigel popped the pill. "But I can't take this anymore. I can't sleep, I can't eat. I haven't shaved. We haven't set foot outside this room."

"They'll think we murdered him!" said Günter. "They have the death penalty in this country!"

"You don't need to remind me. It's all I can think about." The eye went to the window again. "My chest won't stop pounding, like the cops are going to break in any minute."

"We have to get that video back!" said Günter. "As long as it's out there, we'll be looking over our shoulders the rest of our lives!"

"I know, I know, but how?" Nigel rubbed his wino whiskers. "It's impossible to track that Serge guy down, plus he may have already made copies of the tape. I don't want to leave this room."

Günter began crying again, then Nigel.

The tears trickled off. "Okay, we have to get ourselves together," said the producer. "We're big deals, after all. We don't need to be cowering ..." *Sniffle*. "... We need a plan. We need to take action!" He plugged his cell phone into the charger.

"*That's* taking action?"

"It's a start." *Sniffle*. "The main thing is getting organized. When was the last time we bathed? ..."

They took turns in the shower.

Nigel toweled off his hair. "That's better. We're taking control now. We're thinking straight."

"So what's the plan to get the tape back?" asked Günter.

Nigel stood in thought, his brain flipping through mental note cards. He finally shook his head. "I can't come up with anything that will work. What about you?"

"Maybe if we— ... or we could— ..." Eyes began welling again. "It's impossible. Unless we ..."

"Unless we what?"

"The hillbillies. They'll know where he is."

"Except we don't know where *they* are," said Nigel. "We'll never find that cabin, and even if we do, I want to go back there even less than I want to leave this room."

Günter collapsed on the bed. "We're doomed!"

"Hold everything," said Nigel. "I think I've got it."

"Got what?"

"The whole time we've been approaching this from the wrong angle." He picked up an electric razor. "We'll never get the tape back. So what?"

"So we go to death row."

"Don't you see? It's exquisitely simple," said Nigel. "What does the tape show?"

"Us burying a body."

"No, it shows us burying *something*. Who's to say it's even human?"

"The police will discover that when they dig him up."

"Exactly. So we have to make the tape irrelevant," said Nigel.

"What does that mean?"

"We need to fix it so that when the authorities follow that video into the woods and start digging, they don't find anything," said Nigel. "All we need to do is go back and move the body. It solves everything."

Günter's eyes bulged. "No way! I'm not going anywhere near that forest!"

Another peek out the window. "It'll be dark enough soon."

"Especially at night!"

"It's our only hope," said Nigel. "I can't do this alone."

"Even if I agree to come, I don't think I can function," said Günter. "I'll freeze up with nerves. It's hard enough just getting my legs to cooperate in this room."

"We're going to have to stop for shovels anyway, so we'll pick up some beer."

"Might work," said Günter. "It's a long enough drive."

THE GROVES

Afternoon sunlight streamed through a kitchen window. Butterflies circled outside. Squirrels dug for nuts. A hummingbird hovered with unseen wings at a decorative feeder.

Trish smiled at the view. Serge had been right. A good nap and now all the weight pressing down on her was evaporating.

The kitchen began to fill with the smell and sound of frying butter. A mixing bowl poured batter in the skillet. Trish began whistling a merry tune as she sliced Valencia oranges in half and twisted them on a hand-operated juicer.

Coleman plopped down in a seat at the table, his hair in anarchy.

"I'm making pancakes." Trish flipped with a spatula. "Nothing like breakfast when it's not breakfast time. Want any?"

Coleman had a distant stare like he was recovering from a stun gun. "I'm not quite here yet." He began his own breakfast with Schlitz.

"By the way, have you seen Serge since I went to sleep?"

"Ask me again in a few minutes?"

"I wonder where he could be? ..."

... Ten miles east, sunlight sparkled off bright green leaves. A hand snatched a Valencia orange off a tree.

Serge jammed a ninety-nine-cent plastic citrus sipper in the side of the fruit and began sucking as he squeezed. The deflated orange was cast aside and the sipper lovingly stowed in a Velcro pocket of his cargo shorts. "I never get tired of that."

Then he picked up his shopping bags and ventured deeper into the isolated rows of orange trees until arriving at a preordained spot.

He stood alone and pinched his lower lip. "Did I get my coordinates wrong?" He looked down at the ground where there had been some kind of commotion in the dirt. "No, this is definitely where I left him."

There were two irregular grooves in the soil. Serge followed them, pushing branches aside as he climbed into the next row, then the next. "There you are!"

On the ground, a man was tied to a tipped-over chair, frantically digging heels into the earth to push himself along. *"Mmmmm! Mmmmm! ... "*

"Let me give you a hand." Serge uprighted the chair. "Didn't mean to be gone so long, but it was nuts rounding up all the supplies for my new *Route 66* job." He dropped the bags and sat on the ground in front of the chair. A large pictorial book opened in his lap. "This stuff is absolutely fascinating! And I thought I knew everything about crystals, even polycrystals like ice cubes, where individual components of the geometric structure don't carry over to the next cell. Aren't ice cubes insane? That crystal formation is why water *expands* when it freezes—the lifelong enigma is finally solved!"

"Mmmmm! Mmmmm! ..."

"You're right, I'm getting off track." He flipped pages. "The hard-core crystal community believes their rocks vibrate at different energy levels to impart the virtues of joy, energy, creativity, wisdom, protection, sexual prowess ... *Nudge, nudge, wink, wink ...*"

Serge reached into the first shopping bag, removing various clear packets of stones that he arranged chromatically on the ground. "I've totally rededicated my life to the world of crystals. When I was in school, they told us neutrons and protons and electrons were as small as it gets. But now there are quarks, bosons, hadrons, gluons, which means I was seriously gypped!" He rummaged in the other bag, producing a pair of drinking glasses and bottles of spring water. "But here's where all that science brings us to crystals. Most people think that only plants and animals are alive, and everything else isn't. I mean, look at my car keys. Like crystals, they appear completely solid, but inside, all these subatomic particles are racing around like they're late for something. So my keys are actually alive ... Note to self: Don't just throw them on the dresser anymore ..."

"*Mmmmm! Mmmmm! ...*"

Serge turned to a new chapter in his picture book. "Some devotees even swear by dropping large crystals into glasses of water, then drinking it or pouring the 'essence' on their skin. Absolutely true." He turned the book around. "These women are doing it. What do you say we give it a try and find out if they're onto something?"

Serge uncapped the bottles of water and filled their glasses.

"*Mmmmm! Mmmmm! ...*"

"I get it," said Serge. "You don't completely trust me, just because I tied you up and pointed a gun in your face and dragged you into the kind of neglected orange grove that attracts search parties. The real reason I picked these rows of Valencia trees is that in the early days, the spiritualist camp held 'grove services.' A stranger told me ... But don't just take my word that I mean no harm. This here will put your mind at ease. See how all these bags of crystals are clearly marked and factory sealed?" He then stood and placed the book in the captive's lap. "And if you're still worried, read this part on preparation of the magic potions. It explains that none of the crystals actually dissolve and end up in the liquid. The rocks just give off positive vibes, filling the water with 'mystical information' and 'ancient memory.' If you believe it, great, you'll be a new man. If not, the worst-case scenario is you're drinking spring water and bullshit."

"*Mmmmm! Mmmmm!*"

"How about this to sweeten the deal?" said Serge. "If you drink it, I'll set you free. I'll even drink mine first."

The hostage stopped struggling and looked up.

"You want to say something?"

Urgent nodding.

Serge ripped the duct tape off his mouth.

"Ow! ... Will you really let me go? No tricks?"

Serge raised a pair of fingers. "Scout's honor."

"Let me see the book again."

Serge held it to his face. The captive read quickly down the page. "Okay, now let me see those bags."

"Here you are."

The captive read the labels and inspected the seals. "Hell yes, it's a deal! I'll drink as much as you want!"

"That's the spirit."

Serge prepared their respective cocktails, over and over, drinking his own and holding the others to his guest's mouth. More concoctions were poured liberally over their skin.

Then they sat and waited.

Serge's big toe began to vibrate, then his whole foot, his leg, his other leg ... ripples of energy rushing up his chest. He hopped to his feet. "Hot damn! There really is something to this! I feel like dancing!"

Serge jitterbugged from one row of trees to the next, then did cartwheels and somersaults. "I've never felt so young and full of life!"

"Untie me! Untie me! ..."

"Really?" said Serge. "It's working for you, too?"

"Hurry!"

"Well, I *did* give you my word." Serge flicked open a pocket-knife and slashed the bindings.

The ex-husband grabbed his chest. "There's something seriously wrong. What's happening to me?"

Then he suddenly began running in figure eights through the trees, flapping his arms and speaking in tongues: "*Arrrgreeee-bloooghpppfffazzz! ...*"

"I must be getting old," Serge told himself. "I'm not up on the latest dance moves ... On the other hand, it's never too late ..."

Serge joined his captive, chasing after him through the rows, flapping his own arms and babbling: "*Arrrgreeeebloooghpppfffazzz!* ..."

The ex-husband hit the dirt and flopped like a landed fish. "*Blalalalalalalalalalalalala!* ..."

Serge flopped next to him. "*Blalalalalalalalalalalalala!* ..."

The captive leaped up again and took off into the trees, arms now windmilling. "*Yayayayayayayayayayay!* ..."

Serge windmilled his own arms. "*Yayayayayayayayayayay!* ..."

But Gil was now running faster than anyone could keep up.

Serge stopped and listened as the yelling trailed off over a hill. "I'm jealous. He must have gotten luckier crystals than me."

Chapter 20

MIAMI WOMEN'S LEGAL AID CLINIC

Word was getting around. The waiting room had never seen so many clients. They all leaned forward in their chairs and strained to hear the commotion coming from some unseen part of the building. The receptionist got up and closed the door to the hallway.

In the last office, Brook stared slack-jawed at the angry mob on the other side of her desk, quarreling nonstop and spewing epithets.

"Please be quiet ..."

They didn't miss a beat, shouting away.

"Quiet ..."

It only got worse.

"Everyone! Shut the hell up!" Brook's fist hit the desk. "Shut up! Shut up! Shut up!"

Silence. Stunned eyes turned toward her.

"I'm sorry I had to speak to you that way," said Brook. "But you have to listen to me. These are serious offenses. I've spoken with the prosecutor, and if everyone agrees not to file charges, we're only talking about a little community service. Do you understand?"

The combined staffs of the nail and beauty salons began to nod.

"But here's the most important part, and you absolutely have to do exactly as I say," Brook continued. "This war ends now. You'll be on probation, so that means no more vandalized cars, no more dead rats in mailboxes, no more cars doing doughnuts on front lawns, and definitely no more lasers. Are we in agreement?"

The crowd exchanged nasty glances, but reluctantly began to nod again.

"Good." Brook stood up. "Now make the peace ... Go on, hug. It's a non-negotiable condition of me representing you."

The staffs tentatively embraced, then thanked Brook and departed. The door closed.

The door opened.

Jacklyn Lopez escorted Danny into the office.

Brook stood up with a big smile. "Did Jacklyn tell you?"

Danny looked back and forth at the two attorneys. "You really want to hire me?"

"Without a doubt. You're sharper than most law students I know," said Brook. "And you're working your way through Miami-Dade College at what? The food court? We can do better than that."

"You want to pay me for more referrals?"

"No, we're not asking you to chase ambulances," said Jacklyn. "Just stuff around the office."

"I didn't mean it that way," said Danny. "It's just that a lot of my community is under-served in this area, and you take cases others won't touch. But you'll still work with people I bring in on my own?"

"If it's like that, sure, we always want to help," said Brook. "Anyone who comes to you purely of their own volition—"

"Already got a few," said Danny. "Actually a bunch."

"That was fast."

"Word's out about you in the neighborhood. It's all good." She opened her purse. "The business with the forfeiture sealed the deal. The fact that you wouldn't divulge the names of your illegal migrants in open court earned their complete trust in a way no outsider could ever hope for."

"I'm flattered."

Danny pulled her hand from the purse and slid a stub across Brook's desk.

"A lottery ticket?"

"A *winning* ticket."

"Good Lord!" said Jacklyn.

"Don't get too excited," said Danny. "It's one of the smaller pots, Fantasy Five, just several thousand."

"What are you doing with it?" said Brook. "More perplexing, why are you giving it to me?"

"A neighbor of mine wants you to cash it in. And I've got a dozen more in here just like it."

"Why me?"

"Like I said, word's getting around."

"That's not what I meant." Brook examined the ticket in her hands. "Why doesn't your neighbor cash it himself?"

"Because you have to show ID and do all the tax stuff. Except he isn't trying to avoid taxes."

"And I'm guessing deportation," said Jacklyn.

"I keep telling everyone not to waste their hard-earned money on these stupid tickets, and then Hector wins that thing, and the whole block scrambles to the nearest bodega ... His only other option is to go to these shady brokers that run dubious convenience stores, and they take a cut."

"You do realize that I'll be taking a cut, too," said Brook. "Pro bono starts with constitutional violations and ends at lottery winnings."

"But it'll be a smaller cut, and it will go to you."

"Haven't done anything like this before," said Brook. "Never even thought of it."

"I've heard of situations where someone is buying up investment property and wants to shield their identity so the prospective sellers don't raise their prices. So they create some kind of trust where a law firm's name shows up on everything."

"Sharp. That's why I just hired you." Brook set the ticket down. "But this is more than just a name change in a public file. This is actually taking possession of money. I can still wrangle that, but your neighbor will need two lawyers."

"Why?"

"I'll represent the client and draw up the contracts with the other attorney, who will be assigned legal ownership of the ticket and cash it in on behalf of *his* client, which is me," said Brook.

"Sounds awfully complicated."

"We need the firewall created by a second layer of attorney-client privilege," said Brook. "It may even set a precedent."

"Got anyone in mind?"

Brook reached for the phone. "Let me do some calling around."

CASSADAGA

A doorbell chimed.

Trish opened it before the sound had finished. She threw her arms around Serge's neck. "You're back! You're safe! Is everything okay? What happened?"

"I have much to report!" He hurried past her and opened his picture book on the parlor séance table. "These things actually work! Who would have thought?"

"What are you talking about?"

"Crystals! The magic water!" He found the right chapter and jabbed his index finger at an illustration. "I've just had the most intense spiritual experience of my entire life! My soul shot through the cosmos like the ending of a Kubrick movie!"

"You actual drank the water?"

"Of course! And now I need more crystals immediately!" He began stomping his feet like a child. "Must have crystals! But where can I get them? Right, every single place in town! ... Be back in a second ..." He ran for the door.

"Serge, stop! Calm down!" Trish caught up to him from behind and grabbed his arm. "Now just come back to the table with me and point out in the book exactly which crystals you drank."

"Okay, this one ..."—flipping pages—"and this one, and these two over here. That's it."

"You sure you didn't use any other stones?"

"I'm certain."

Trish sat back in her chair. "Hate to tell you this, but those stones are completely benign and without any effects, pro or con."

"But my complete transformation!"

"Just the power of suggestion." She broke into a smile. "And your great natural energy level."

"But the book said—"

"I'll let you in on a secret," said Trish. "The unspoken rule around here is don't speak about it."

"About what?"

"Believe in crystals or not, it's all harmless fun and games," said Trish. "Nobody gets hurt."

Serge pouted. "So I didn't attain a higher plane of consciousness?"

"I think you're already there." She chuckled. "Someday you'll have to tell some of us around here *your* secret."

"Crap." Serge picked up a broken piece of his Eight Ball. "First I got cheated out of quarks and now this travesty."

Trish was about to say something, but suddenly paused with a nagging feeling. She was forgetting something. But not for long.

Up on her feet: "Serge, what happened to my ex-husband?"

"Oh, him?" He picked up the dislodged and dripping Eight Ball message nugget. "Had a great talk. He's fine."

"You let him go?" Heart racing again. "I mean, I didn't want you to— ... but I thought at least—" She ran to the window. "Where the hell is he?"

"Could be anywhere," said Serge. "You sure these crystals are just paperweights? I really think I felt something."

She hysterically grabbed his shoulders. "What am I supposed to do? He could be coming back here right now!"

"Seriously doubt it." Serge dabbed a finger into the Eight Ball water on the table and touched it to his tongue. "Maybe this stuff will work."

"Stop it! I'm really freaking out!" Trish heaved in a cascading anxiety attack. "Why do you say you 'seriously doubt it'?"

He held up the geodesic nugget. "I was quoting the Eight Ball, or what's left of it."

"Dammit, Serge, I'm having a heart attack!" She fell into a chair with hands over a crying face.

"Whoa, easy now," said Serge. "He sincerely seemed to have a thorough change of personality after sharing gem water."

"Like that's supposed to reassure me." Trish grabbed a tissue and blew her nose. "I told you those crystals you used don't do anything!"

"Well, we did drink different crystals."

"Different?" She wiped her eyes. "Which ones?"

"Well, the turquoise variety in this picture looks familiar, except it also came in a yellowish-green clump that looked nice in the light. And this one, and this one ..."

Trish's blood pressure whipsawed as she turned glossy pages. "What else?"

"That baby for sure," said Serge. "Couldn't resist the translucent burnt-orange hue. And this one."

She turned more pages. "Is that all?"

"And that ruby-red baby," said Serge. "Reminded me of pink grapefruit juice."

"Holy—" Trish stood and stared at a wall in general. "This may be a first for the crystal community."

"What's wrong?"

"Serge, you couldn't have picked a worse assortment of rocks if you had tried."

"Worse? But I thought you said they didn't do anything?"

She sat rod straight and flipped to the back of the book. "The crystal culture might be a lot of make-believe powers and practices, but you're still dealing with actual minerals that react in the physical world according to the laws of science. Even the guy who wrote this book knows that."

"I'm not following."

"While these authors are cashing in by telling people that drinking crystal waters will make them glow with good fortune and spiritual balance, they still have to worry about lawsuits." She found a page with a giant exclamation point inside a big red warning circle. "Here's a list of crystals that under no circumstances should you ever drink, or even pour on your skin. All the ones you gave him are here. For instance, adamite, which is zinc arsenate hydroxide."

"Are you saying it contains arsenic?" said Serge. "Interesting."

"Here's lópezite, an even bigger no-no. Galena here contains lead, and cinnabar is a pleasantly unassuming name for mercury sulfide."

"I gave him mercury?" said Serge.

"Plus, torbernite is radioactive," said Trish. "It's another dirty little secret of crystals: many contain heavy metals, which are some of the most toxic substances you can introduce into the human body. That's why all professional spiritualists keep one foot in the real world and know which stones to handle with care or avoid altogether."

"Utterly riveting," said Serge. "I never got that far in the book. Please tell me more!"

"As opposed to mystical powers, each of the crystals on this no-fly list has its own documented adverse neurological reaction," said Trish. "Administered in that kitchen-sink batch you gave him, and it's all uncharted waters, if you'll excuse the pun."

"That's quite an eye-opener."

"Wait," said Trish. "What's this?"

"What?"

"You told me you didn't get this far in the book." She held it up. "So why is the warning page dog-eared?"

"It is?" said Serge. "Then I must demand a refund. Some browsing customer obviously did that in the store."

A pause to stare. "If you say so."

"Hey, guys, check this out!"

Serge looked down the hall. "Coleman's up?"

"Drinking Schlitz and watching cartoons."

"Hurry or you'll miss it!"

"Hold your horses!" Serge slowly rose with a strain of patience. "Coleman's one of the few people to voluntarily pursue an assisted-living lifestyle ..."

The pair entered the kitchen. "What's so important?"

Coleman giggled and pointed at the TV with his beer.

"That isn't cartoons," said Serge. "You never watch the local news."

"I was flipping channels, and they had amateur cell-phone videos of something that happened today. They're about to show it again."

They all gathered round. The news station ran a banner across the top of the screen: FLORIDA MAN EXCLUSIVE. Beneath it—with spots strategically blurred out—a naked man ran through traffic, flapping arms, banging on windows and babbling incoherently.

Trish gave a wary glance sideways.

"Hey, it's not like I forced him to drink it at gunpoint," said Serge. "Some people just see a gun and automatically infer."

The man on the screen was now scrambling over hoods of cars and clawing at his skin, before darting into the intersection. The station stopped the video clip just before the moment of impact with the dump truck. It cut to a location shot:

"This is Ashley Zahn reporting live from the scene of today's tragedy on the outskirts of Cassadaga. And while toxicology reports are still pending, police sources suspect the epidemic of the new designer drug flakka ..."

"Trish," said Serge. "You didn't mention he was also a drug abuser."

Chapter 21

AFTER DARK

High beams of a black SUV split the ominous night on Highway 98. Nothing but trees and lawlessness. An oncoming semi truck whizzed by on the two-laner, rattling the car. Then wisps of fog. Every now and then, eyes glowed on the center line before darting off into the brush.

It became less isolated as they saw more and more headlights. The vehicle crested a hill and found the reason. A country store near the Wakulla River. Only place open for miles at this hour.

The SUV pulled into a parking lot full of pickup trucks with abnormally large tires. They went inside, and Nigel headed for the beer case. "You get the shovels."

They approached the counter.

"Shovels and beer?" said the grizzled clerk. "You boys burying something?"

"No!"

He scanned in the purchase. "Then you must be digging something *up*."

"W-w-why do you say that?"

The clerk shrugged. "It's Friday night."

Nigel and Günter rushed out of the store.

The next customers stepped up to the counter.

"Anything else?" asked the clerk.

"Just the shovels and beer."

The SUV took off into the woods. Günter popped the cap off a Beck's and began chugging.

"Give me one of those," said Nigel. A green bottle upended.

The Suburban flew over hills and screeched around desolate turns, deeper into nature. Deeper into the beer. They took the fork at Tate's Hell. A bottle flew out the window and shattered on the sign. "*Fuckin' A!...* That's what they say around here, right?"

Nigel turned up the brightness on the vehicle's instrument panel and watched the odometer, counting down the last 5.7 miles to X-marks-the-spot. They slowed to a crawl when the last tenth turned over. "We're here!"

"*A-Ooooooooo!*" Günter bayed at the moon. "*Werewolves of London!*"

It had been a twelve-pack. The contents of ten were back in the mist, with the final two in their hands as they opened the back of the vehicle for digging implements.

"Just a second," said Nigel, pulling back the mat over the wheel well. "Take this."

"A gun?"

Nigel tucked his own pistol in his waistband. "They sell them everywhere in the state. I bought these last week during our confrontational exposé on the dangers of gun shows."

"Why?"

"To be on the safe side." Nigel popped his last beer and staggered toward the woods. "Those gun people were scary."

The pair plunged down the road's embankment through mossy ground cover, aided by a D-cell baton flashlight.

"This way, I think," said Nigel. "Günter? ... *Günter!* What are you doing waving that gun?"

"Thought I heard something." He crouched and took aim. "Shine that light over there."

The beam hit a tree and an unimpressed bird.

Bang.

The bird took flight.

"Why'd you shoot at an owl?"

"His intentions were unclear."

"Well, knock it off. We might need those bullets. These automatics only hold sixteen."

Onward. Scraping themselves on branches. Falling down, tearing their pants.

"What's so funny?" asked Nigel.

The cameraman stifled giggles. "This whole mess. Now that we've calmed down, it's pretty hilarious if you think about it."

"Günter! We're not out of this yet! ..." Snort. "We still have to—" Then he was cracking up as well. "You're right. It *is* funny."

Günter held his last bottle up to the moonlight. "How much you got left?"

"About half."

"Same here ... On three: one, two, *three*!"

They guzzled the last of their beers together, followed by the sound of bottles breaking on trees. Laughter again as they threw arms over each other's shoulders like war buddies, blustering forward dragging shovels.

They found themselves in a clearing. An erratic flashlight beam bounced around trees and dirt.

Günter turned in a circle. "Where's the grave?"

"Remember, it was by a clump of trees?" said Nigel, curiously pointing the flashlight at his own face. "And a fallen log?"

"I'm starting to get worried again." Günter leaned on his shovel. "What if the cops— ... Can't even think about it."

"I feel the same. The beer isn't cutting it." Nigel reached in his back pocket for a sterling-silver flask.

"What's that?"

"Emergency supply to fortify our nerves." Nigel took a swig and cringed. "Wasn't sure how hairy this would get. Try some ..."

Günter sniffed the pungent open cap. "What is it?"

"Sour mash, from someplace they called Tennessee."

"Never tried it," said Günter. "I'm a gin man."

"So am I, but they told me everyone in the state drinks this stuff."

"Where'd you hear that?"

"At the gun show."

Günter glugged and coughed. "That'll sure clear your sinuses. Which way?"

"Let's try this direction," said Nigel, setting off north.

The pair wove through the woods for a half hour, meaning they were ten minutes from the road.

"That way looks familiar ..."

They staggered southwest, then east, northwest, south—"Why can't we find it?"—north again, southeast. If you could chart the flight of a moth, that was the course of their search.

The two stopped again. "Where's that flask?" asked Günter.

"Me first." Nigel took a slug before passing it. "Stuff grows on you."

Günter drew a big sip, looked around and scratched his head. "It's the damnedest thing. We were just here the other day."

"I could have sworn I'd never forget the spot," said Günter. "All that digging."

"No way the forest could have covered it up so soon. It should be easy to identify with all that freshly disturbed ground." Nigel stomped his foot, tamping down loose soil, and pointed the flashlight at the ground. "Like this place right here. There's a clump of trees and a log. It should look exactly like this."

"Okay," said Günter. "We need to find a spot that looks like the one we're at."

"Let's go." They set off on another serpentine quest with a zigzagging beam of light that grew dimmer with depleting batteries. After a few cloverleaf patterns in the forest, they returned to where they had just started.

"Check it out!" Nigel aimed the beam. "It's a spot that's just like the other one."

"And look! Fresh footprints where someone was just tamping it down!" said Günter, spinning in place. "Who else can be out here? I'm a nervous wreck."

"Here's the whiskey."

"Right."

They began digging. The task was much easier this time around, since the soil had recently been unpacked. It was sloppy as digs go, but precision wasn't required. They were down to their hips, then chests ...

Günter thrust his spade. "Think I just hit something. Turn on the flashlight."

"It *is* on." Nigel shook it next to his ear. "I think the batteries are dead. Dig with your hands."

The German dropped to his knees and scooped. "Yeah, it's definitely him. Here's his nose."

"This calls for a drink ..."

They cleared a trench around the body, then stood at opposite ends and lifted him by ankles and armpits. "All right, throw him up there onto the ground."

The swung the body from side to side to build momentum— "On three. *Three!*"—and threw him into the side of the hole.

"What happened?" asked Günter.

"This isn't working." They finished off the flask, and Nigel flung his shovel over the edge. "Okay, I'll climb out, and you prop him up against the side. Then you join me, and we'll pull him out together."

Heavy grunting, but they finally extracted the corpse, then fell to the ground with it to catch their breath.

"What now?" asked Günter.

"I think we're supposed to take him somewhere else."

"Okay, I got his ankles."

"I got the other end. Let's go that way."

"Wish that flashlight was still working."

"Me, too. Start walking ... *Ahhhh!*"

Thud, thud.

"Ouch! Shit! ..."

"Nigel, I think we're back in the hole again."

They pulled the body out a second time and picked him up. "Let's go a different direction—"

It was quiet except for a mild rustling of leaves under their feet. They heard a louder rustling, approaching fast from behind.

Günter's head whipped around. "What's that?"

Blinding lights came on as a cameraman rushed toward them. An Australian voice: "Why did you kill him?"

"Ahhhhhh!"

They dropped the body and fled in different directions.

"Follow them!" directed Cricket Brisbane.

The cameraman named Dundee gave chase. "I think one of them went this way ..."

Bang, bang, bang.

Brisbane hit the ground. "Who's shooting?"

Dundee killed the lights, ran back and flattened himself next to his producer. "I think they are."

Now another direction: *bang, bang, bang.*

"*Nigel!*" Günter called out from behind a tree. "*They're shooting at us!*"

"*I know!*" yelled another tree. "*Where are you?*"

"*Over here! Let's make a break for the car!*"

"*Okay, but we'll have to cover each other!*"

"*Now!*"

The pair charged out into the dark forest like Butch Cassidy and Sundance. *Bang, bang, bang ...*

"Dundee!" whispered the producer from Perth. "They're coming back this way. Make sure you get this."

"I'm ready."

Bang, bang, bang ...

Dundee turned on the camera lights, capturing the rival reality team in full stride and blinding them.

Bang, bang, bang ...

And just like that, nothing.

"Where'd they go?" asked Brisbane.

"I don't know." Dundee cut the lights again.

Bang, bang, bang, bang, bang, bang ...

Muzzle flashes flickered up out of the hole in the ground.

"What the hell?"

Then a long silence as tendrils of gun smoke dissipated into the trees.

The Australians cautiously rose. Camera lights came on again as they walked over and stared down into the grave.

"Are they dead?"

"Get a close-up."

EPISODE FOUR

Chapter 22

THE GOLD COAST

Another hot and bustling day along U.S. 1 in Miami. Sidewalks full of businesspeople on lunch and aimless people on parole. Broken headlight glass in the street, and the rest of the fender bender at the curb. An old man worked the intersections with a cardboard sign: WHY LIE? I WANT TO BUY BEER. A tent sale with balloons, a bicycle with dangling iguanas, a hooker past her sell-by date.

At every corner, waiting customers spilled out of convenience stores. Above, perpetually updating billboards where the workers might as well just camp out.

A silver Corvette sat at a red light. Coleman popped a Pabst and stared. "What's the deal with all those people in line? Did a Stones concert go on sale?"

"Shhhhh! I'm trying to listen." Serge turned up the radio. "Lottery's now projected to break another record by Saturday. I always monitor the lottery when it gets this high."

"But you hate the lottery." Coleman burped. "You said it preys on people least able to afford it."

"Plus, my coffee gets cold waiting in line at the counter." The light turned green, and Serge passed another daunting assemblage that extended into an alley. "But even if you don't play the numbers, you have to follow the jackpots as a matter of survival down here."

Another swig. "How so?"

"If you live in Florida, a major jackpot is like a hurricane about to make landfall," said Serge. "Society looks no different than during the final hours of storm preparation. The lottery lines screw up all major infrastructure for basic needs, so frantic people fight through snarled intersections to stock up on water and food, get prescriptions filled, hit ATM machines, and keep their cars full of gas, because God knows if you can't pay at the pump and have to go inside, you better be wearing comfortable shoes."

"Never thought of it that way."

"The closer you come to the official drawing of the Ping-Pong balls, the lower the state's IQ."

"But why all the fuss now?" asked Coleman.

"That stupid Powerball jackpot a couple years ago that broke a billion dollars. Since then, everyone's had lottery fever. But the Powerball prizes are back down, and Florida's are up, so we get all the commotion."

"Lucky us," said Coleman.

"But it's also the perfect setting for our next episode," said Serge.

Coleman looked down at a ripped spot on his shirt, where an employee name tag had been unceremoniously removed a half hour earlier. "At least we got our new jobs out of the way. Working at that supermarket was nerve-racking."

"Getting fired after thirty minutes doesn't count toward an episode," said Serge.

"I think it does."

"You don't get to make the call," said Serge. "You were the one drinking at the register and messing up the lottery tickets."

"And you're the one telling everybody in line not to buy them, then shoving the manager," said Coleman.

"That was tough love," said Serge. "I did another statistical analysis. Did you realize that among all the millions of people who played the lottery last week, there were no winners, yet seven others will be struck by lightning in their lifetimes?"

"For losing the lottery?" said Coleman. "That's harsh."

"No, that's not what— ... forget it."

Coleman glanced down again. "Do you think they're going to want their shirts back?"

"I'm taking a wild guess that 'Get the hell out before I call the police' means the shirts are our severance package." Serge hit a blinker. "But it's all for the best. I just came up with a much better idea for our next gig."

"What is it?"

"You'll find out when we get to the Party Store."

"The Party Store?" said Coleman. "They have everything! ..."

... An hour after their shopping spree, the silver Corvette sat at another typical South Florida strip mall anchored by a tattoo parlor and a Hungry Howie's pizza place. Serge stood on the edge of the parking lot with a megaphone. "You're fantastic! Just keep it up!"

"I'm having trouble breathing," said Coleman. "And I'm getting really hot."

"That means you're doing it right," Serge barked. "Now execute a camel foot and the pancake spin, then a big finish with the inverted butterfly."

"Okay, here goes."

"Whoa!" yelled Serge. "That's way too fast!"

"What do I do?"

"Slow down!"

"I can't!"

A heavy cardboard sign flew into the air and came down, bonking Coleman on the head. "Ow!"

Serge ran over and helped his fallen friend up into a sitting position. Then he removed the giant, furry costume head. "Coleman, speak to me."

"This sucks." He rubbed his forehead. "How come I'm the one who has to dress like a panda and twirl a sign for the Chinese lunch buffet?"

"Because I'm your manager," said Serge. "Sign-spinning has become an increasingly competitive field. They now even hold conventions with their own version of the X Games. If I don't teach you the newest technique, there's no way you'll survive out here ..." He pointed across the highway at a gorilla executing a triple Lutz to promote international calling minutes.

"Can't I just stand still and wave at cars?"

"No!" Serge grabbed the panda head. "Now put this back on. There's much work to do. Many crowd-pleasing routines to learn: the swim, the flop, the gator, the reverse axle, the Heimlich maneuver, the DUI field test, the restless leg syndrome, the Czechoslovakian Dance of Death ..."

"I'm just going to wave at cars."

Serge seized him by the shoulders. "Get a grip on yourself!"

Coleman held out a paw. "I think it's starting to rain."

Serge looked up. "Crap, you're right ... Hurry! To the bus-stop shelter before your sign starts to smear!"

They dashed under the metal overhang and the sky cut loose, as it is known to do every afternoon in the Florida summer for fifteen minutes.

Coleman took a seat with the panda head in his lap. The bench had an advertisement for corrupt personal injury attorneys: NO PAIN? NO PROBLEM! Across the street, a gorilla glared at them from another bench advertising a credit repair service that just made it worse.

A fingernail scraped at a mustard spot on the panda's chest. "Serge?"

"Yes, Ling Ling?"

"How come it rains every afternoon in the summer?"

"Temperature differential because land heats up faster than the sea as the sun climbs into the sky, creating a pressure drop and pulling air and moisture in from the ocean." Serge chugged a giant cup of coffee and gave the gorilla across the street the bird; the gorilla beat its chest. "The rain effect is most pronounced in the summer."

"Huh?"

"It's above your need-to-know." Serge reached in his pocket and began fiddling with a new cell phone. "But don't worry. It stops as fast as it starts."

"Rain makes me sticky inside this suit."

"What are you complaining about? I'm pissed off at filling out official forms."

"Forms? Where? When were you filling out forms?"

"Inside my head. Another flashback." Serge pressed phone buttons. "I forgot that I'm really angry at all the forms we're forced to complete. Name, address, emergency contact, page after page, checking off tiny boxes that you're a U.S. citizen, don't have artificial joints and understand the terms of agreement."

"Who makes you fill them out?"

"Everyone with more money," said Serge. "It's the American Dream, version six-point-oh: Some dude finally makes it big, and the first day he drives up to his new mansion, 'Excellent, now I get to make the *others* fill out forms.'"

"It's just not right."

Serge nodded with conviction. "I'll be standing at that counter with the sliding-glass window where they hand you a clipboard, and I say, 'I've been here before,' and they say they have a new filing system, and I respond, 'But my doctor referred me—he already has all this info. Can't you share?' They say, 'That's a different office,' and I say, 'It's the same building, in fact it's right next door. For heaven's sake, you have state-of-the-art imaging machines that can produce cross sections of every organ practically down to the cellular level, and yet that wall behind you is a baffling barrier to my date of birth?'"

"What happened?" asked Coleman.

"The same glare every time, like *I'm* the one who's crazy," said Serge. "But I'm hip to their mind-control scheme. The whole process is no accident. The receptionist herself owns a personal phone with a thousand times the computing power of the entire Apollo program, and yet the clipboard she just handed me has a crappy pen hanging from twisted-up rubber bands, not to mention that all the forms are primitive, tenth-generation Xeroxes so grainy that people haven't seen resolution this poor since Three Dog Night was big."

"Jeremiah was a bullfrog! ..."

"Man! Keep it together! ... So I finally acquiesce, taking a seat in the waiting room to fill out this same shit for the millionth time, and they've set me up for failure again! I know they're all hiding behind the counter giggling: 'Look! Look! He's trying to write his e-mail address on that line that's only a half-inch long! This is too much! Now he's trying to write his Social Security number on the line that's only a *quarter*-inch! I'm laughing so hard my sides hurt!' ..."

"Serge?"

"Wait! Wait! Wait! ... Then the receptionist tells the others: 'Shhh! Pipe down! He's coming back up here. You guys keep hiding and I'll stand up and take care of this ... Ahem, yes, Mr. Storms, thank you for filling out— ... Wait, you missed this one part, the address of your primary physician ... Yes, I know he's next door ... Yes, I understand it's the same address as ours ... No, sir, I'm sure that line on the form is longer than a half-inch ...' Then they send me into the bathroom: 'Look! Look! We asked him to pee again in a cup that's way too small! And we told him not to eat anything after midnight when it doesn't matter! This is priceless!'"

"Serge?"

"Huh?" He looked around with a glazed stare. "Why are we here? What are you doing in that costume?"

"The new sign-spinning job."

"Oh, right. It's coming back now."

"Serge, when was the last time you filled out a form?"

"I don't know, two years? Three? But that's the thing about trauma."

A panda arm extended from under the bus shelter's overhang. "I think the rain is letting up like you said."

"But the streets will stay flooded for hours." Serge deftly navigated a small touch screen.

"You sure love your new cell phone."

"These new babies are now called *smart*phones. I don't know how I've managed to get along without one!" *Tap, tap, tap.* "I've never possessed a cooler gadget in my life, and I've only begun to scratch the surface of its potential. But from what I've seen so far, these phones are the pinnacle of human achievement. Forget nuclear fission and stem-cell research. Every culture on every continent now has instant, around-the-clock, multiple media platforms to share with the rest of the globe that cats like to sit in boxes."

"There's an app for everything."

"And here's the crucial reason I needed it for our mission. While we're crisscrossing the state tilting at lighthouses, we can watch all the old episodes of *Route 66* that were filmed in Florida ... Hold on, I'm trying to pull one up now."

"I'm still having trouble believing the two main characters could land a new job every week."

"It was a golden age," said Serge. "The baby-boom economy became so robust that people had no trouble getting any job in any city at any time if they were the stars of a hit TV series."

"Wow."

Vehicles on U.S. 1 continued speeding by with a rhythmic whoosh of tires on the slick roadway. Clouds began to part. Pedestrians folded umbrellas.

"Okay, check it out," said Serge. "I just finished a show from season four where Martin Milner—who would later star in *Adam-12*—gets hired as a safety diver for the mermaids at Weeki Wachee. And here's one from season three, when they're over in Punta Gorda doing yard work, and the town rises up after Linc is falsely accused of injuring a family dog with pruning shears. Back then the viewing public required less stimulus."

Coleman peeked over Serge's shoulder at the phone. "I don't see anything."

"That's because it's not finished loading," said Serge. "Just keep watching the screen! This is going to seriously rock! I'm getting the tingles! It just finished loading! It's starting! ..."

A taxicab went by, followed by a red Porsche just off the factory line. The Porsche's driver spotted the bus shelter and cut the wheel at the last second, swinging over for the lane closest to the curb. The motorist timed his skid perfectly, hitting a deep roadside puddle like a slaloming water-skier.

The wave of spray drenched a pair of people at the bus bench.

Serge stared silently at the road as bulbous droplets fell off his eyelashes and streamed down his cheeks. The departing Porsche had a vanity plate: SCRW U.

Coleman tapped his shoulder. "Hey, Serge, you were just about to show me something really cool on your new phone. Why'd you turn it off?"

FLORIDA CABLE NEWS

The assignment editor saw Reevis heading across the newsroom and waved him into the office.

"I just caught it on TV," said Reevis. "I can't believe they're dead. What happened?"

"Accidentally shot each other while disposing of a body in the Apalachicola Forest," said an Australian accent.

Reevis turned to find two people he hadn't noticed sitting against the wall. "Who are you?"—then, turning to the editor's desk, "Who *are* they?"

"Reevis," said Shug. "I'd like you to meet your new film crew. This is the acclaimed producer Cricket Brisbane and the equally renowned videographer Dundee."

Reevis covered his face. "It doesn't end."

"I know you're still in shock," said the editor. "But I think you'll have a much better working relationship. After all, they broke the story about Nigel and Günter's violent demise. That's the kind of hard news you've been begging for."

Brisbane tipped his bushman's hat. "We also went back and reviewed their work. Tonight we're airing a segment that discredits them professionally. They manufactured a hoax story."

"I'm getting dizzy," said Reevis. "They hoaxed about a hoax?"

"Who knows? But we ran it by the focus groups."

"The important thing," said the editor, "is that all of you get to know each other and find a chemistry."

Brisbane stood. "No time like the present. Saddle up, buckaroo!"

Reevis meekly turned to his editor. "Help ..."

... When the SUV arrived on the scene, U.S. 1 was backed up all the way to downtown Miami. It wasn't congestion. It was rubbernecking.

Drivers slowed and stuck their heads out windows and stared up. No fewer than five news trucks were already there. Reevis climbed out of the sixth. "Dear God!"

Cameraman Dundee got down on one knee so he could film Reevis at an upward angle, framing the source of all the curiosity.

"Look this way," Brisbane told the reporter.

"But we can't film this," said Reevis.

"Why not?"

He pointed skyward. "Because the body is still hanging up there. We never show victims on TV when they're still— ... I mean, look!"

The three of them did. It was one of the countless lottery billboards across the state with an insane new jackpot number ... and not the figure that was up there when the body was discovered, but the one state officials in Tallahassee had ordered put up while he was still swinging, because police interviews of witnesses were taking too long. And hanging by a noose in front of the digits was a lifeless state employee in a short-sleeve dress shirt with a laminated badge clipped to his pocket. The badge said DAGWOOD FOOTE. Can't buy that kind of publicity.

"Ready when you are," directed Brisbane.

"I told you, we don't show corpses!" said Reevis.

"New directive." Brisbane flapped a sheet of paper as proof. "This is the future. We posted crime scene photos on the Internet and took a poll, promising to 'like' the page of anyone who approved. They couldn't get enough, the more grisly the better, especially if there were sexual overtones or the victims had funny haircuts ... Just look at all the people around us taking selfies with the billboard over their shoulders."

"Because there's something deeply wrong with them," said Reevis.

"That's our specialty," said Brisbane. "All of my audiences have problems. That's why they watch."

"But journalism is supposed to lead the way," said Reevis. "Not follow."

"Not anymore." Brisbane held up a page with another directive. "I'll feed you your opening line: *Has lottery fever claimed its first victim?*"

"I'm not saying that!"

"Is there a problem?"

"Yes! It's distastefully flip! The man probably has a wife and kids, for heaven's sake."

"Do I need to call your assignment editor?"

"Fuck you! Fuck all these callous people!"

Brisbane leaned sideways to his cameraman. "Did you get that?"

"Every word." Dundee adjusted the lens for a close-up.

"Good!" said Reevis. "Go show it to my supervisor, for all I care. Now you have your evidence that I'm insubordinate."

"No," said Brisbane, high-fiving his cameraman. "You nailed it!"

"Nailed what?"

"The confrontation that was essential for the segment." Brisbane nodded. "They said you were a genius. Forget feeding scripted lines. From now on, you work best organically."

"But that was just a confrontation between you and me."

"That's why they call it editing."

Chapter 23

THE NEXT DAY

A mom-and-pop motel sat on a corner of Biscayne Boulevard between Miami and Fort Lauderdale. A simple turquoise court topped with white barrel tiles. It was once a sparkling postcard oasis where families on a budget drove two days in station wagons from Illinois and Indiana to enjoy a safe and happy vacation in paradise. Manicured lawn, shrubbery trimmed to strict angles, an intoxicating tropical palette of azalea, jacaranda, bougainvillea, poinciana. Children splashed in the pool, newfangled window air-conditioning units dripped on the sidewalk, and everyone bought ice cream next door from a stand in the shape of a large sugar cone. It was actually called the Florida Motel, with a neon sign in the shape of the state, bragging about color TV and shuffleboard.

That was then.

Today it clung to life as one of the countless old joints tucked among pawnshops, liquor stores and victim clinics, with its own constellation of the undead orbiting at all hours. The swimming pool had an aggressive aroma of chlorine ever since the crime tape came down, and police required the office to supply photocopies of driver's licenses from everyone who checked in, except the manager let that slide for ten bucks.

The sun was at that point just below the horizon where approximately half the cars whizzing by had their lights on. A taxi pulled over and picked up a gorilla. Most of the motel rooms were dark, but number four had a glimmer of life. Inside it was quiet. The wall over the bed featured a faded Edward Hopper painting of a lonely person staring out a motel window at a lot of wheat. On the other side of the room, a lanky man stood intense and motionless at the sink, as he had for an obsessively lengthy time.

"Serge," said Coleman. "Why do you keep staring at that bag of uncooked rice?"

"Because my new cell phone is in it."

"Why?"

"Rice is supposed to absorb the moisture if you get your phone wet." Serge crouched down and inspected the bag two inches from his face. "This is the coolest gadget I've ever owned, so I'm going balls out with household tips. The most crucial step is not to turn your cell back on too soon. If you do and there's any wetness still inside, the power surge will fry the circuitry. It's a test of patience now."

Coleman popped the cap off a beer bottle. "Why am I wearing a skin-diver suit with rubber gloves, boots and a mask?"

"More on that later." He checked his wristwatch. "Hmm, I wonder if I've waited long enough. I must have waited long enough because my feet are starting to throb."

"I say go for it." *Fart.*

"That means I better wait ... What are you drinking now?"

"Miller High Life!" Coleman thrust the bottle above his head in triumph. "The champagne of beers!"

"Coleman, do you realize what a ridiculous advertising slogan that is? Had all the executives just chugged a case of the stuff before green-lighting that chestnut?"

"What are you talking about?"

"In marketing, it's not just what you call attention to, but what you don't," said Serge. "I mean, 'the champagne of beers'? That's like 'Miami Mass Transit: The Rolls-Royce of riding the bus.'"

"Miller gets me fucked up. That's all I know."

"Now *that's* a slogan."

Serge raised the bag of rice and shook it. Coleman popped another beer, using the drawer handle on the nightstand. A police officer left the motel office with a stack of photocopied driver's licenses. Someone screamed and clawed their eyes after jumping in the swimming pool. Coleman threw up in the nightstand's drawer and closed it. "I say the phone's ready."

Serge slowly began to nod in agreement. "I've definitely given it more than enough time. Now I'm just wasting my life." He swiftly yanked the phone out of the bag and turned it on.

Coleman walked over with a squeaking of neoprene. "Look! It's working!"

"So it is," Serge said with a satisfied grin.

Coleman pointed as the tiny screen suddenly zapped to black. "What just happened?"

"*Son of a bitch!*" Serge flung the broken device in a rage, and now the room's Edward Hopper painting featured a lonely person looking out at a field of wheat with a giant cell phone in the middle.

"That was pretty interesting," said Coleman.

Serge walked over to the window and peered outside. "It's almost dark enough."

"What for?"

"Back to the wet suit you're wearing."

"Almost forgot I had it on."

"How does it feel?"

"Wet again inside."

"Hold this in front of you."

"Why?"

"Because the panda costume wasn't cutting it."

"You don't mean ..."

"That's right." Serge nodded again. "We're taking sign-spinning *big*!"

Fifteen minutes later, Serge and Coleman stood in front of a narrow storefront with extra burglar bars and reinforced concrete pylons to prevent smash-and-grabs using stolen vehicles to ram the entrance. A cardboard sign lay at their feet: WE BUY GOLD.

"It finally stopped raining," said Serge.

"The streets are flooded again."

"Doesn't affect your big debut." Serge grabbed a plastic atomizer bottle. "Now hold out the left arm again."

Coleman reluctantly complied. "I don't know about this. What if something goes wrong?"

"I'm a professional. What can possibly go wrong? ... Now stick out your right leg ..."

"There's got to be another way."

"Trust me," said Serge. "We're about to turn the sign-spinning world on its head!"

"Then why don't *you* wear the wet suit?"

"Stop whining! You're about to become an Internet rock star!" Serge reached in his pocket. "If anything, *I'm* the one making the sacrifice ... Stay still. The only thing you have to remember is not to panic ..."

Thirty seconds later, Coleman ran shrieking in terrified circles in the parking lot.

"You're panicking," yelled Serge.

Motorists on U.S. 1 slammed their brakes and dialed emergency numbers, watching in disbelief as a person fully engulfed in flames ran around a parking lot with a burning cardboard sign.

"Look at all the attention you're getting!" said Serge.

Coleman sprinted by. "I'm all on fire!"

"I told you I used low-burn-temperature cooking alcohol," said Serge. "It's just a little bit of fire."

Coleman dashed back the other way. "*Aaaaauuuuuhhhhhh!*"

"Shit, he's running into traffic." Serge grabbed an extinguisher. "Coleman, stop moving so I can put you out."

Cars jumped curbs and rear-ended each other as Serge chased his friend around the street with blasts of foam.

Coleman eventually stopped in the intersection, removed his mask and looked at the steam coming off his arms. "Am I out?"

"Except for that foot. Stick it in that puddle on the edge of the street."

Sizzle.

Serge gave the smoldering black suit a final blast of foam. "There, good as new. Now don't you feel silly?"

"Holy turds," said Coleman. "Look at all the people pulling into our strip mall to sell their gold."

A horrible squealing of tires. *Crash.*

A horn continuously blared from the wrecked car.

"Uh-oh," said Serge. "That guy just had an accident, and of course he's probably going to try and blame us."

"Some people," said Coleman.

"We better go help ..." Serge ran up to the side of the convertible. "Sir, are you okay?"

The woozy driver raised his head off the steering wheel. "What happened?"

"You smashed up your car because you weren't paying attention."

Coleman pulled off charred rubber gloves. "Nothing we did."

A mother with two small children ran over. Serge looked them up and down. "What happened to you?"

"That jerk drenched us! He deliberately swung over from the center lane to hit a deep puddle while we were waiting in the bus shelter. I just bought this phone!"

Serge turned back to the car. "Wait a second ..." He took a step back to appraise the color and model-year of the Porsche. Then walked around back to check the license plate.

SCRW U.

"Sir." Serge opened the driver's door. "On second thought, you need to come with us."

"Why?"

"As a safety precaution, you should be held for observation."

250

JUST UP THE STREET

The stitching above the pocket on the oily shirt said JEREMY. The auto mechanic looked down into the glass case. "I'll take the Big Bucks scratch-off, Money Bags, Huge Loot, the Price Is Right, a Lotto quick-pick, a pack of Winstons and the beer."

The convenience-store clerk rang him up while arguing with his girlfriend on the phone.

"Oh, and can you check if this one's a winner?"

The clerk scanned an old ticket and handed the mechanic a crumpled five-dollar bill. The next customer stepped up. "Let me have a Ruby Riches, King's Gold, Bejeweled Diamonds ..."

Outside in the surveillance van, the supervising agent leaned over a shoulder at a computer screen. "So this one store is responsible for how many, now?"

The tech pressed buttons. "Twelve different straw buyers have each won at least fifty times in the last year, all over five hundred a throw. But that's a tough prosecution with complicit customers, so we have to nab them ripping off the unsuspecting ones."

The undercover agent in a mechanic's shirt climbed into the van. "Only gave me five dollars."

"We saw it on your pinhole camera."

"What's the status?"

"Still waiting— ... Hold on." The computer tech watched the numbers change in a live feed from the lottery's main computers in Tallahassee. "That's it! He just cashed it in for five hundred!"

The supervising agent grabbed the radio. "All units, go! Repeat, go!"

A half-dozen vans whipped around the corner. Side doors flew open. Agents in black vests hit the ground running.

"Everyone out of the store! ... You! Away from the counter! ..."

The clerk was arrested, and the lottery machines unplugged. But neither was moved yet because the officers were waiting for the TV stations they had called. When the satellite trucks arrived and all the cameras were in place, out came the handcuffed employee and the hand truck with the lottery machine. On top of the machine, strategically positioned for the benefit of the home audience: glistening rolls of scratch-off tickets from the glass case. The idea was to increase sales that night.

"This is Reevis Tome reporting live for Florida Cable News in Fort Lauderdale, where an independent convenience store has just been raided by state lottery officials after an undercover agent caught a clerk red-handed..."

"Dundee," said Brisbane. "Zoom in on those shiny rolls."

"... Meanwhile, simultaneous raids occurred today at sixteen other outlets across Broward and Miami-Dade counties in a coordinated sting operation dubbed 'Millionaire Cash Frenzy' after the latest instant game being heavily promoted..."

By the end of the evening, all the hubbub had died down, the clerk made bail, and the good people of the community were dozing off to the late news that concluded with a piece about a Miami revitalization committee seeking funds to clean up the city, and submitted a downtown map with icons documenting where people had pooped in unauthorized locations. Completely true.

The clerk who had just gotten out of jail returned to the convenience store for double duty on the late shift, because the owner was pissed. Business fell to a trickle since the store no longer had lottery tickets and people took their beer and cigarette money elsewhere. Just after midnight, a white Jaguar pulled up outside. A tall man with dreadlocks entered and looked down into the empty glass case. His right hand rested on the counter, fingers tapping in rhythm. The back of the hand had a tattoo of a flaming skull that said MOTHER. He didn't speak, and the employee didn't care because he was on the phone. Finally, the clerk covered up his cell.

"Can I help you with something?"

"Where are the scratch-off tickets?"

"We don't sell them anymore."

"Why not?"

"We just don't."

"I like the scratch-offs."

"There are plenty of other places around here that still sell them."

"But I want to buy some here."

"I just told you, we don't have any." The clerk looked closer. "Do I know you?"

"Don't think so."

"Yes, I've seen you in here with the owner a few times."

The customer looked up at a small black dome in the middle of the ceiling. "Is that a real security camera, or just a dummy?"

"It's real. And I would like you to leave."

"Hang up the phone."

"Listen, asshole—"

A pistol with a silencer came out. The black dome shattered. "It was a dummy. Why did you lie to me?"

The clerk dropped the phone as he backed up and raised his hands. "Take all the money. It's yours."

"I already knew that." He walked around behind the counter and crushed the dropped cell phone with the heel of a snakeskin boot ...

... House lights went dark in bedrooms across the bedroom neighborhoods, and revolving red ones came on outside a convenience store on U.S. 1.

Before it was over, the street outside Mart-Mart was again full of police vehicles and TV vans. They found the body in the alley behind the Dumpster, hands tied behind the back. They needn't wait for identification. The victim's face had just been all over the news when he was paraded out of the convenience store in handcuffs just a few hours earlier. The ruling wasn't official yet, but the cause of death would eventually be classified as asphyxiation from the victim's head being completely wrapped numerous times with rolls of scratch-off tickets.

Chapter 24

MIDNIGHT

The vintage Florida-shaped sign was dark at the motel, which meant it was open.

Coleman dumped a bag of weed on the dresser of room four. "What are you looking at?"

Serge gazed out the window at the part of the sign advertising color TV. It was one of the old signs where each letter of the word *color* was a different color. Serge liked that every time. Then he looked back across the room at their own television with thirteen channels of black-and-white snow.

"Mmmm! Mmmm! Mmmm! ..."

Coleman removed pot stems and glanced over his shoulder. "I think he wants to tell you something."

"Almost forgot about him." Serge returned to the center of the room and the aisle between the two beds, where a chair had been repositioned. In it sat a trim and tanned young man in a golf shirt. Not exactly by choice. Nylon rope fastened his arms and ankles to the chair with complicated nautical knots.

"You talking to me?" asked Serge.

The captive nodded anxiously.

Serge grabbed a corner of the duct tape and quickly ripped it off the mouth. There was a brief scream, but Serge didn't even notice anymore.

"Please don't hurt me!"

"Why would I hurt you, boss?"

"I, uh, well, I'm tied up."

"That's right, boss." Serge whacked him upside the head with a rolled newspaper. "Being tied to a chair is a subtle hint that your day probably isn't building toward the usual laugh track."

"But why me? What did I ever do to you?"

"Gee, I wonder." Serge placed a fresh stretch of duct tape across the mouth. "Concentrate hard, boss."

Coleman began puffing up a spliff as thick as a roll of quarters. "I don't think calling him boss will make him like you this time."

"You can never allow jerks to take you out of your game." Serge set a clipboard down and placed orange cones around the chair.

"Mmmm! Mmmm!"

"Shut the hell up!" Serge pressed the barrel of a pistol against the man's nose. "Can't you see I'm conversing!"

Coleman stuck his eye in the opening of an empty prescription bottle. "Serge, you got any more of your pills?"

"You know I never keep count of that junk."

"Damn." Coleman began going through a suitcase.

"Why do you take those things anyway?" asked Serge. "It's my anti-psychotic medication, completely lacking in recreational value."

"That's where you're wrong," said Coleman. "One of the first rules of the drug culture: A pill is a pill."

"Mmmmm!"

Serge violently ripped the tape off again. "What now!"

"Y-y-you take anti-psychotic medication?"

"Not for weeks, boss. Nothing to worry about." Serge pulled something from his pocket. "Now, back to your obvious confusion about this little pinch you've found yourself in. Recognize this?"

"Uh, it's pieces of a cell phone?"

"I smashed it pretty good, but that was post-mortem."

"Don't understand."

"A couple days ago, we were in a bus-stop shelter to escape the rain, and you deliberately swerved your car to spray us with water."

"I did?"

Another whack with the newspaper. "I can't begin to emphasize how important that phone was to me. I could look up any Florida historical fact, retrieve photos of the most obscure landmarks, hover over the remotest scenic roads in three dimensions, receive ten parameters of live telemetry from weather buoys in the Gulf Stream, and I even heard a rumor it makes phone calls."

"Wait a minute," said the hostage. "*You're* the guys I drenched? This is all about a wet phone?"

"I recognized your license plate when you crashed earlier tonight," said Serge. "'SCRW U'? So I'm guessing you're a regular on the dickhead rodeo circuit."

"It was just a joke."

"I'm in stitches. Especially the part where you also drenched that mother and her kids." Serge reached in the dresser and pulled out a plastic spray bottle. "But since you love the art of comedy, I've got a better joke."

"W-what's in the bottle?"

"Just harmless water." Serge reached into the dresser again.

"Hey!" yelled the captive. "That's my new Galactic Quadrennial XLZ5000 smartphone with Triple Vagueness Technology!"

"So it is." Serge held the phone in one hand and aimed the spray bottle.

Squirt.

"No! Not that!" yelled the man. "I'll give you anything!"

Squirt.

"Wait! Stop! Before it's too late!"

"Why should I?"

"Because I have all my contact information in there."

"My phone did, too," said Serge.

"Yes, but ... I'm important."

Squirt, squirt, squirt, squirt ...

"No! Stop! It burns!"

Squirt, squirt ... "Hey, boss," said Serge. "Did you forget to charge the battery today? The screen just went black."

"*Nooooooooooo!*" The man hung his head in sorrow. "You destroyed it. You're mean."

"Mean?" Serge picked up the pistol again and pointed at himself. "You will soon wax nostalgic for that kind of tenderness."

"Okay, you got me back. You destroyed my phone." The captive looked down at the rope around his chest. "We're even now, so you can untie me."

"You really are a comedian," said Serge. "We've only begun your lesson."

Coleman chugged a bottle of Old Crow. "Can I watch this time?"

"Don't see why not."

"Cool!" For the occasion, Coleman began constructing an even bigger spliff with a quilt of eight gummed-together rolling papers. "This is going to be so excellent!"

"But you might want to pace yourself," said Serge. "This is going to take a while."

"Then we should throw him a going-away party."

"Brilliant idea!"

Coleman froze. "The world must be coming to an end."

"Why do you say that?"

"I'm two-for-two. First, you almost never let me watch. And now, during one of your experiments, we're also going to party?"

"I always say to enjoy your work." Serge grabbed his keys. "We need to go shopping. Lead the way."

"To the Party Store! ..."

MEANWHILE ...

The condo was new construction with lots of reflective glass that, at the proper angle, appeared a metallic shade of sapphire. In the sales brochures, the window material was touted to cut down on harmful UV rays and unwanted glare so lucky residents could enjoy views of the Atlantic Ocean and Port Everglades. It didn't mention that in another direction was a very loud international airport.

The current owner of the top-floor penthouse suite was about to have a sit-down meeting. Actually more of a throw-down.

The front door opened with the bluster of involuntary circumstance. "Let go of me!"

Goons held the man fast by both arms. He was a bald sixty-year-old, just under five feet tall, with bronze, cracked skin. He recently learned on an Internet ancestry website that he had one-quarter Argentine blood, which was a pint and half. His doctor told him to eat more fish for iodine. His name was Jacinto. He was still wearing his work shirt with a pink flamingo button: PLAY THE FLORIDA LOTTERY.

The goons slung him to the floor.

"What's the meaning of this?" said the old man, sitting up and rubbing his ribs.

The alpha male in the room stood at the tinted windows with his back to everyone, looking out across the ocean. He wore a lightweight pale suit and was known for his dramatic pauses in conversation. His name was Rogan. His dreadlocks reached the middle of his back.

Everyone else knew that this was the part where you didn't say anything until Rogan spoke first.

Rogan liked ships, for some reason, and kept the rest of the room waiting as he watched a freighter with a Liberian flag clear the inlet. Still looking out the window: "What took you guys so long?"

"Had to search everywhere for him," said one of the goons. "Found him in an Argentinean seafood restaurant."

Rogan took a seat on a leather sofa and stared down at his involuntary guest for a short eternity. Finally, an educated voice with a British accent: "You look like you want to say something."

"You! ... You killed my nephew!"

"Didn't realize he was a relation."

"It's all over the news," said Jacinto. "His head wrapped in lottery tickets!"

"My guess would be that someone was trying to send a message."

The goons chuckled, and Rogan squinted at them from behind designer prescription glasses. They settled down. He removed the glasses, which put the goons in motion. One helped the diminutive man into a chair while the other poured him a stiff three fingers of rum.

Jacinto took the glass in trembling hands and sipped. "I can't believe he's dead."

Rogan leaned quietly. "What part of our agreement did you not understand?"

"He was just making a little on the side." Jacinto blew his nose. "All the other stores do the same ticket-scan trick."

"I'm sure you remember our agreement. And the agreement hinged on making sure that everything else you did would be totally legal, beyond scrutiny, because the last thing in the world we wanted was even the slightest bit of attention," said Rogan. "It might just be me, but I thought I had made myself quite clear on the importance of that particular detail."

Jacinto nodded obediently. "You did."

A fist came down hard on the arm of the sofa. "Then why the fuck am I out seventeen stores that are on every TV channel? And you have the stones to accuse me about your cousin?"

"His nephew," said a goon.

"Shut up!"

The goon lowered his chin, trying to hide in his chest.

"Now then, Jacinto, do I not pay you enough? Do I stutter? Do I look funny to you? I'm just trying to understand the lack of respect."

Jacinto sat mute, offering up respect in spades.

"Let's get back to live programming," said Rogan. "The only reason that it's just your nephew—and not you as well—who's unavailable to join us so enjoyably today is because you have other stores. I need those stores. And I need all the *other* stores. I need you to see how serious I am."

Indeed, those stores conducted a bustling brokerage business in buying up winning tickets for a percentage. But they also accomplished something of greater importance to Rogan.

Money laundering.

There are a number of reasons why people launder money: avoid taxes, creditors, ex-spouses who threw all their clothes on the lawn. But Rogan was happily married, had no debt and paid the IRS in full. Rogan made his particular fortune from the import-export business. Drugs came in; money went the other way. It was all part of a larger Jamaican organization out of Kingston, which had embedded Rogan in the Fort Lauderdale condo. He specialized exclusively in making dirty cash sparkle.

Rogan had begun by washing his funds the traditional way through various banks around Miami, because that's what they were there for. Then drug enforcement agents clamped down, and the white-collar class who kept bankers' hours caught a severe case of testifying. So Rogan and the others in his field had to improvise. First they moved down the financial food chain to check-cashing parlors, but that still generated too wide a paper trail for the growing law enforcement field called forensic accounting. A colleague named Hingis was doing life in the Atlanta federal pen for that one. They tried used-car lots and sandwich shops and dry cleaners, and that worked to a point—that point being more people went to jail.

Then came the lottery explosion. It all began by act of legislature in 1988, which seemed to dovetail nicely with the end of the cocaine explosion. Even the state wasn't prepared. They started with a small series of simple games, and had to keep adding and adding to feed the insatiable appetite of a gambling tapeworm the size of the monsters from *Dune*. More games debuted. Lucky Money, Mega Millions, Cash 3. And extra drawings during the week, and more drawings within a single day, and so many scratch-off tickets that they were ending up in birthday cards and Christmas stockings. Nothing was ever enough.

This is how serious the fever got. It was enough to sustain a lottery magazine on how to beat the odds. At first blush, it sounds absurd because as any roulette player can tell you, past performance has no bearing on future random outcome. So here's what the editors did: They bought all kinds of Ping-Pong balls and extremely accurate scientific scales. They were able to detect excruciatingly tiny, but nevertheless distinguishable manufacturing variations in the weights of the balls. Then they tracked the frequency of winning numbers, correlated weights, and published the results. Over the long haul, the numbers became less random. Jacinto carried the magazines in his stores.

And now, with so many people playing the legal numbers racket at such a crazed rate, money launderers had the perfect cash blizzard to hide inside. What better way to explain unexplained income? Word spread from Miami to Bogotá, Barranquilla and Bolivia. Planes began landing.

"... One thing you probably didn't realize," Rogan told Jacinto. "The day your store was raided, some agents also paid me a visit. Can you comprehend how upset that makes me? ... Please nod once for yes."

Jacinto did.

"They asked many prying questions about my livelihood," said Rogan. "I do not regularly have people interrupt my lunch with such questions. Do you know why?"

Jacinto shook his head.

"Because I'm a careful man. I have a careful life. Such a thing requires much time and effort," said Rogan. "And all that work was undone the minute you started scamming scratch-offs. They've identified most of our straw buyers and are attempting to connect them back to me. But in the end, they will have nothing. Do you know why they will have nothing?"

"Uh, because you're a careful man?"

"Because they will no longer be able to locate any of the straw buyers."

Gulp.

"You are beginning to understand," said Rogan. "I simply asked that my instructions be followed, but you did not follow them, and now somewhere in some office, they have started a file with my name on it. I like that even less than interrupted lunch. From now on you will follow my instructions, and you will not be told again ... You may nod now."

Jacinto nodded fast.

"That is very good," said Rogan. "You may stop nodding ... Now then, I have another piece of business in which you might be useful. I have begun noticing a drop in brokered tickets, even before all these raids. Not much of a decrease, but enough that it's no accident. And in my business experience, that usually means one thing. Someone is moving in on my territory. That is not a good thing. You wouldn't happen to be involved, would you?"

"No! I swear!" Trembling again as Jacinto downed the rest of his drink. "I would never! ..."

Time for one of Rogan's dramatic pauses, which caused the old man to suddenly become verbally incontinent. "On my mother's grave! I give you my word! Please! Listen! I heard some talk on the street! Some people *are* going elsewhere! I don't know where! I didn't know anything. You have to believe me!"

"Talk on the street?" Rogan said calmly. "That is very interesting. What else did this talk indicate?"

"Nothing!" said Jacinto. "All I heard is that some lawyer is supposedly behind it. Someone trusted in the Latin community. That's it!"

"See how easy that was?" Rogan turned toward two of the goons. "Check out this talk on the street. I would like to have an appointment with this attorney."

The pair raced out of the room.

"My day is improving," Rogan told the old man. "That is a good thing ... But you still seem to have a look on your face."

Jacinto desperately tried to change the look on his face so that it was no look, but that just made it a bigger look.

"I think I get it now," said Rogan. "You have one last question: Of all the stores that were raided, why did my nephew have to be the one to pay? ... Go ahead, ask."

"W-w-why did my nephew have to pay?"

"Because he was on TV."

Chapter 25

ONE HOUR LATER

Coleman chugged. Serge scribbled on a clipboard. A boom box blared.

"... *Get down tonight! Get down tonight! ...*"

Serge hopped up on a bed and fastened something to the drop ceiling with string and thumbtacks. "The Party Store has everything!" He jumped down as a small disco ball began to twirl, sending hundreds of flecks of light across the walls. Other parts of the room were decorated with balloons and crepe-paper streamers and a piñata. A box of cupcakes sat on the nightstand.

"... *Do a little dance ...*"

Coleman gyrated off balance in a Chubby Checker twist, swinging a bottle of whiskey by the neck. Serge repeatedly sprang up and down around the room in a hyper-spastic version of the pogo.

The captive sat in motionless terror. Wide eyes swung back and forth—Coleman wearing only his undershorts and a panda head, boogying past the TV set; Serge with a beauty-contestant sash from the Party Store across his chest, jitterbugging the other way, waving a gleaming hatchet.

"This is some party!" said Coleman.

"Reminds me of my sixth birthday," said Serge, attacking the piñata with the small ax. "Die, motherfucker!"

Candy scattered. Serge and Coleman dove on the floor and began wrestling. "I saw the Pez dispenser first!" "It's mine!" "Give it to me!" "Ow, my hair!" "Ow, you're bending my finger back!" "I'll hit you with my whiskey bottle!" "I have a hatchet! ..."

They released each other and sat on the carpet, gathering Milk Duds and Hershey's Kisses. "That was fun," said Coleman. "Can we do it again?"

"We still need to pace ourselves," said Serge. "This is how Elvis went."

The candy-collecting jamboree continued. A Baby Ruth stuck out of the panda's mouth. "What a party!"

"It's how we roll."

"Mmm! Mmm! Mmm! ... "

Coleman pointed. "Our guest doesn't seem to be having fun. In fact, he looks scared shitless."

"Probably worried about us because he's not used to seeing people rock out with Roman warrior stamina."

Serge walked over to the captive's chair with the hatchet.

"MMM! MMM! MMM!"

"Oh, that. Sorry." Serge tossed the ax aside. "Where are my manners! You're the guest of honor, but we've been having all the fun." He tore the duct tape off the man's face, mashing a cupcake in his mouth and sticking something on his head like a hat. "That's your celebration tiara." Then he replaced the tape.

Knock, knock, knock.

"Someone's at the door!" Coleman jumped back. "Who can it be?"

"Relax." Serge unlocked the dead bolt. "We ordered a pizza. It's automatic with a hostage, remember?"

The door opened and a man with a name tag stepped inside.

"Watch your step," said Serge. "There's candy everywhere."

The delivery guy was about to place the pizza on the bed when he suddenly stopped. He looked Coleman over, then Serge, the disco ball, the hatchet, and finally a bound-and-gagged man with frosting up his nose and an orange traffic cone on his head like a high-visibility dunce cap.

Serge took the pizza and handed over some cash. "There's a little extra for you in there." Then he pointed at the candy-strewn floor. "The piñata was bigger than I thought. Need anything?"

"I'm good."

"Mmm! Mmm! Mmm! ..."

The delivery guy pointed at the chair. "What's the deal with him?"

"Just getting his freak on," said Serge, adjusting his beauty-contestant sash. "Why? Does something seem weird in here?"

"No, I deliver to Miami motel rooms all the time. Have a good one.

"Thanks for the prompt response."

The delivery guy was about to leave when he stopped again and looked back in the room. "Wait a second. Didn't I deliver a pizza to you a few years ago on Collins Avenue?"

"I doubt it."

"Yeah, you told me it was the Goldfinger Suite or something."

"You must be thinking of another room where everything was completely okay."

The pizza man shrugged. "It's Miami."

"Thanks for your service."

The door closed.

Serge stared back at the hostage chair and rubbed his palms together. "Alone at last. And have I got the perfect lesson to help with your people skills. It just came to me ... Which is why we didn't only go to the Party Store. We also stopped at the Home Depot! You're probably wondering why? Because Lowe's has a color scheme to attract chicks, and that's a slippery slope. Wait here ..."

Serge made a few quick trips to the car, returning with a custom-cut piece of plywood and a bunch of cement blocks. "... We also went to Sam's Club ..." More excursions outside, each time Serge laboring with an outrageously heavy sack, until ten were stacked against the wall. "I know I'm not supposed to like Sam's Club, but the quantity prices are insane!"

"Another science experiment?" asked Coleman. "What is it?"

"Actually our guest gave me the idea." Serge ripped the tape off again and got face-to-face with the captive. "I don't know how I can ever thank you. Actually I do, but that's not in the cards. Sorry, dealer's choice. The best you can hope for now is the bonus round."

"W-w-what's the bonus round?" asked the hostage.

"I'm so glad you asked!" Serge patted him on the shoulder. "If you thought you were in a quandary before, it's going to get exciting in a big hurry. And the bonus round is this: I used a spray-mist bottle on your cell phone instead of, say, dropping it in the toilet. That way there's still the possibility it can come back to life. Or maybe not. Who knows or even cares? You obviously didn't when you splashed me." He playfully pinched the man's cheek. "That's the whole joy of the bonus round! It so unpredictable! ... If that thing eventually comes back on, you can call 911 before it's too late. And the bonus round takes points off for lateness." Serge shivered at the thought. "So here's the most important part that you must remember above all else. If you turn your phone back on too soon, before it's sufficiently dry, it'll fry the circuits. You taught me that concept as well, so additional kudos if I don't see you again. And if the phone fries, it's game over. Game over is really bad ... Well, that's about it. Welcome to my latest science project!" The tape went back over the mouth for the last time.

A finger pressed a button on the boom box. Sly and the Family Stone came on.

"... Dance to the music! ..."

Serge and Coleman locked arms for a do-si-do square dance, twirling in a circle.

Serge singing: *"Welcome to the science world ..."*
Coleman: *"Let's give it up for science world ..."*
"Edison, Newton, the periodic chart ..."
"Did you know you can light a fart? ..."

The pair continued crooning as they spun the chair around and tilted it backward until the man's feet left the floor. Then they began dragging it backward toward the bathroom.

"Mmmmmmmm! Mmmmmmm! ..."

"Will he survive the bonus round? ..."

"No one freaking knows ..."

The bathroom door slammed shut.

Chapter 26

THE NEXT DAY

A knock on a door in the Miami Women's Legal Aid Clinic.

"Come on in."

The office assistant named Danny took a seat. "I just wanted to thank you for all your help again on the lottery-ticket thing." She opened her purse and pulled out a large plastic bag full of paper stubs.

"Jesus!" said Brook.

Danny placed the bag on the desk. "There's so much goodwill toward you in the community that if you ever moved there, you'd never pay for another meal the rest of your life."

Brook stuck the bag of tickets in a briefcase. "I'll get moving on this right away."

"Thanks. There's plenty more where that came from."

Danny left and the phone rang.

"This is Brook Campanella ... Wait, *what* kind of case? ... He's being held *where*? ..." She got out a yellow pad and pen. "Okay, back up to the beginning, and don't leave anything out ..."

... The Florida Keys are unto themselves. No point in trying to make sense. They're just the Keys being the Keys.

The only road to the string of islands is U.S. 1 out of Florida City. In 1982, the U.S. Border Patrol established a checkpoint on this route outside the Last Chance Saloon, looking for illegal immigrants and drugs. If you know anything about local geography, the bottleneck at Mile Marker 126 is bad enough as it is, the worst possible site for a federal choke point. Traveling by car to the Keys became unworkable. The tourism-dollar lifeblood was cut off. Objections from area officials went ignored.

So they declared independence from the United States.

No kidding. But this time Keys logic actually was logical: If there was a border-crossing station for anyone attempting to either enter or leave the islands, then they were essentially being treated as a separate sovereign state. So they called themselves the Conch Republic. It was all tongue-in-cheek, very silly and quite savvy. The mock celebrations were tailored for TV, and the story made news across the country and overseas. There were T-shirts and hats and beer koozies and even fake passports. The official blue flag with a conch shell began flapping from flagpoles. The U.S. government bowed under the pressure of embarrassment, and the border station was closed.

But the movement became such a hit that sales of Conch Republic keepsakes remain brisk to this day. A huge sign on the runway at the Key West airport welcomes visitors to the fictitious nation. And locals began a contest of sorts. The souvenir passports didn't just look kind of official; they were dead on. The goal was to see how many times you could use it to enter a foreign country without detection and get it officially stamped. It was great fun and games, especially when showing them off in bars.

There was no official tally, but a man named Ennis Keefe was arguably in the lead with twenty-two official stamps.

Then came 9/11. Homeland Security. The Patriot Act.

Ennis was still sailing smoothly, until he decided to go for the most coveted customs stamp of all. The United States of America.

A twin-prop commuter flight from the Bahamas landed at Miami International on a quiet Tuesday afternoon. Ennis arrived at the international air side and presented a small leatherlike booklet from the Conch Republic. He was still smiling when they slapped on the cuffs.

"It's just a joke," said Ennis. "I'm really a U.S. citizen and my regular passport is in that bag, so you can release me now."

Customs people were on phones and walkie-talkies. More agents arrived. Then a transport van.

"Seriously, guys, I do this all the time," said Ennis. "It's harmless."

"I'm listening," said a senior agent. "What exactly do you *do* all the time?"

Ennis exhaled with relief. "Thank you! Finally someone reasonable! Just call anyone in Key West. It's this game we play in the bars to see how many stamps we can collect."

The agent flipped the pages of the ersatz passport. "How many foreign stamps have you collected in this game?"

"Twenty-two! I was in the lead but someone just tied me," said Ennis. "So if you'd be kind enough to just hit that thing with your own stamp, it would really make my day."

"Let me see if I have this straight," said the agent. "For a couple of decades now, you've been traveling all over the world and entering these countries illegally with a forged document?"

"No, not forged," said Ennis. "They sell them in the T-shirt shops all over Duval Street."

His luggage was quarantined and taken out to a remote field. They had determined that the suitcases posed no threat, but blew them up anyway because it was fun. Frightened eyes stared out the metal screen in the back of an INS van as it drove through the barbed-wire entrance gates of a sprawling, fortified facility surrounded by the equally sprawling migrant farmlands near Homestead. Ennis became the only U.S. citizen detained in the infamous Krome Detention Center ...

... Brook finished scribbling. "Thanks ... Yeah, I have a pretty good idea where to get started. Just tell your brother not to say another word."

She hung up and dialed again. "Reevis, it's me, Brook ... Yeah, I've been busy. How about dinner tomorrow night? ... Listen, you know how you're always asking me if I've got a good story and press coverage will help my client? ... Oh, it's a real beauty ..."

A FEW MILES SOUTH

A plump man sat on a bus bench along U.S. Highway 1 in North Miami, angrily folding furry black-and-white arms.

"Coleman, I thought we talked about this," said Serge. "Pandas are out."

"I don't want to be set on fire again."

"It was a controlled burn," said Serge. "You saw all the business we brought in."

"My lips still hurt," said Coleman. "And my hair is singed!"

"It'll grow back. Here's some ChapStick."

Coleman looked away in a rare stand of defiance to his lifelong friend.

"Don't you see what is happening across the street?" said Serge.

"Yeah, the gorilla."

"He's twirling flaming batons," said Serge. "He stole that from *us*. I'm telling you, fire is the future! The first caveman who said that also got blowback."

"Pandas are as far as I go." Coleman rubbed his fluffy white chest. "If you like fire so much, why don't *you* do it?"

"You think I'm afraid of a little fire?" Serge jumped up. "I'll show you!"

He went over to the trunk of his car, pulled out a bag and began slipping his legs into a suit.

Coleman wandered over in curiosity. "Where'd you get that outfit?"

"At the Party Store. You were busy checking out the beer funnels."

Coleman scratched an armpit as Serge finished climbing into the costume.

"A cheetah?"

"Not just any cheetah." Serge put on the head. "Chester Cheetah."

"Who's that?"

Serge pulled more equipment from the trunk. "The Cheetos mascot." He began connecting a series of curved metal tubes.

Coleman removed his head as he watched his pal insert the assembly into a large metal base. "You like cheetahs?"

"I like *Cheetos*." Serge grabbed a bottle that said FLAMMABLE. "Besides, the cheetah is the perfect animal to match my wiry, spring-loaded persona."

"But you said you didn't have time to do the costume thing— that I was the talent and you were the manager."

"It's this economy," said Serge. "Business is booming. I just got a lead on a pair of high-paying gigs at a nearby strip mall, so I'm forced to step off the sidelines." He poured the contents of the bottle into a hole at the top of the contraption.

"Where'd you get that thing?"

"Also from the Party Store. They have everything!"

Coleman glanced around furtively, then lit a short joint and put the panda head back on.

People on the sidewalk stopped to watch as Serge dragged his assembly to the middle of the lot. He went back to his trunk, retrieving a pair of gymnastic tumbling mats that he placed in strategic positions. Other onlookers began peering out store windows.

"Coleman, do something useful and hand me your lighter."

Marijuana smoke streamed out the panda's eyes and ears. He tossed Serge his Bic.

Serge flicked it, and the ring of fire came to life. He leaned a cardboard sign against the support post: KWIK LUBE, NO WAITING. Large cheetah feet carefully paced off steps. Then he got down in a sprinter's crouch. Customers stepped out of stores and became silent during the tense anticipation.

"Now!" Serge took off running and dove through the ring of flames, landing with a somersault on a padded mat. He hopped up to a smattering of polite applause.

"See?" He spread big white hands. "Nothing to it."

Coleman spit out the joint. "Serge ..."

"Wait, the audience wants more." He paced backward on the opposite side before running and diving again. Cars honked. The crowd grew.

"Serge ..."

"Not now! I owe it to my fans!" He took off running.

The panda shrugged. He uncapped a longneck Budweiser and stuck it through the mouth hole.

Serge landed again to more applause. Another dive, and another.

"Serge ..."

"Dammit, Coleman! What is so important?"

"You're on fire."

"I know! The public loves me!" Serge suddenly stopped and sniffed inside his costume head. "What's that smell? Why is my ass hot?"

Coleman pointed with the beer bottle. "Your tail."

"Shit, I'm on fire!" He began running in frantic circles, trying to reach behind and swat his backside with furry paws. "Coleman, do something!"

More people gathered as Serge ran screaming in a circle, chased by a panda splashing beer on his butt.

Fifteen minutes later, all was quiet again. A panda and a cheetah sat on a bus bench. Serge held the end of his charred tail. "Crap, I was really starting to like this outfit."

A black stretch limo pulled up across the street. A gorilla threw his sign in the backseat and got in.

Coleman watched as the vehicle pulled away. "What's that about?"

"The scenarios are endless." Serge stopped to reflect. He looked at the smoldering metal ring in the parking lot and the gymnastics mats, and then down again at his blackened tail. "The economy can't be this complicated. Am I overthinking this? Coleman, tell the truth: Am I acting appropriate?"

Another panda shrug. "Look at all the people getting their oil changed."

A cheetah head began to nod. "I thought so. I just like to regularly perform self-awareness checks to make sure my behavior is still coloring inside the lines. Once again, the all-clear signal."

"You mentioned some higher-paying gigs."

"We start tomorrow," said Serge. "And if you insist on being a panda, you're going to need a gimmick."

The limo returned and pulled to a stop in front of the bus bench. The tinted back window rolled down. A gorilla head stuck out. "Aren't you going to the Furries' Ball?"

"What?" asked Coleman.

"I mean, you're not *just* sign-spinners," asked the ape, "right?"

"I would agree with that statement," said Serge.

"Knew it," said the gorilla. "There aren't many spinners out here in full costume. So you're actually into the whole lifestyle?"

"Panda for life," said Coleman.

"Got a Cheetos monkey on my back," said Serge.

"I'll give you a ride." The back door opened. "There's plenty of room."

Coleman looked at Serge. "What do you think?"

"A gorilla unexpectedly offering a ride in a limo. In some cultures, that's a sign of good luck."

They climbed inside. The limo drove off.

"It's got a full wet bar!" yelled Coleman. His head whipped toward the gorilla. "Please tell me it's free."

"Of course."

"Hot damn! This is definitely good luck."

"Hold on." Serge looked at the gorilla again. "Your voice. It was muffled when you were talking to us at the curb. Are you a ...?"

"Girl?" said the ape. "Yeah, I get that a lot because of the masculine animal choice. Most of the other gals go for softer stuff like puppies or bunnies ... Whew, it's getting a little hot." She removed the primate head.

"Dear God!" yelled Coleman. "She's, she's ..."

Yes, she was. A drop-dead beauty with sandy-blond hair and dark brown eyes.

Coleman rushed back with a drink and wedged himself between Serge and the girl.

Panda and cheetah heads came off. A black-and-white paw extended. "My name's Coleman."

She shook. "Liv." Then she leaned closer. "You like to yiff?"

"Yippie!"

"No, silly." She laughed. "You know, *yiffing*. I pegged you two as yiffers. I'm a pretty good judge of these things. I just love men who yiff. So am I right?"

"Yiffie ki yay!" yelled Coleman.

"Life's short," said Liv. She took Coleman by the paw. "Let's go."

"Where?"

"If you're new to it, just follow my lead."

"Anything you say."

She looked back at Serge. "Want to join us?"

"I'm still processing."

Liv grinned. "Feel free to jump in anytime." She led his pudgy pal to the middle of the limo and got down on the floor.

"What do I do?" asked Coleman.

"First, put your head back on," Liv said as she donned her own. "It doesn't work without the head."

"I totally agree."

"Okay, now ..." She felt around his costume.

"Whoa!" said Coleman.

"Wait, where is it?" She continued probing between Coleman's legs. "Something's wrong."

"Everything's A-OK here."

"If you yiff, you've got to have a flap." Liv indicated a spot in the middle of the gorilla suit. "Here's mine."

Coleman became woozy. "I—I—I ..."

"No problem," said Liv. "There's a small paring knife at the wet bar ... and I'll just cut a little slit here, where you can add Velcro later for when you go back to work the street." She put the knife away. "There. Now you have your yiffing flap."

"I—I—I ..."

"I really like the top," said Liv. "Do you mind?"

"I—I—I ..."

It was a clumsy start getting everything aligned, but soon the limo's chassis began to rock.

Serge's eye bugged out and he braced himself with both arms against the edge of his seat, watching a silverback gorilla furiously hump a panda on the floor. "Christ on a surfboard! What kind of strangeness am I looking at?"

Chapter 27

SUNSET

Limos arrived for the festivities along a trendy section of South Beach. There was a ridiculous selection of clubs along Collins Avenue, but many in the late-night set chose one particular art deco building that featured dinner shows. They filed inside and were escorted through the dark to tables dimly lit with those old-style candle lamps with that plastic netting. It was a spirited crowd, as dinner shows go. The nightclub was called Hips, and the sign was trimmed in pink neon.

Dry martinis, cosmopolitans, pork loins with wild mushrooms, laughter, conversation that needed to be loud to compete with other conversation. Topics ranged from shoes to revenge. Some tables were full of friends not talking to each other so they could text people also not talking to their friends in a different club.

The stage lights came on, and blue velvet curtains parted to rousing applause. The first act was a performer in a tight sequined costume with a riot of feathers that extended almost to the ceiling and looked like something out of a parade in Rio de Janeiro. When that subtleness was over, the room filled with the familiar strains of "Somewhere Over the Rainbow" and "Everything's Coming Up Roses," sung respectively by impersonators of Judy Garland and Ethel Merman.

Finally, the moment they'd all been waiting for. The stage lighting tightened to a single spot in the middle of the blue curtains. A platinum-blond head coyly poked through, followed by the rest of the performer named Marilyn. A four-song set reached its finale.

"Happy birthday, Mr. President ..."

... Later in the dressing room. Cabaret lightbulbs surrounded the mirrors, and autographed photos lined the walls. Marilyn came in, took off her wig and began brushing it out. His real name was Chuck, and his hair was black.

"Darling, you were great tonight," said Liza.

"Thanks," said Chuck, wiggling out of a slinky silver dress.

A sudden commotion at the door. "You can't come in here!"

"But I have to see Marilyn!"

"You've been warned before!" said Ethel. "Get out!"

"I brought her roses! ... Marilyn! Tell them you want to see me!"

Chuck retreated to the back of the dressing room as the rest of the "girls" formed a protective pack. "Leave now before you get hurt!"

"She sang that song especially for me! I really *am* the president," said a man with thick brown hair who partially resembled JFK.

The bouncers arrived. Red flowers went flying.

"Let go of me!"

He was dragged out and told never to come back.

"Marilyn! I love you! ..."

Chuck collapsed in a makeup chair, tears down his cheeks. The others gathered around for support.

"Honey, are you okay?"

"No." Chuck was shaking. "It just keeps getting worse! He sits in his car for hours outside my apartment, follows me to the grocery store, keeps calling even though I've changed my number six times now."

"You need to go to the police, girl."

"I'm afraid to provoke him," said Chuck. "Police warnings only work if someone is at least remotely rational, but he's certifiably insane."

"Because he's an obsessed stalker?"

"No, because he really thinks he's the president," said Chuck. "When we first met and I didn't know he was off his rocker, he showed me family photos in his wallet of Jacqueline and Caroline and John-John. He drives an old black Lincoln convertible like in Dallas, and once I even saw him on a street corner setting up a portable podium with the presidential seal and delivering a speech about America going to the moon."

"You can't sit and do nothing," said Garland.

"I know, I know," said Chuck. "I just haven't figured it out yet."

DANIA

The players trotted out in athletic jerseys for the introduction.

The seating at the sports arena was largely empty. Weekdays even more so. At the east end of the facility, high above everything else, stood the glassed-in luxury section. It was the most affordable skybox in all the state. The dining tables were tiered steeply to see all the action. Each had its own closed-circuit television.

A couple sat across from each other with open menus and concentration.

"Dinner at the Dania Jai Alai Fronton," said Brook. "How many times does this make?"

"I asked if you were okay with it," said Reevis. "If this bores you, we can go—"

"It's more than fine," said Brook. "But you're starting to worry me. I've never seen you so tense."

"It was a tough day. Tough *month*." Reevis scanned the menu. "That's why I needed to come here. It's one of my comfort zones."

A curved basket swung. A kill shot echoed off the wall with a violent clack.

Reevis jumped to his feet. "What the hell was that?"

"Just a jai alai ball hitting the wall." Brook sat back and appraised her beau. "You sure you're okay?"

"No!" He grabbed his menu extra tight. "I just finished interviewing a guy in the hospital after he was bitten on the face by a water moccasin he slept with, and yesterday it was the suspect arrested on wildlife charges for bringing a small alligator to a convenience store to trade for beer. You know how I hate covering weird Florida stories."

"That's just annoying," said Brook. "The change in your mood runs deeper than that."

Reevis considered the prime rib. "I'll be fine."

Jai alai players swung cestas. *Clack, clack.*

Reevis didn't jump up again, but his shoulders flinched each time.

"You're far from fine," said Brook. "You're not telling me something."

"Maybe it's all this craziness with the state lottery," said Reevis. "It's like a damn hurricane season, except those storms don't usually have raided convenience stores, a dead guy hanging from a billboard and another with his head wrapped in scratch-offs."

"Oh, that reminds me," said Brook. "I might have a story for you, and it's a good bet to get those producers off your back. Everyone loves stories about the lottery."

"What is it?"

And she explained the whole new legal field of fencing winning tickets.

"You're right," said Reevis. "Those producers will definitely go belly-up. I'm calling them right now."

"Can't it wait?"

"No, it can't. I'm in pain ... Hi, Cricket, do you have a pen handy? ..."

Brook watched more balls clack off the wall as Reevis laid out the story to the receptive Australian. He briefly covered the phone. "What was that address again?" Brook told him, and he passed it along.

A new set of players took the court. Reevis stuck the phone back in his pocket.

"Feel better?" asked Brook.

"Immensely," said the reporter. "He was so excited about the story, they might leave me alone for days ... By the way, who is this other attorney that you're working with? Do I know him?"

Brook just smiled mischievously. "Ziggy."

"Ziggy!" Reevis leaped to his feet and took a step back from the table. "Ziggy *Blade*?"

"Yes, Ziggy Blade," said Brook. "And I thought you'd find it funny, but what's with this wild reaction? Now I know you're hiding something."

Jai alai players climbed the wall. *Clack, clack.*

"Okay, I'll tell you." Reevis slowly sat back down and lowered his head. "I talked with Serge."

This time Brook sprang to her feet. "What!"

Other diners turned around.

"Lower your voice," said Reevis.

"How? When? Where?" Brook gripped the edge of the table with white knuckles. "What happened?"

"He turned up on some feature footage that didn't air," said Reevis. "I wanted to give him a heads-up. Who would have thought that his old cell number still worked?"

"What was the footage?"

"He was a psychic using a Magic Eight Ball," said Reevis.

"Can't believe that slipped your mind."

"It didn't," said Reevis. "I wanted to save you the worry. My heart's been pounding ever since that call. I think I have post-traumatic stress from the last time we were with Serge. And since Ziggy was also there, when you mentioned his name, well ..."

A player rolled on the court and came up flinging the ball. *Clack.*

Brook took a deep breath and looked at her menu again. "Wow. I wasn't expecting that."

"I'm not the superstitious type, but I'm getting this really bad feeling like some disaster is about to happen again."

"Why?"

"You and I are already together, and I've recently talked to Serge, while you've been in touch with Ziggy. Not to mention Ziggy's brother, Coleman, who's a good bet to be attached to Serge's hip. It's like the whole cast of that major fiasco back in Key West is getting together for an explosive reunion."

"You *are* being superstitious," said Brook. "You know Serge. He's probably off pinballing around the state hundreds of miles away."

New players in yellow-and-red jerseys took the court. *Clack, clack, clack.*

"I don't know," said Reevis. "It just seems like this is the last normal evening we're going to have for a long time. It's a strong premonition in the pit of my stomach."

"Because your stomach's empty."

Clack, clack, clack. The waiter returned.

Reevis handed back his menu. "I'll have the prime rib."

"The pompano," said Brook, then smiled at the reporter. "You'll feel better once you eat."

"You're right." *Clack, clack, clack.* "Serge is probably a million miles away right now."

MEANWHILE ...

A man in a cheetah costume stared out the back window of a limousine as the Dania Jai Alai Fronton went by. The vehicle continued a few more miles until it arrived at a small, windowless nightclub that was hosting a private event.

Others were already there, the sidewalk full of people in line dressed like animals. They formed a veritable Noah's ark procession of every conceivable creature before entering the club.

The cheetah and panda climbed out of a backseat. Coleman seized Serge by the arm. "Tell me I'm not hallucinating! Did I really just get laid?"

"A more amazing development than if gravity quit."

"So I really did have sex! Yes!" A panda fist punched the air. "That's the first time in at least a decade!"

"What about this morning?" asked Serge.

"I mean with someone else."

Serge pulled out his replacement smartphone. "Coleman, do you realize what's going on?"

"Good luck?"

"I checked on the Internet." He tapped the phone's screen. "We've accidentally stumbled into some bizarre fringe element that has a fetish for animal costumes, the furrier the better."

"Fetish?"

"That's right. And 'yiffing' is their slang for screwing in their costumes. In fact, some of them can *only* have sex with the costumes on."

Coleman nodded emphatically. "I can wear a costume."

They went inside the dim club. Anthropomorphic animals paired off everywhere. Livestock, house pets, zoo attractions, beasts of burden, Disney characters. Everyone making small talk and trying to hook up. Most had learned how to drink with straws through the costume heads. Two people in a pony suit made their way to the dance floor. Serge wandered the room in a surreal daze. "I had no idea this was going on ... Coleman ... *Coleman?* ... Dammit, another manhunt."

Serge searched the entire club and ended up in the empty men's room. "Where can that idiot be?" Then a notion. He stepped into the hall and stared at the door to the women's room. "What the heck, I'm a cheetah."

An orange-and-white paw pushed the door open. Much nicer accommodations. Sparkling clean with automatic air-freshening dispensers. Oil paintings on the walls. Serge stared at attractive potted flowers along the sink. "I had no idea this was going on."

A unicorn departed and Serge was left alone, or so he thought. One of the stalls began to rattle. He got down on paws and knees and looked under the door. Two pairs of feet. Panda, gorilla. He momentarily closed his eyes in frustration, then went and leaned against the sink to wait.

A few minutes later, the rattling stopped and the door opened. Coleman saw his pal standing with impatiently folded arms. "Serge, what are you doing in the ladies' room? Can you believe these flowers?"

"You knucklehead!"

Coleman whispered close to Serge's ear. "Twice in one day. That's like a record! And with a really hot one."

"I'm sure she shits rainbows," said Serge. "But you did just give me a great idea."

"Really?"

"Remember when I said you needed a gimmick for our new gig tomorrow? Excuse me a moment." He walked over to Liv, who'd removed her costume head to freshen up at the sink. "I've got a proposition for you."

She winked. "I knew you'd come around."

"This is a business proposition."

Chapter 28

THE NEXT DAY

Fluorescent yellow crime tape was back up at the Florida Motel in Miami. This time, stretched around the general vicinity of room number four. The parking lot filled with marked and unmarked police cars.

Someone dusted the DO NOT DISTURB sign for fingerprints. A detective scribbled in a notepad as he questioned the whiskered manager in a bowling shirt for the Biscayne Guttersnipes.

"You say you didn't have much contact with them?"

"Not really." He swatted a love bug off his arm. "Kept to themselves, some of the best tenants I've had. Paid cash up front for the last three days."

"Did you notice anything unusual about forty-eight hours ago?"

"Not really, except for some music by K.C. and the Sunshine Band, if that helps. Plus, hundreds of twirling spots of light on the curtains."

The detective looked up from his notebook. "What?"

"Probably a disco ball."

"And that's normal to you?"

"Do you know how many meth labs and portable sex dungeons we've had to clean up at this place? I see a disco ball, I say, 'Go with God.'"

"Okay." The detective flipped his pad closed. "Just one more thing. We'll need to check your guest registry against the stack of Xeroxed driver's licenses you provided us by law."

The manager stared at his shoes, which were Keds, then at the detective's shoes, which weren't.

"You did make copies of their licenses, didn't you?" said the officer.

"Oh, of course, of course," said the manager.

"Because if you didn't, that's a serious offense," said the detective. "We've already arrested several managers along this strip for taking bribes not to make copies."

"I remember very clearly now. I definitely asked for their licenses."

"That's better."

The manager headed toward his office. "Just give me a few minutes to find them."

Another patrol car arrived. An officer opened the back door, and a pizza deliveryman got out.

"What's going on?"

"We'll ask the questions here." A detective flipped to a fresh page. "I understand you made a delivery to room four a couple nights ago."

"So?"

"Did you notice anything unusual?"

"Not really."

"Do you recall what they were wearing?"

"The thin one had a beauty contest sash, the chubby guy was in a panda head, and the dude tied up in the chair wore an orange safety cone on his head."

"And all this seemed normal to you?"

"You must be new in town," said the driver. "Have you ever delivered a triple-cheese meat special to an orangutan-smuggling ring?

Inside room number four, more detectives milled with Styrofoam cups of coffee. One of them eyed a box of cupcakes, but knew it would be wrong. Camera flashes strobed out of the bathroom. A forensic technician emerged with a phone in a sealed evidence bag.

"Is that the cell he used to call 911?"

"We'll know as soon as we get it to the lab. But it's a safe bet ... It's kind of a shame."

"How's that?"

"More and more people are making emergency calls from cell phones," said the technician. "If they came from landlines, we could pinpoint the exact locations. But if the person is incapacitated and can't communicate—like our victim in there—we can only get a general location by triangulating pings off cell towers. He might have made it."

"Why couldn't he communicate?"

A stretcher rolled past them with a zippered body bag. The forensic tech glanced back at the bathroom. "See for yourself. It's clear to go in now."

A pair of detectives arrived in the doorway as the last photographer left. The medical examiner made notes on a clipboard. He noticed them staring at the plywood and cement blocks that had been moved to the side. "Those were used to keep him from getting out of the tub."

"You mean someone drowned him?"

"Just the opposite." The examiner sadly shook his head. "This was so tediously planned in sadistic detail that it could be nothing other than the result of extreme, prolonged rage. Whoever did this had a serious grudge with this guy."

"But if he didn't drown in the tub," asked the first detective, "then how did they kill him?"

The examiner bent down and retrieved a few tiny granules near the drain.

"What's that?" asked the second detective.

"Rice," said the examiner. "My staff just carted away several huge bags of the stuff. The tub was filled to the brim, completely covering the naked victim. We're going to do a chromatograph to see where it was bought, but in this quantity, my guess is Sam's Club. We're still trying to figure out why the killers left him with a cell phone taped to his hand."

The first detective crunched his eyebrows. "Rice killed him? But how?"

"Dehydration," said the examiner. "Rice pulled a bunch of water out of him in a major rush. First leg cramps and delirium, migraine-level headaches, speech loss and, at the end, a falling domino line of organ failure."

"Rice does that?"

"You know how you'll sometimes buy a moisture-sensitive piece of electronics, and you open the box and there's a little porous bag that tells idiots not to eat it? That's a chemical substance similar to rice to keep your product dry. Or you might have heard that if your cell phone gets wet, you can stick it in a bag of rice to save it?" He glanced back at the tub. "Doesn't work so well on people."

"Thanks, Jerry."

"I'll send over my final report by the end of the week, but you already have the main talking points."

The two detectives left the room and strolled across the parking lot. "Rice. Just when you think you've seen everything."

"What was he yapping about with the cell phones?"

"That's true. I accidentally splashed some water on my phone near the sink, and rice fixed it," said the first detective. "One of my kids told me about the tip. Apparently they're constantly getting their phones wet and have to deal with it before their parents find out."

They entered the motel office. The manager stood behind the counter and handed over a Xerox. "That's him. That's the guy who paid for the room."

"Are you positive?"

"I'll never forget the face."

"Thank you for your time."

The detectives drove away from the motel, hot on the trail of a retired couple from Peoria.

HIALEAH

A stereo blared.

A bong bubbled.

Ziggy stared in disbelief at all the lottery tickets on his desk. Like Brook had told him at the beginning, word was definitely getting out on the street. All relatively small amounts, but it added up.

Knock, knock, knock.

Ziggy took another enormous hit and ruminated about instant scratch-offs, the Cuban bolita, the Harlem rackets, and other numbers games throughout history.

Knock, knock, knock.

Ziggy leaned his head back with his Visine—"Damn, I am way too high. I hope I don't have any appointments"—and turned Joplin up on the stereo.

"... *Another little piece of my heart ...*"

The knocking at the front door became banging.

Ziggy jumped and dove under his desk. "What the hell was that? Have they finally come for me? ... Okay, you know the drill. It's just the pot. Get yourself back on the rails! How do they keep making this shit stronger? Maybe I just *imagined* I heard something ..."

Bang! Bang! Bang!

"No, I definitely heard it that time. Someone's at the door. I'm in no condition to deal with the public. They always *know*. If I make myself as small as possible, they will go away ..." He tightened himself into a ball.

Bang! Bang! Bang!

Teeth gnashed under the desk. "They're not going away. This is a crisis ... Try to think: It's probably just a courier with more lottery tickets. You've gotten through this kind of thing before. The key is rehearsal. What is acceptable behavior? Take the package and say thank you. That's only two things to remember. You can handle it. Two things, two things, two things. Take package, thank you, take package, thank you ..."

Bang! Bang! Bang!

"... Take package, thank you. Take package ... What was the third thing? I think it was a variation on the other two numbers. Numbers, numbers, numbers ... Roman numerals? Why do they always come up at the end of a movie? MCMLXXII ... What the fuck is that about? ..."

Bang! Bang! Bang!

Ziggy took a deep breath and began crawling out from under the desk. "... Here goes nothing: Say thank you and give him the package ..." He stopped crawling. "Give him the package? Where's the package? Did I lose something again?"

Bang! Bang! Bang!

"I'm coming!" yelled Ziggy. "Be there in just a minute!"

From behind the desk, a head slowly rose until bloodshot eyes were even with the edge. Ziggy forced frozen legs to march to the door. He began undoing a sequence of locks. "Thank you for the package, coming or going. You're welcome. Peace, out."

He opened the door.

Bright lights blinded him. Dundee stuck the TV camera in his face, and Brisbane thrust a microphone: "What kind of lottery scam are you trying to hide?"

They chased Ziggy as he ran squealing like a ferret and dove back under his desk.

MIAMI WOMEN'S LEGAL AID CLINIC

Brook sat behind her desk, staring in new thought.

On the other side was her latest client, wearing a moose costume and holding the head demurely in his lap.

"Mr. Rabinowitz, these are very serious charges," said Brook. "Lewdness in front of minors, attempted sexual battery, creating a public nuisance resulting in injuries."

"It's all a big misunderstanding," said the accountant. "I was at the mall and saw this other moose. I could have sworn she was one of *us*."

"So what you're saying is you didn't realize she was actually entertainment for a children's birthday party when you mounted her from behind?"

Mr. Rabinowitz stuck two fingers through openings in the costume head in his lap. "My eyeholes were too small. Like I said, an honest mistake."

Brook finished writing on a legal pad. "If you don't mind me asking, why did you wear a moose costume to the mall in the first place?"

"To hook up."

"Okay, no promises, but I'm fairly confident we can work out a plea." Brook smiled as naturally as she could under the circumstances and shuffled papers in the client's file, indicating the meeting was winding down. "Uh, you don't happen to have a change of clothes, do you?"

The client looked down at antlers. "Only the moose. Why?"

"A condition of being released on bail was not to wear any costumes in public. Inside your own house, have at it."

A sad voice: "Okay."

"Then wait in the lobby until I can have my assistant get something appropriate. Don't want you pulled over on the drive home." She picked up the phone. "Danny, I've got an odd request ..."

The moose excused himself. Brook was filling out a motion to preclude when Danny burst in. "Brook! You have to see this!"

"I'm in the middle of something."

"It's important! Hurry!"

Brook got up and followed Danny into the break area with a microwave and fridge. And a TV. The broadcast showed a jiggling camera approaching a squat concrete office in Hialeah.

"I delivered some lottery tickets there," said Danny. "Isn't that the office of the other attorney—"

"Shhhh!"

Fists banged on the door until a frumpy lawyer finally answered and bright lights hit his stoned face like high beams. *"Ahhhhhhhhhh!"*

He scampered away as the camera chased Ziggy through a curtain of purple beads.

"What kind of lottery scam are you trying to hide?"

Ziggy shrieked and ran right over the top of his desk, scattering winning tickets and marijuana roaches. Then he slithered underneath and hid.

The cameraman quickly rounded the furniture and got down on the floor. TV sets across South Florida were filled with the image of Ziggy balled up under his desk, clutching his knees to his chest and rocking back and forth with eyes closed. "If I make myself really small, they will go away."

Brook covered her face. "Can this get any worse?"

A cell phone rang. "Brook Campanella. How may I help you?"

"I can explain," said Ziggy. "They violated my rights, but it's fixable."

"Don't do anything!" yelled Brook. "Stay inside and keep your mouth shut!"

"No, I messed up and need to make this right."

"Ziggy, stop!"

"TV is the global campfire," said Ziggy. "So I'm going to fight fire with fire."

"I don't even know what that means," said Brook. "Just stay put!"

"Sorry, got to split." *Click.*

"Ziggy! ..."

Brook slowly hung up in defeat.

"What's going on?" asked Danny.

"It just got worse."

The two women walked together toward the front of the law office. As they did, a faint noise grew louder from the street.

"Do you hear that?" asked Brook.

"Yeah, but I can't make out what it is," said Danny.

The more they walked, the louder the noise, until it was an outright clamor.

"Darn it!" said Brook. "What do those salon people not understand about being on probation? The last thing I need right now is another rumble in the parking lot."

Danny ran ahead and peeked out the blinds of the waiting room. "Relax, it's nothing to worry about."

Brook picked up her pace. "Then what's all that noise?"

"The audience."

"What?"

"The salons apparently have hired rival sign-spinners," said Danny. "You have to see it to believe it."

Brook joined her at the window. "What in the name of creation?"

Down below in the parking lot, a cheetah with a bandaged tail repeatedly dove through a ring of fire while a gorilla humped a panda.

A moose walked out of the legal clinic: "Can I cut in?"

"No!" said the gorilla.

"This is the best job ever!" said the panda.

Chapter 29

THE NEXT DAY

The official press conference announced another lottery rollover, resulting in the biggest jackpot yet of the already record-breaking year, but nobody knew how high it would go before Saturday night's drawing.

At that very moment in a South Florida penthouse, a Jamaican man with dreadlocks hit the pause button on the remote control. He leaned and stared at the tall numbers on the official lottery tote board. "If only I could get hold of one of those tickets ..." Then Rogan resumed channel surfing. *Click, click, click.* Rerun, rerun, rerun. *Three's Company, One Day at a Time, Different Strokes,* credit-card travel perks, flooring installed, online education for less. Something caught his attention. He stopped clicking. On the screen:

A potbellied man in a tie-dyed T-shirt swayed Zen-like to sitar music. He had a scraggly beatnik beard and John Lennon glasses.

"You think most lawyers are scum? I agree! So score the karmic representation you deserve at the cosmic court where the age of Aquarius is still alive ..." He began singing off-key: *"'... Please allow meeee ... to introduce myselffff ...'"* Singing stopped. *"Ziggy Blade here. DUI? Bankruptcy? Divorce? Hash pipe found during routine traffic stop? Who says it was yours? Come on down and let yourself move to the*

smooth legal groove with the Blade-man ..." He thrust his fingertips to within inches of the camera in a trippy, 3-D effect, except the camera wasn't 3-D, so there was no effect. *"... And as always, we legally cash in all lottery tickets. No appointment necessary in downtown Hialeah. Call the number below now!"* Ziggy pointed down at red flashing digits superimposed across his legs.

"You've got to be kidding me," Rogan told himself. "This is my competition? *This* is the lawyer who's been horning in on my territory?" The man with the dreadlocks put pen to paper to write down the phone number, but it quickly disappeared. "Damn, I wish he'd show that number again."

"That number again ..."

It began flashing and Rogan began writing. He underlined the name Blade three times and got on a burner phone.

NIGHTFALL

Another dinner engagement with Brook.

Reevis was picking her up at her office. He waited in his car, catching up on e-mail. His mind drifted back to thoughts of an Easter pageant in first grade when his mom made him wear a stupid hat that was a basket of little chickadees, held in place by a large pink ribbon tied under his chin. He told himself: *Let it go.*

Reevis stared out the windshield at nothing in particular, just idly in the direction of the nail salon. There was a reflection off the window, so he didn't notice it at first. He slowly leaned forward. "What the—?"

Inside the salon, cardboard arrows leaned against two chairs. A panda and a cheetah getting pedicures.

"Are you sure you want to keep the heads on?" asked the nail specialist. "It must be stuffy in there."

"We're Method actors," said the cheetah. "We must stay in character."

"Serge," said the panda. "Why are we getting this done anyway? You always bite your nails. I mean your fingernails."

"I'm always fascinated when I don't understand a major cultural phenomenon," said the cheetah. "I've seen hundreds of these nail places everywhere and can't grasp how they survive. Yet customers are always coming and going. Why would anyone pay good money when they can just bite?"

"They can't reach their feet?" said Coleman.

"But I'm starting to understand the allure of the pampering treatment."

"They are being pretty nice to me."

"Especially considering the condition of your toes."

"What's wrong with my toes?"

"Coleman, my toes are no picnic, but yours are a house of horrors. The big one's going the wrong way like a hit man's nose, and the mutant little one's like a blind mole rat, not to mention the volume and composition of all the material you've been storing up between them. What *is* that?"

"Just stuff."

"The poor woman working on you is like a dental hygienist with a patient who didn't brush after barbecue and corn on the cob."

Two women looked up from their feet and smiled. A bright pinpoint of light swept across a wall.

"Did you see that?" asked Coleman. "What was it?"

"A laser," said Serge.

"What would they use a laser for in here?" asked Coleman.

"I don't care, but I'm next in line for it." He checked a wall clock. "And we have just enough time before that appointment to meet our new client."

"What client?"

"Don't you remember anything? I got a call from Mahoney."

"The private detective?" asked Coleman. "What did he say?"

"He was talking to himself in the third person, but I was able to translate that he had an important case for us."

"I thought that being furry sign-spinners was our job for this *Route 66* episode."

"Sometimes they had two jobs when Line and Tod went separate ways, except I'm not letting you out of my sight," said Serge. "Besides, in the end everything always pieced together ..."

... Out in the parking lot, journalistic curiosity got the better of Reevis. He left his car and stepped inside the salon.

The panda turned. "Look who just walked in."

"Reevis!" said the cheetah.

Being on TV was starting to get Reevis recognized on the street, so it wasn't that unusual. "Uh, do I know you?"

The cheetah's head came off. "It's me, Serge!"

"Ahhhhhhhh!" Reevis fell back against the plate-glass window.

Serge hopped out of his chair with cotton balls between his toes.

"Mister," said the pedicurist, "I'm not done."

"I'll pay in full anyway," said Serge. "Something's come up and I have to put my cheetah feet back on."

Reevis ran over. "Serge, Jesus!" He suspiciously glanced out the window. "What are you doing showing your face around here?"

"Thought you'd be more happy to see me."

"It's not that." Reevis watched a police car drive by. "We need to get you out of sight!"

Serge passed a few twenties to the nearest woman. "Keep the laser warm."

Reevis tugged a furry arm as they left the salon. "Let's get going. You can duck down in my backseat until I can think of something."

"Hold your horses," said Serge. "Why should you be so worried if I'm not?"

"That's what worries me."

From another direction: "Reevis, who are your friends?"

"Ahhhhhhh!" He spun around. It was Jacklyn, leaving for the day.

"Something I said?" asked the lawyer.

"No, you just startled me."

"Don't be so nervous," said Jacklyn. "So what's the deal? You're now striking up conversations with sign-spinners?"

"No," said Serge. "Reevis and I go way back, very long history between us ... Isn't that right, Reevis?"

A look of terror.

Jacklyn got out her car keys. "Where do you know Reevis from?"

Serge nonchalantly twirled his cheetah tail. "Here, there, solved a mystery together in the Keys, tracked down landmark movie locations, fled ruthless murderers, got hit with fish falling from the sky, nothing special."

Reevis slipped into a full-scale panic attack, but Jacklyn began laughing. "Nice sense of humor on you ... and not a bad ring-of-fire trick."

Serge looked over at the blackened ring still standing in the parking lot. "I can do a special performance, if you'd like."

"No, I have to get going." She hitched up the strap on her purse. "Late for a class."

"Class? What are you taking?"

"Actually I teach."

"Like at a college?"

She shook her head. "Women's self-defense."

"Now I'm seriously impressed," said Serge. "That's so important these days. Most men don't realize it, but women are living in an entirely different world—a whole extra level of danger that requires constant vigilance and precautions that men never have to think about. Mainly because we're the problem. On behalf of my gender: Our bad."

"Now *I'm* impressed," said Jacklyn. "You're right, most men don't realize it, but you seem to understand."

"The things I've seen!" Serge waved a white paw in the air. "Every day you probably pass a dozen bone-deep crazies out in public, maybe even stop and talk to one in a parking lot. A guy can look perfectly normal and charming, but you never know which dinner date will end in a cloud of Mace. Us men, on the other hand, have it so easy. If a woman turns out to be batshit, you can just tip over a rack of potpourri jars in the Pottery Barn and run away."

Jacklyn had been taking new notice of Serge as he talked. His banter, his eyes, and of course the Latin thing. "I have an idea. Why don't you come with me to my class?"

"Unfortunately I have to get to my own self-defense class," said Serge.

"You take self-defense?"

"No, that's where I'm meeting a new client. She's a stalking victim." He threw up his paws. "Men again."

"Where's this class?"

"Gold Coast Mixed-Arts Academy."

"That's *my* class," said Jacklyn. "Listen, if you don't mind and have any extra time, could you guys also stand in as live partners for the women to practice on? It's so much better than stuffed dummies."

"Say no more," said Serge. "Anything we can do to make up for *everything*."

"Then let's go."

The silver Corvette followed Jacklyn's MINI Cooper south on U.S. 1 until it arrived at another strip mall. In the middle of the building, a large plate-glass window filled with sweaty activity.

After changing into her spandex workout suit, Jacklyn looked out over a room of chaotic bobbing and jumping. "Okay, girls, let's get started! ..."

The kinetic energy ceased, and the women formed disciplined rows. They came in all shapes and sizes and ages, but most had ponytails.

"I'll start tonight by going back over the basics that you've already heard a hundred times, because it's all about repetition and practice until everything's second nature." Jacklyn formed an aggressive posture. "First, never ever let yourself be taken to a secondary crime scene. That indicates he has intentions with a very low order of survival. Even if you're facing a gun or knife, there's a better chance making a stand right where you are, kicking, scratching, screaming. Next—and this is for the same reasons as the first—do not let yourself be bound. No handcuffs, plastic wrist ties, rope, duct tape. You must explode like a wildcat because your life depends on it ..."

"Jesus," Coleman whispered to Serge. "Is this stuff really going on?"

"Unfortunately, more often than you'd think."

"... Third, this is not a fight. The moment you're able to incapacitate your assailant using our training techniques, run and yell like crazy. Getting in extra punches and kicks out of anger is movie bullshit that increases your exposure." Jacklyn waved for Serge and Coleman to join her. "And speaking of incapacitating, I have a couple of volunteers who have graciously agreed to help us tonight."

A woman in a blood-drive T-shirt raised her hand. "Are animal costumes something new we should be watching out for?"

Jacklyn chuckled. "No, they just got off work. So while they're changing, why don't you start on the regular bags."

The women lined up in front of three human-shaped sacks dangling from chains. Serge flinched at the battle cries that accompanied violent thrusts.

"*Yahhh!*" "*Yahhh!*" "*Yahhh!* ..." Punching throats, stabbing eyes, kneeing groins.

"Screw it," said Coleman. "I'm keeping the suit on. Padding."

"At least use this helmet and mouth guard," said Jacklyn.

Minutes later, they all quietly gathered around their instructor. "The benefit of using live volunteers is that you never know how your attacker will grab you, so some of their vulnerable spots won't always be open," said Jacklyn. "You need to train your reflexes to automatically find what's available. But remember, they're *live* volunteers, which means no full follow-through ... Michelle, can you come up here? ... Turn around ... Coleman, stand behind her and pick a random way to grab her."

"Like this?" he mumbled through the mouth guard, seizing her around the waist.

"Yahhh! Yahhh! Yahhh!"

Coleman curled up on the floor. "My nuts."

"Okay, maybe this isn't such a great idea," said Jacklyn. "Girls, go back to the other bags for now."

The front door opened, and one of the larger members of the class came in with a gym bag. "Sorry I'm late."

Serge looked puzzled at Jacklyn. "I thought this class was just for women."

"It is, but she's a drag queen. We don't judge." The instructor helped Coleman up from the floor. "He's been having some problems with a fan lately."

"By any chance would his stage name happen to be Marilyn?"

"How'd you know?" asked Jacklyn.

"I just found my client." Serge trotted across the room and extended a hand. "Marilyn, my name's Serge, and I was sent by the private eye you hired." He saluted. "Ready to provide extreme help."

"Nice to meet you. My real name's Chuck."

"So some asshole is bothering you?"

"I can't sleep! I can't eat! Do you have any idea how stressful it is dealing with a lunatic?"

"Not personally. But I've met a lot of people who've told me." Serge slapped Chuck's back. "Why don't you fill me in on the details."

"It started about two months ago— ... Oh my God!" He ran around and hid behind Serge. "There he is now!"

"Where?"

"In the parking lot!"

"You mean that JFK-looking dude sitting in the Lincoln convertible with a dozen roses?"

"That's him! He follows me everywhere, but I didn't think he knew about this class. That's why I asked you to meet me here."

"So what's his shtick? A presidential impersonator?"

Chuck shook his head. "He actually thinks he's the president."

"You mean he's abnormally deep into the role, like those Civil War reenactors who take it way too far and forget to have sex?"

"No, listen to me: He's completely unhinged," said Chuck. "That's what makes me so scared. He's under a full-blown delusion that he's Kennedy!"

"Delusional? Why didn't you say so in the first place?" Serge pumped fists in the air. "Delusions are my specialty. This will be fun!"

"Fun?" said Chuck. "I'm under siege! All the bouncers at my club have his picture, so he can't get in there anymore. But the rest of my life is a nightmare!"

"When do you perform next?"

"Tomorrow night at ten."

"Tell the bouncers to let him back in the club."

"What!"

"All your problems will soon be over," said Serge. "Trust me."

Chapter 30

THE NEXT MORNING

A late-model arctic-white Mercedes-Benz was an odd sight in the neighborhood. In fact, the largely abandoned industrial area didn't see much traffic at all, except the twenty-four-hour pedestrians moving with less verve and direction than zombies. Dobermans barked behind fences topped with barbed wire to protect tanks and drums of manufacturing chemicals.

The Mercedes pulled into a parking lot that baked in the unfiltered sun. Five Jamaicans with dreadlocks got out. It was the job of the last one to unfold a silver reflective screen and place it in the windshield.

A small concrete-block building with burglar bars sat in the back of the lot. A hand knocked on the door.

"Be right there!"

For once, it was answered promptly. Ziggy Blade was all smiles as he held the door. "Come in! Come in! Thank you for calling! Pleasure to meet you! ... My secretary's out sick today ..."

Ziggy parted a curtain of beads and led them into the back half of the one-room office. He quickly unfolded Samsonite chairs. "*Mi casa es su casa*. Please, all of you have a seat ..."

They remained on their feet and stared with vacant eyes.

"Or stand," said Ziggy.

They sat down in unison.

Ziggy took a deep breath and found his own chair behind his desk. "Now then, you mentioned on the phone something about lottery tickets. I'm not sure I completely understood."

"We want to buy winning lottery tickets," said Rogan.

"That's what I heard on the phone," said Ziggy. "I'm not sure how long you've been in the country—and by the way, we're so glad to have you despite what you might have heard—but how it works is you buy your tickets at the stores. Supermarket, convenience, they're all over the place."

"We've lived here a long time," Rogan said evenly. "And we know how to play the lottery in the stores."

"Then I'm not exactly sure what my role is."

"We've seen you on TV. You cash in lottery tickets for people who can't come forward. We highly respect your discretion. We've asked around."

"Well ..." Ziggy chuckled. "The glowing testimonials can get a little embarrassing when you're at the top, but they're always appreciated."

Rogan opened his jacket to remove an Uzi, and the rest of the men followed his lead.

"Whoa!" said Ziggy. "What are all the guns for?"

"We know about cashing in other people's lottery tickets because that's our line of work," said Rogan, stretching out his arm with the machine gun. His voice raised in volume and menace: "You simply decided to move in on my territory? Just who in the fuck do you think you are?"

Ziggy stared motionless with wide, bloodshot eyes. Then he cracked up with uncontrollable giggles. He held up a hand—"Sorry, just give me a second"—the laughter subsided and he wiped away tears. "As your attorney, this is probably unprofessional, but you have dreadlocks, so I'm sure you'll understand. I just scored some radioactive hydroponic pot and it's kicking my ass. I'm practically hallucinating and hearing things I'm sure you didn't say. But put any worries aside—when it's time to get cracking, I'm all business."

"Motherfucker!" screamed Rogan. "How dare you mock me! Anyone else insulting me like you have has ended up praying for death!"

Ziggy cracked up again and began slapping his desk. "Stop! You're killing me! ... I'm definitely calling my weed guy and getting some more of this shit ..."

Rogan's shooting arm became rod-straight, as did all the others.

Ziggy held out a plastic tube. "Bong hit?"

"What?"

"Of course, you're driving." Ziggy concealed the smoking tube back under his desk. "Now then, what can I do for you?"

Rogan abruptly changed the trajectory of his thoughts. He sat back in his chair and studied the attorney, thinking to himself: *I was wrong about the bozo in that TV commercial. Now it's obvious how he was able to muscle in on my turf. He has balls the size of coconuts.*

The Uzi was stowed back inside his jacket, and the others followed again. "You have my respect. I hope I have yours."

Suppressed laughter. "Totally."

Rogan gave a slight nod, a signal to the others.

Ziggy had been tripping out on the sight of the guns so that he completely forgot about all the briefcases the men had carried into his office. And now they were popping open on his desk to reveal an obscene amount of cash.

"Whoa!" said the lawyer. "I'm definitely calling that weed guy back."

Rogan allowed the effect of the money to settle in. "I wanted you to see how serious I am."

"About what?"

"We are going to become business partners. It's not negotiable."

Ziggy had never seen so much cash, even on TV. "You sure you have the right lawyer?"

The leader nodded. "You come highly recommended."

"I do?"

"On TV, you advertised that you cash in winning lottery tickets," said the leader. "And as I mentioned earlier, we do the same, but our connections have become unreliable as of late. I'd like to start bringing you our winning tickets."

"Why would you want to do that?"

"To launder money."

Ziggy covered his ears and made a high-pitched beeping sound—"Didn't hear that, didn't hear that, *beep, beep, beep* ..."

The leader looked around oddly at the others.

Ziggy dropped his hands. "Let me explain attorney-client privilege. You're free to tell me anything you've done in the past, but the privilege doesn't extend to unlawful acts you're planning in the future."

"But you will do this thing for us?"

"Like ringing a bell."

"One more item," said Rogan. "This is my territory. Any other tickets that come your way from your TV commercials or otherwise are mine. You'll still receive a cut. I'm sure a businessman of your stature will see the mutual benefit."

Another fit of giggles. "Why not?"

"That's very good. That's what we like to hear." He pulled a brown envelope from his jacket and tossed it on the desk. It slid into Ziggy's lap.

"What's this?" He looked inside. "Trippy!"

"Your retainer," said Rogan. "How much flow do you get?"

"Depends on how lucky people are." Ziggy thumbed through the cash. "Some hit the Fantasy Five, or one of the big scratch-offs. A few thousand on a slow week, maybe five figures on the better-than-average, unless someone hits a really big one, then we're looking north."

"You're probably already taking five percent off the front end." Rogan began standing. "We'll give you another five. Buy some furniture."

"How will I get in touch with you?"

"You won't. You'll hear from us." He walked toward the bead curtain and turned around. "When you do business with us, your word is your bond. From now on, you will not cash in anyone else's tickets without running them through us ... I will take your silence as your word."

Giggles.

Rogan rolled his eyes. "I will take that as silence."

They let themselves out.

Ziggy went to the front window and watched the Benz drive away. "Where's that number for the weed guy?"

BISCAYNE BOULEVARD

The same perpetual rhythmic sound came from a dozen directions at two-second intervals. It filled the store. *Chss-chss, chss-chss, chss-chss, chss-chss.*

It was one of those new copy shops where you could do almost anything. Send faxes, mail overnight packages, buy colorful gift bags and greeting cards, order posters, connect to wireless Internet. You could even make copies.

Coleman was stoned and tipsy at a display for office supplies. He repeatedly discharged a staple gun into the air until an employee asked what he was doing.

"Nothin'."

He wandered over to an unoccupied copy machine. There were buttons to press. He changed all the settings for the next customer—darkness, contrast, magnification. There were little organizers next to each printer with scissors and tape and complimentary paper clips. Coleman decided to load up on rubber bands.

Serge stood at the service counter, handing over cash and running a program on his phone. Someone bumped into him from behind.

"Coleman, there you are. What have you been doing?"

Coleman reached into his pocket, producing a wad of rubber circles, and put them back.

"Case solved," said Serge.

"What are *you* doing?" asked Coleman.

"I explained back in the nail salon," said Serge. "Working on that case for Mahoney."

"But why a copy shop?"

"It's the coolest thing ever!" Serge clasped his hands in effervescence. "This place has one of those new 3-D printers that I've been reading about. I found all kinds of tips online about what you can make with them. Shot glasses, birdhouses, clips to seal opened bags of pretzels, combs, *Star Wars* figures, dildos, and combinations of the last two. But I'm thinking, where's the imagination? The possibilities are mind-numbing, so I decided to brainstorm and download some images to my phone, which I just sent to this store. For only a few bucks, that guy in the back room is whipping up my idea right now!"

"What is it?"

"A surprise," said Serge. "But think historical significance."

"Far out."

"And I'm going to need some of your rubber bands."

"But they're mine."

"What possible use could you have for that many?"

Coleman swayed and looked toward his pocket. "Play with 'em."

"We'll negotiate later." Serge turned around and leaned with his back against the counter. "I love copy shops! Know why?"

"Paper?"

"Multi-cultural harmony." Serge nodded to himself. "I might just be the first person to recognize it, but copy shops are the ultimate bellwether of ethnic relations. We may eat different food, wear different clothes, but every race and creed needs copies."

"Never thought about it that way."

"And that's the mistake CNN makes. Every time there's some civil unrest somewhere, reporters descend and visit all kinds of businesses for interviews with the common man—breakfast diners, Starbucks, massage parlors—but never a copy shop." Serge waved an arm over the room. "Look at the arching bridge of humanity! Those Muslim women over there, that Asian guy, the African Americans, Latinos, whites and, not pictured, Eskimos. See, everyone receives shit in the mail that needs duplication, and we're all bonding under that oppression together, brothers and sisters! At least until there aren't enough available copy machines, then it could get tribal."

"... Sir? ... *Sir!* ..."

Serge turned around. "What?"

"Here's your purchase."

"Oh, thank you." Serge looked down into the bag. "Excellent work. May I ask you a question?"

"I guess."

"What happens when there aren't enough copy machines? What do the people do?"

"Uh, wait?"

"God bless America! ... Come on, Coleman!"

They hopped back in the Corvette and headed south to Miami Beach as night fell. The lights of the Miami skyline filled the air with electricity as Serge picked up the MacArthur Causeway.

Coleman chugged a bottle of Mad Dog. "So that dude back at the self-defense class is really being stalked?"

Serge gritted his teeth. "I *hate* stalkers!"

Stretch limos jammed Collins Avenue all the way up nightclub row. Serge accepted a ticket from the valet and went inside a dinner-show lounge called Hips. They waited for their eyes to adjust in an ultra-dark room with a flickering array of candle lamps, martini glasses and lobster. Faces glowed with anticipation. Stage lights came on, curtains parted. Applause for the Barbra Streisand experience.

"Is that also a dude?" asked Coleman.

"You'll get the Audubon field guide later."

"... *The way we were* ..."

The show swelled toward a highly anticipated climax. A brown-haired man sat quietly in the dark as a baby spotlight hit the curtains and a head of platinum-blond hair.

"... *Diamonds are a girl's best friend* ..."

Serge elbowed Coleman. "It's time."

The vocals dropped to a sensuous whisper. "... *Happy birthday, Mr. President. Happy birrrrrrrrrthday to youuuuuuuu ...*"

The crowd was on its feet as Marilyn disappeared through the curtains, and the house lights came up.

The gals crowded around Chuck in the dressing room. "That was incredible." "Honey, you keep getting better with age." "You're back to your old self!"

Knock, knock, knock.

One of the performers opened up. "Who are you?"

"I need to see Marilyn," said the stranger. "She's expecting us."

From behind: "It's okay, Liza," said Chuck. "They're friends."

Serge strolled over. "Just remember what I told you. From this point forward, there's nothing to worry about."

"I can't thank you enough—"

Suddenly an explosive commotion at the door.

"I have to see Marilyn!"

"Hey, you can't just barge in here like that."

"Marilyn! I brought these roses for you."

Streisand blocked his path. "Get out before you get hurt!"

Serge glanced down. "Coleman, quick, give me rubber bands." Serge reached into the bag from the copy shop.

"So that's what that thing is."

"Marilyn, tell them it's okay! You sang that song again for me! ..."

The gals formed a protective phalanx. "We'll call the police!"

Coleman laughed. "Serge, where did you get the idea?"

"Soon as I saw those three-D printers, I said to myself, 'History has just come alive.'"

"Marilyn, I love you! ..."

Serge approached the defensive formation from the back. "Girls, I've got it from here." They parted and let him through, wearing a plastic Halloween-style mask held over his face with the skimpy rubber bands.

He stepped up to the man with the roses. "I've been looking all over for your presidential ass! Figured if I hung around Marilyn long enough, you were bound to show up."

The brown-haired man stumbled backward in terror. "Oh my God! ... Not *you*!"

"That's right," said Serge. "Lee Harvey Oswald."

"Get away from me!"

"We've got business. How about a pamphlet? 'Fair Play for Cuba.'"

The bouquet flew into the air, and JFK took off through the club, crashing into people and knocking over tables.

Serge was right behind him leaping over chairs. "Destiny knocks!"

"Stop following me!"

Serge pulled up short at the front door and cupped hands around his mouth. "Meet you at the grassy knoll."

Chapter 31

SETTING THE TABLE FOR THE CLIMAX

News of yet another lottery rollover spread like only lottery news can, and the greed typhoon whipped from Florida to the rest of the country and Latin America.

It was still the wee hours before dawn, but a group of men in the nation of Costa Gorda were paying particular attention to a big-screen TV. The luggage had remained packed and waiting since their last unsuccessful visit to Miami.

The new jackpot was announced, and all heads in the room turned toward the same person.

He gave a curt nod, which scrambled the others into a military-style operation. The dark of night had begun to dissipate when the men trotted briskly across a mountainside plateau. A Learjet lifted off, climbing into the orange light of the sun still below the horizon. The passenger manifest was in the name of one Ocho Pelota.

The last time around he had been caught off guard by an inability to buy the whole board in one fell swoop. Insufficient time or boots on the ground. And a tidy sum down the drain. He would not make the same mistake twice.

"Pablo, come here," said Pelota, sipping a mimosa. That's how it worked. Don't speak until spoken to.

Pablo took a seat in the jet next to his leader. "What are you reading?"

"This cheap lottery magazine. I bought it in a convenience store on our previous trip." Pelota flipped back to show him the cover. "It gives advice on how to increase your odds of winning."

"But mathematically you can't predict randomness."

"Usually," said Pelota. "But one thing that's not random is the weight of the Ping-Pong balls. This fascinating article explains why there have so many record-breaking jackpots in a row this year, like when they had that unprecedented conga line of hurricanes back in '05."

"What's it say?" asked Pelota.

"That the lottery changes its set of balls from time to time, and they did so again at the beginning of the year. The magazine statistically analyzed the new set and determined that the balls with the most favorable weights were high numbers."

"How does that cause a bunch of big jackpots?" asked Pablo.

"The lottery numbers are one to fifty-three, but this article says most people like to play birthdays—their own, spouses', children's—or anniversaries and other occasions. The months limit the numbers to twelve, and the days of the month to thirty-one. Hence, lots of rollovers."

"That makes sense," said Pablo. "We lost last time on a high-number drawing."

"So we do it in reverse this time." Pelota stirred his drink. "Start buying combinations of the biggest numbers and work backward. That way if we can't complete the board in time, we'll at least be in a better position ..."

The Lear touched down at Miami International in time for brunch. Pelota and his coterie cleared customs. He had called ahead from the plane, and a luxury motor coach was already full of cheap Latin labor.

After his earlier failure, Pelota had done the math five ways. It was all about the proper design of an organizational pyramid. Each of the men who had flown down with him would supervise ten local associates with their own crews. And each of them was given a specific spread of permutations descending from fifty-three. It worked on paper and, unbeknownst to Pelota, had actually been done before in the nineties by a group of legitimate venture capitalists who, as they say, hit the jackpot.

Pelota's gang all met in the conference room of an extended-stay business hotel near the airport, and the local bank vice president even accompanied the armored car that delivered the needed currency.

"So happy to see you again in Miami," said the executive. "With all this cash, will you be needing any protection?"

Pelota gave him the look.

"Oh, right." The vice president left.

Ocho's lieutenants fanned out across the city to put their plan in motion. Underlings were dispatched in geometrically precise quadrants. They worked all day and well into night, then the next day, and the next. They cut in line. They sped on the highway. Parked in handicapped spots. Rushed back to the hotel to refill with cash on hand. Then back out again.

Pelota remained in his suite, receiving hourly rounds of phone calls with progress reports. Traffic was thick and the crowds thicker. Ticket machines crashing from the volume.

By the last evening, they were still on schedule, and then they weren't. It came down to the wire. One way or another they would know by the end of the night ...

10:40 p.m., sales cut off.

10:46, last piles of Pelota's tickets collected.

10:51, rental sedans raced back to the extended-stay hotel near the airport.

Crime lieutenants crowded into the elevator for the top-floor suite. Pelota was already sitting at the table when they whipped out notebooks and entered results on the master spreadsheet.

Much, much better than the last time. But ...

"You didn't get all the tickets?" Pelota asked the first lieutenant.

"It was impossible ..."

"I don't pay you for *impossible*." He turned to the next one for an answer.

"The places were crazy ..."

On down the line, same story.

Pelota had adopted a saying he'd picked up in prison. Don't get mad until it's time to get mad. He was roundly feared for his erratic and ruthless temper, but in truth his emotions were a highly polished chest of tools, and he orchestrated erraticism to an advantage. He had known these men going back forever, his most trusted and dependable. If none of them was able to fully complete the task, then maybe he was asking too much, but it was not something to admit. He folded his hands in pregnant thought. He quietly raised his eyes. "How much?"

It was all entered into a calculator, and the equal sign punched. "We were able to buy ninety-two percent of the board."

Not perfect, but definitely better than last time around. As long as the numbers didn't fall into the low end. Pelota downed a double of Johnnie Walker Blue to stop the anxious calculus in his head. Nobody spoke during the last five minutes as they waited in front of the television. Pelota was closest to the set, sitting on the front edge of a padded lounger. The rest stood in a semi-circle around the back of his chair.

11:15 p.m.

Hyper-optimistic game-show music came on as a pink flamingo logo swirled to the center of the screen. The Miami skyline lit up the back of the studio as Ping-Pong balls ricocheted around a clear chamber. Vacuum tubes sucked up a half dozen of the balls in succession as the emcee read them off: "Eighteen, twenty-nine, thirty-six, forty-five, forty-eight, fifty-two ... Thank you and good night from the Florida Lottery!"

Silence.

Everyone in the room knew.

The men standing around the chair began jumping and whooping and hugging. Pelota simply shut his eyes in relief.

The only question now was how many other winning tickets, and that data would come the next day. With jackpots this large, there was often more than one, but the split would still be exceedingly ample. The celebration in the hotel suite lasted almost till dawn. Big cigars puffed out on the ninth-floor balcony. Cart after cart of room service arrived, and the mini-bar guy was called in to restock. They ignored front-desk complaints about the blaring TV. A local commercial came on with sitar music and a swaying lawyer in a tie-dyed T-shirt.

Covering 92 percent of the board is a lot of tickets, but you wouldn't believe how much actual physical space they take up until you saw it. Almost twenty briefcases sat in neat rows in Pelota's closet. Considering whose suite they were in, security was no issue. The cases weren't going to get as much as a fingerprint.

The sky gave its initial hint that the black of night was beginning to fade, and the last of the lieutenants adjourned to their own rooms.

Ocho Pelota was left alone on his balcony in a personal orb of cigar smoke and accomplishment. Tiny lights blinked on the western sky as the first of the red-eyes began their landing approaches from Los Angeles and San Diego. Pelota stubbed out his cigar and went to bed.

Chapter 32

JACKPOT

> **Jack-pot (noun)** 1. The top prize in a game of stakes, such as bingo, poker, slots, lottery. 2. A significant fortune. 3. Large, unexpected success. *Syn:* pool, kitty, bonanza. *Hitting the jackpot.*
>
> *Idiom:* (chiefly western, southern) Suddenly and without warning entering into a position of extreme distress or peril. *Syn:* jam, pickle, crisis. *Find oneself in a jackpot.*

MONDAY MORNING

Ziggy Blade was fresh off a two-joint breakfast as he tapped his steering wheel to the not-so-ageless tunes of Iron Butterfly. There was a reason for his jaunty outlook besides chemicals. A recent uptick in his lottery resale business. He attempted to do the math in his head, but the pot made it like trying to spray molasses from an aerosol can. *Let's see, those tickets and the other ones, multiplied by this and divided by that and, well, it's a lot.* The twelve-year-old Toyota turned in the parking lot at his office, and Ziggy saw a sign that the new week was indeed going to be special.

A new customer was already waiting outside his door.

"Peace," said Ziggy, trotting up the steps with keys in hand. "Been waiting long?"

A head whipped this way and that, and back again. "Can we just get inside?"

"Chill," said Ziggy, leading him through the office. "Most defendants are nervous like you when they first arrive, but your troubles are over now that you're with the Z-ster—as long as you haven't signed any confessions." An eyebrow raised.

"No confession," said the client.

"Great!" Ziggy took a seat behind his desk. "How can I help you today?"

The man's hands trembled as he reached inside his jacket for a large envelope, which contained a medium envelope, that held a small envelope, protecting an even smaller one ... It was like all the secret doors at the beginning of *Get Smart*. Ziggy blinked hard.

The new client finally reached the end of his low-tech security system. He stood and placed a small rectangle of thick paper in front of the lawyer.

"Oh, another winning ticket," said Ziggy. "How many numbers did you hit? Four? Please tell me it's five ..." A widening smile.

The man continued twitching as he placed a folded-over page from the *Miami Herald* on the desk. Ziggy held it side by side with the ticket, eyes moving back and forth, number after number. The smile disappeared. Ziggy didn't trust his cannabis eyes. He checked all six numbers again, then backward, then slowly set the ticket down like a Fabergé egg. "You *won*?"

"I know."

Emotions rocketed in opposite directions. First Ziggy was elated at his cut of the take. *Hooray!* ... Immediately followed by: *I could be holding hundreds of millions in my hands, in this neighborhood.* "I need another joint." Rapid-fire toking. "Now I'm paranoid."

And now they were both twitching and jerking around. "We have to get this to a safer place pronto!" said Ziggy. "My wheels aren't reliable enough for this kind of gig. What are you driving?"

"New Chrysler 300."

"You're driving."

They repackaged the ticket in all the envelopes and stuck it in Ziggy's soft-sided hemp briefcase. They crept to the front of the office and peeked out the window. "All clear!"

"Run!"

A Chrysler slung a cloud of dust as they sped away.

MIAMI WOMEN'S LEGAL AID CLINIC

Brook sat behind her desk. The client on the other side wore a camo baseball cap.

They were quiet for the moment, the attorney trying to decipher new data.

"Let me see if I understand this correctly," said Brook. "You took a small alligator in a cardboard box to the convenience store to trade for beer and lottery tickets."

"That's right. I was all over the TV."

"But ... why?"

Shrug. "The other guy was getting the better deal."

Brook paused again. "You do understand that stores don't make trades."

"I do now."

A sigh. "Okay, then what happened?"

"State wildlife officials arrested me and took the gator."

"If they took the gator," said Brook, "then what's in the cardboard box in your lap?"

"I had others," said the client. "I wanted to see if we could work out a trade concerning your fee."

The phone rang.

"Hold that thought." She picked up the receiver. "Brook Campanella, how may I— ... Oh, hi ... Wait, slow down. What's wrong? ... You're not serious ... You *are* serious? ... Okay, I have to think this through. Meanwhile, you need to come here right now and don't stop anywhere ... You're already driving over as fast as you can? Good, but not too fast ... Oh, and one more thing: Whatever you do, don't talk to anyone else."

She set the receiver down and looked at her client. "Sorry, but something's come up. Can you wait in the waiting room?"

Her client left and Brook picked up the phone again ...

A Chrysler 300 raced east across greater Miami. Ziggy got off the phone.

Pablo turned in the driver's seat. "The other attorney?"

Ziggy nodded. "One of the best. Everything will be fine." He began dialing again.

"I could overhear," said Pablo. "I thought you weren't supposed to talk to anyone else."

"I know what I'm doing." He put the phone to his head. "Hello, it's me, the Blade-man ..."

A young reporter stood bedside in a recovery room at Miami General Hospital. A cameraman filmed a patient whose head had swollen up like a basketball.

"But why were you sleeping with a cottonmouth water moccasin?" asked Reevis.

"Mgfhjadsd ..."

"There are reports that you regularly kissed it."

"Mgjireifdek ..."

"Is that when it bit you on the face?"

"Midfkgkls ..."

A cell phone rang, and Reevis checked the caller ID. "Hold on, I have to take this ... Hello, Brook, what's going on? ... What! ... Okay, don't go anywhere. I'll be right over ..."

"Mjjjfggsys ..."

"Sorry, but something's come up," said the reporter. "I have to go."

"Another big story?" asked Brisbane.

"No, a personal matter," said Reevis. "I need to get over to the legal clinic." He began dialing again as he rushed out of the room.

Brisbane and Dundee glanced at each other and nodded. They ran out the door.

A couple of satisfied customers had returned and occupied a pair of chairs in a nail salon.

An Asian woman smiled at a cheetah. "But you don't need the laser treatment."

"Doesn't matter," said Serge. "I'm all about lasers. Bring it on."

She smiled again and went to work, giving him extra pampering because of his massive tip from the last visit. She was starting to get a crush.

A cell phone rang, and rang. It took extra time to take off the paw and fish inside the costume. "Serge here ... What! ... Slow down, what's wrong? ... Don't move. I'll take care of everything ..."

"Is something the matter?" asked the woman walking over with a narrow beam of light.

"Sorry, but something's come up." He jumped out of the chair and peeled off twenties. "Come on, Coleman! ..."

It was a frantic search that became so desperate it ventured into irrational territory. In the top floor of an extended-stay hotel near the airport, all the briefcases lay open on the beds as men ripped apart pillows and pulled paintings off the walls.

Ocho Pelota stood in the middle of the room with a crimson face.

Reports came back from various parts of the suite: *"I can't find it." "It's not anywhere." "What could have happened to that ticket?"*

"Shut the fuck up!" Pelota took a deep, violent breath. "Who's not here?"

They looked around. "Pablo."

"Pablo!" repeated Pelota. "He's the last person I would have—Goddammit!" He pulled out his cell phone and dialed. And dialed.

"He's not answering?"

"What about 'shut up' do you not get?" Then he began pressing other buttons, pulling up a map in the screen. "All the cell phones I gave you guys are GPS enabled ... There's Pablo, and he's on the move. Everyone, strap up!"

They grabbed all the weapons they could lay their hands on and ran for the door.

In a Fort Lauderdale condo, a man with dreadlocks and a bathrobe stared out at the ocean with a phone in his hand. "... I understand ... Yes, you did the right thing ... Your word is your bond ... We'll meet you there."

He hung up.

"Who was that?" asked a trusted assistant.

"Our new lawyer," said Rogan. "Get everyone together as fast as you can, and pack heavy."

A Chrysler 300 screeched into the strip-mall parking lot. Ziggy and Pablo ran up the stairs to the law clinic as another vehicle jumped the curb. Reevis leaped out.

Brook was waiting at the top. "To my office!"

They piled inside. Then the tedious process of going through the layers of protective envelopes until the ticket lay in the middle of her desk. Everyone stood around staring silently like it was a piece of the Dead Sea Scrolls.

Brook flipped to a page in the *Miami Herald* and compared numbers one by one. Over and over. She began hyperventilating. "It's for real."

A cell phone rang. Pablo jumped. He checked the caller ID and started shaking uncontrollably. He hurriedly completed a forgotten task: turning off his GPS.

"You better have a seat," said Brook. "And you better tell me right now why you can't come forward with this ticket. Most of my clients are jittery, but something's more than not right here. And it isn't just the size of the jackpot."

Pablo just continued vibrating as the color drained from his face.

"The whole story," said Brook. "Or we don't go any further."

Pablo stuttered through most of it, but he eventually finished the wild tale.

Brook and Reevis locked eyes. "Dear God!"

The reporter pulled out his cell phone.

"Reevis, who are you calling? ..."

A silver Corvette skidded into the parking lot. The pals jumped out and dashed inside.

"Serge, thank heavens you're here! I didn't know what else to do!"

"You can calm down now," said Serge. "I've got this under control."

"I couldn't believe he came back," said Marilyn. "He's been sitting in his car across the street all morning."

Serge glanced out the curtains at a brown-haired man in an old convertible black Lincoln. "The mask is in my car. This won't take long."

Marilyn didn't want Serge to leave her side, and she tiptoed behind him. Serge popped the trunk and grabbed the disguise. A cell phone rang. "Serge here ... Reevis, slow down, you're talking too fast ... What! ... Don't move. I'll be right over." Then to Marilyn: "Something's come up ..."

"Wait!" said a terrified drag queen. "You can't leave me!"

"Wouldn't think of it." Serge slammed the trunk. "You'll be safe with us. Come on!"

The trio ran to the Corvette. The sky began to darken, wind picked up. Coleman sat in Marilyn's lap as Serge tossed the Oswald mask on the dashboard. He gave it the gas and took off down the street, followed by a black Lincoln. They both took the on-ramp to the Palmetto Expressway.

The full-scale freak-out was contagious. Everyone in Brook's office felt hearts pounding through their chests. They kept checking out the window as purple thunderheads rolled in.

Then other pounding, feet coming up the stairs. Serge burst into the office with Coleman and Marilyn in tow.

"Thanks for coming," said a shaken Reevis. "I wasn't sure I'd be able to reach you."

"Everyone can relax now," said Serge. "But we have to move fast. If events are already in motion like I think, we're not safe here. Who has the ticket?"

Ziggy grabbed it off the desk. "Me." No time for the envelopes; he tucked it in his wallet.

"Whose Chrysler out front?"

"Mine," said Pablo.

"Coleman rides with me," said Serge. "Everyone else in the other car. If we can reach the Palmetto, we should be in the clear."

They all scampered down the stairs. Serge stopped at the door for a quick recon before the final sprint to the cars. The sky cut loose in a downpour, but the coast was clear.

"Now!"

The gang ran for their vehicles as a pair of Mercedes flew into the parking lot. Pelota and his boys jumped out, forming a line and pointing Uzis. "Nobody's going anywhere!"

They froze where they stood, rain dripping down their faces.

"Now, who has the ticket?" demanded Pelota.

A cheetah stepped forward. "I do," lied Serge.

"Just hand it over and nobody will get hurt," said Pelota. "Except Pablo. He's coming with us."

"You look like a reasonable person," said Serge. "Don't you think a finder's fee is in order?"

"Serge!" snapped Brook.

"Shhh, I'm negotiating here."

Pelota smiled, but it wasn't friendly. "You've got some nerve. That I respect. So I'll make an exception and ask a second time, and only a second time. Give me the ticket."

Tires squealed. A Jaguar and a Cadillac braked to a stop on the other side of the parking lot. Rogan's dreadlock gang got out and formed another row, pointing MAC-10s.

Silence.

As fast as the rain had started, it ceased. Only the sound of water quickly draining off the parking lot into the storm drains and rushing through concrete pipes to the sea.

"I believe someone has my ticket," said Rogan.

"*Your* ticket?" Pelota laughed with derision. "I believe you are seriously mistaken."

"You're the one who's making a mistake." Rogan tilted his head slightly, and all his men raised their weapons. Instantly, Pelota's crew raised theirs. Fingers twitched on triggers.

Standoff.

The O.K. Corral comes to Miami.

Nobody moved. Two parallel firing lines faced each other twenty yards apart, with Serge and his hapless friends caught in the middle.

All the women from the salons were at the windows. It was a simple equation of timing now. Whoever got the drop and shot first at the perfect moment. But no sooner or it would be an un-coordinated spray.

The innocent people glanced one way and the other at the death squads. The looks in the gunmen's eyes told them exactly what they were considered to be: collateral damage.

Goons in each camp slowly began squeezing triggers.

Suddenly another squeal of tires. A black Lincoln convertible raced into the parking lot. "*Marilyn, I love you!*"

"Oh no," said Serge.

An SUV sped in from another direction. Dundee jumped out with his camera, and Brisbane made a fist. "*Action!*"

"Oh no," said Reevis.

"Who the fuck are all these people?" said Pelota.

"The ticket," said Rogan.

The squeezing fingers were a hair from dropping the firing pins.

The door of the law office opened, and an oblivious man with a camo hat and a cardboard box wandered into the fire zone.

All guns swung toward him.

He looked up. "*Ahhhhhhh!*" And dropped the box. A reptile scampered.

"Alligator!"

Every trigger pulled.

Bang, bang, bang, bang, bang, bang, bang, bang...

The crowd in the middle flattened themselves to the ground as chunks of parking lot exploded around the gator. But all the shots were wildly off target because the gunmen had learned how to shoot from TV. The reptile emerged unscathed.

Bang, bang, bang, bang, bang, bang...

But bullets do have a habit of ricocheting. Lead flew up from the pavement.

A scream as one of Pelota's men went down, then one of Rogan's.

Bang, bang, bang...

More screams.

"Cease fire!" Pelota waved both arms in the air. "Everyone knock it off! It's just a stupid little alligator! We don't have the ticket yet!"

When the smoke cleared, bodies lay still, and each of the gangs was down to three.

A bicycle rolled by on the sidewalk with reptiles dangling from the handlebars.

"Iguanas!"

Bang, bang, bang.

"Stop shooting at everything!" yelled Pelota.

Sirens, police cars, dozens. The heavy artillery told them to hang back a block and form a perimeter until the tactical armored trucks arrived. Officers drew weapons and squatted behind open squad-car doors.

The warring factions grabbed clips to reload, and Serge used the opportunity to inch closer to the Corvette. He glanced toward the window of the nail salon and furtively formed his thumb and forefinger into a letter of the alphabet. One of the nail women nodded.

The guns were racked and raised. Squinting, quiet, itchy fingers.

Serge slowly reached for the dashboard and put on the Oswald mask.

"*Ahhhhhhh!*"

JFK took off running.

Bang, bang, bang, bang, bang, bang ...

The brown-haired man high-stepped it through the flying chunks of pavement and dove back into his convertible Lincoln.

More ricochets, more screams, more bodies fell.

Bang, bang, bang, bang, bang ...

"Stop shooting! Stop shooting!" screamed Pelota.

But he was only talking to himself. The crowd in the middle looked around. Rogan's crew had been entirely wiped out, and Pelota's gang was down to, well, Pelota.

A woman ran out of the nail salon and hugged Serge. "Don't shoot him! Don't shoot him!"

"Are you out of your mind?" yelled Pelota. "Get back in the store."

She ran off and took shelter.

Ocho Pelota rolled his eyes at the sky. "The fucking ticket? *Please?*"

"I can't take this anymore," said Ziggy. "I'm way too high ... *I* have the ticket."

"That's more like it," said Pelota. "Just pass it over and we'll be out of your hair."

Now that Pelota's eyes had turned to Ziggy, Serge worked a hand behind his back, manipulating what the nail salon lady had been able to slip him.

Ziggy's trembling fingers fished the ticket from his wallet, and he shook even more as he extended his arm toward the gunman. The stress was too much. The ticket fell from his grasp.

It seemed like it was happening in slow motion as the tiny piece of paper fluttered down. Everyone watched in shock as it slipped through the grating of a storm drain, where a raging subterranean river of runoff began taking it on its journey to the sea.

"*Ahhhhh!*" screamed Pelota, losing control with ungoverned anger. He quickly raised his weapon to kill every last one of them.

Just as he did, Serge hit him in the eyes with a laser from the nail salon. "*Ahhhhhh!*"

The natural reflex is for the hands to go to the face, kind of like a blink response.

When Pelota did, he shot himself in the head five times.

Everyone jumped back as Pelota momentarily stood lifeless before toppling over.

A parking lot full of silent, open mouths and big white eyes. *Did that just happen?*

Then the street came alive again with sirens and tires. All the police cars converged on the strip mall. Officers rushed toward the carnage.

"Serge," said Brook. "What are you going to do? They've got the place surrounded!"

"Just like I planned it."

"Planned?"

Cops kicked guns away from the hands of fallen bad guys. Others ran toward the survivors. Serge popped the Corvette's trunk, grabbed something for himself and handed another to Coleman.

Just as the officers arrived, the pair finished slipping into their Windbreakers.

"You're the hostage negotiators?" asked a sergeant.

"I'll be doing the paperwork on this for a month," said Serge.

"What's with the cheetah and panda outfits."

"Undercover. Sign-spinners." Serge pointed vaguely up the road. "I've got to coordinate with headquarters and seal the airport. Others on the watch list might be trying to get away."

"Homeland Security? FBI?"

"It's a task force." Serge put a hand on the sergeant's shoulder. "But I respect your jurisdiction, so the person you need to talk to is that attorney over there. She'll give you the whole story. And make sure you spell your name for the press release."

"You got it." The sergeant waved for a couple of officers guarding the edge of the parking lot to pull back and make space so the silver Corvette could get through.

Serge headed south on Biscayne Boulevard, wearing a cheetah costume and hostage-negotiator Windbreaker, sitting next to a panda as they passed a bicyclist with dangling iguanas, looking in the rearview mirror as officers interviewed Korean salon workers, an Australian film crew, Marilyn Monroe and JFK, while a man in a camo hat ran through a dozen bodies chasing a small alligator. Serge shook his head to himself. "Life goes by way too fast when it's the same thing every day."

Epilogue

THE FLORIDA KEYS

A silver Corvette glinted in the sun as it crossed the Seven Mile Bridge.

"Where are we going for our next *Route 66* episode?" asked Coleman.

"That was the series finale. When you hit a high note, leave the stage."

They were speaking to each other on walkie-talkies. Because Coleman was in the trunk.

"You sure you're comfortable back there?"

"I like it. Got my beer, munchies, smoke. Cool."

It helped make room in the front seat for the nail-salon woman snuggling up next to Serge.

A walkie-talkie squawked again. "So what are the new plans for now?"

Serge glanced down at his lap and an official summons that he had poached from a mailbox. "I've always wanted to serve on a jury."

MIAMI

A bleached-out lottery ticket with no visible numbers emerged from a spillway and floated off into the Atlantic Ocean.

In the history of the Florida Lottery, there have been a number of unclaimed tickets. The largest jackpot that wasn't cashed by the 180-day deadline came in 2003 at $53.7 million.

The soggy white rectangle of paper continued drifting toward the Bahamas in an offshore seaweed bloom, before a loggerhead turtle nibbled on it until it was gone.

Back ashore, lottery officials were holding another press conference to announce that Saturday night's drawing had actually produced two winners.

In a modest retirement condo along a more affordable stretch of old North Miami Beach, a heated argument broke out among four ninety-something-year-old roommates.

"Give me the ticket!" shouted Eunice.

"I bought it!" yelled Edith. "It's mine!"

"We always go in on it together!" screamed Ethel.

"That was last week!" shrieked Edith.

"The rule automatically carries over," yelled Edna.

"No, it doesn't!" cried Edith. "Ow! Let go of my hair! I just had a permanent!"

"I got the ticket!" said Ethel. "Let's go buy a speedboat!"

Also Available

Local trivia buff Serge Storms loves eliminating jerks and pests. His drug-addled partner Coleman loves cartoons. Hot stripper Sharon Rhodes loves cocaine, especially when purchased with rich dead men's money.

On the other hand, there's Sean and David, who love fishing and are kind to animals -- and who are about to cross paths with a suitcase filled with stolen insurance money. Serge wants the suitcase. Sharon wants the suitcase. Coleman wants more drugs . . . and the suitcase. In the meantime, there's murder by gun, Space Shuttle, Barbie doll, and Levi's 501s.

The first Serge Storms adventure

OUT NOW

About the Serge Storms series

Part spree killer, part local historian, Serge A. Storms and his human narcotic partner Coleman have carved a trail of destruction and marijuana roaches through Florida, and he's just getting started.

Warning: If you sight this man, please contact the police immediately.

Further titles in the series—

Florida Roadkill

Hammerhead Ranch Motel

Orange Crush

Triggerfish Twist

The Stingray Shuffle

Cadillac Beach

Torpedo Juice

The Big Bamboo

Electric Barracuda

When Elves Attack

Pineapple Grenade

The Rip Tide Ultra-Glide

Tiger Shrimp Tango

Shark Skin Suite

Coconut Cowboy

Clownfish Blues

About the Author

Tim Dorsey was born in Indiana, moved to Florida at the age of 1, and grew up in a small town about an hour north of Miami called Riviera Beach. He worked as a reporter and editor for the Tampa Tribune from 1987 to 1999, after which he left to write full time.

He lives in Tampa with his family.

Note from the Publisher

To receive updates on next releases in the Serge Storms series, sign up at farragobooks.com/serge-storms-signup

www.ingramcontent.com/pod-product-compliance
Ingram Content Group UK Ltd.
Pitfield, Milton Keynes, MK11 3LW, UK
UKHW041714250326
469269UK00004B/14